The
Emotional Life
of the
Toddler

Updated Edition

Alicia F. Lieberman

Simon & Schuster
New York   London   Toronto   Sydney   New Delhi

Simon & Schuster
1230 Avenue of the Americas
New York, NY 10020

Interior design by Carly Loman

Manufactured in the United States of America

1   3   5   7   9   10   8   6   4   2

Library of Congress Cataloging-in-Publication Data

Lieberman, Alicia F., author.
The emotional life of the toddler / Alicia F. Lieberman.
Second edition. | New York : Simon & Schuster, [2018] | Includes bibliographical references and index. LCCN 2017035054 | LCSH: Toddlers. | Toddlers—Psychology. | Child rearing. LCC HQ774.5 .L54 2018 | DDC 649/.122—dc23
LC record available at https://lccn.loc.gov/2017035054

ISBN 978-1-4767-9203-3
ISBN 978-1-4767-9204-0 (ebook)

New Praise for
The Emotional Life of the Toddler

"*The Emotional Life of the Toddler* is a wise and kind book about a fascinating and sometimes exhausting stage of life; it will help parents understand and appreciate all that is happening as their young children develop, and it will also help them navigate the complexities of life with toddlers."

—Perri Klass, MD, professor of journalism and pediatrics, NYU

"Alicia Lieberman is a toddler whisperer, illuminating the art and science of this important period of life in informative ways that will enable parents to gain important insights into the mind and behavior of their child. With clear and concise summaries of research findings highlighting developmental milestones of this age woven with practical examples families face in everyday life, this second edition of her classic work is a gift to parents and children alike."

—Daniel J. Siegel, MD, clinical professor, UCLA School of Medicine

"Dr. Alicia Lieberman is a brilliant clinician and one of the most sage voices of our era in the field of early childhood development. As we learn more and more about the critical nature of the earliest years in forming the foundation of lifelong health, this second edition of *The Emotional Life of the Toddler* could not come at a more important time. Clear and wise, *The Emotional Life of the Toddler* is an essential guide for clinicians, parents, caregivers and anyone who has a little one in their lives. For me, a pediatrician and the parent of a toddler, this book is a blessing."

—Nadine Burke Harris, MD, founder and CEO, Center for Youth Wellness

"A *gift* to all—not only to today's parents—but to all those who work with toddlers and their parents. From tantrums to screen time, from toilet training to trauma—and so much more, Lieberman illuminates every aspect of toddlerhood with understanding, empathy, care, experience, research, and wisdom, while at the same time respecting cultural differences and values and the fast-paced lives of today's families."

—Robie H. Harris, celebrated children's book author of
It's Perfectly Normal and *It's So Amazing*

To my parents,
Dr. Manuel Fridman
Dr. Rosa Asrilevich de Fridman

To my son,
Michael Morris Lieberman

And to my grandson,
Samuel Joseph Lieberman

Roots, branch, fruit
Raices, rama, fruto

Contents

Acknowledgments

(Second Edition)

Twenty-five years have passed since the publication of this book's first edition, and much has happened in the world and in my life during this time. I am now the grandmother of a much cherished toddler. Being with him during the many facets of his rich emotional life renews my appreciation for how deeply toddlers feel and how urgently they need us to understand them. Observing his loving parents as they balance their commitment to him with the multiple demands of their adult lives teaches me how much has changed and how much remains the same for young children and those who care for them. I hope the new edition of this book continues to be a trusted companion for parents and caregivers of today as they find their own ways of raising toddlers in an increasingly fast-paced culture. The magic of small, everyday moments with young children continues to be close at hand when we can create the space for it.

My gratitude to all those I thanked in the introduction to the first edition remains strong. That gratitude now extends to more recent partners who join in creating concentric circles of collaboration around the central goal of helping young children and their families. At the UCSF Child Trauma Research Program, I am fortunate to have the invaluable presence of Nancy Compton, Miriam Hernandez Dimmler, and Chandra Ghosh Ippen in the leadership of our training program, our community initiatives, our national and international dissemination, and our research. Our team of caring and talented clinicians is steadfast in its commitment to developing, implementing, and improving our treatment models: Laura Castro, Gloria Castro, Markita

Mays, Griselda Oliver Bucio, Vilma Reyes, Maria Torres. We could not succeed in our research goals without the skills and devotion of Emily Cohodes, Luisa Rivera, Tuesday Ray, and Aru Gonzalez. The National Child Traumatic Stress Network, under the leadership of Robert Pynoos and John Fairbank, gives us a community of practice to help children whose lives are marred by violence and adversity. My friends and partners William Harris, Frank Putnam, Lisa Amaya-Jackson, and Karen Putnam are generous with their wisdom as we endeavor to translate knowledge into action.

I thank my editor, Marysue Rucci, for her enthusiastic support. Her able office, particularly Zachary Knoll, has been creatively responsive to all aspects of the production. I am grateful to my agent, Geri Thoma, for her wisdom and skill. Robie Harris has been the best possible guide in showing me the power of books to change children's lives. Leah Sodowick's help with many aspects of the book was nothing less than inspired. Special thanks to the toddlers whose photos grace this book and to their parents for sharing the wonderful images that bring the text to life. Erika Dimmler is the photographer for many of them, and I am grateful for her wonderful art and generosity in sharing it.

The many years of shoulder-to-shoulder togetherness with my dear Patricia Van Horn continue to imbue everything I do. May her memory be for a blessing.

As in the past, most of this new edition was written at home, after hours, in the sustaining company of my husband, Dr. David N. Richman, whose depth of thought and feeling continues to enrich my own. He gives me the grace of companionship even while in solitude, and through the years I remain grateful to him for that and for much more.

Acknowledgments

(First Edition)

Every book is a tribute to those who made it possible. Many people accompanied me in the writing of this book, and their voices are often intertwined with my own.

Three extraordinary women were my early teachers and helped me to discover who I wanted to be.

Mary Ainsworth took me on as a graduate student when I was a newcomer in this country. She introduced me to research, taught me how to observe babies and parents, and gave me the vocabulary of attachment theory, which grows ever more useful with the years. She provided guidance through my doctoral thesis and helped to unlock the pleasures of writing in a new language. She equipped me for the journey ahead and has remained a trusted and reliable secure base.

From Selma Fraiberg I learned about healing. She knew how pain can be transmitted from generation to generation, from parent to child, and she knew how to speak sensibly, openly, and tactfully to break the cycle of alienation and restore intimacy and love. She taught with joy, and her teachings live on as a result.

Marjorie Harley showed me the world beyond infancy. She gave much and expected much, and I am richer for it.

Two superb supervisors pointed me on my current course. Joseph Adelson encouraged me to write and, even more to the point, challenged me to think. Peter Blos Jr., showed by example. His clinical skills are an ongoing reminder of what is possible when we know how to listen.

I had the good fortune of finding my first job under the direction of

Stanley Greenspan, whose ebullient pursuit of knowledge is matched only by his enthusiasm in sharing it. His understanding of constitutional sensitivities in infants ushered in important advances in preventive intervention, and it was a privilege to work with him at the cutting edge of this field.

The present deserves as much appreciation as the past. The Infant-Parent Program, where I now work, is my second home in every sense of the word. I owe Jeree Pawl, its director, a debt of gratitude for many years of inspired and inspiring leadership. This book carries the imprint of many happy hours spent together musing over, discussing, reconstructing, remembering, and sometimes simply imagining the inner world of the toddler.

I am fortunate to work with colleagues who are also dear friends. I wish to thank Judith Pekarsky, Graeme Hanson, Barbara Kalmanson, and Stephen Seligman for infusing the activities of teaching, clinical work, and even administration with a spirit of camaraderie and intellectual curiosity that enlivens the daily routine.

Cherished colleagues read earlier versions of this book and were generous with their advice. I want to thank Mary Ainsworth, Berry Brazelton, Emily Fenichel, Jeanne Miranda, and Arietta Slade for their careful reading and their thoughtful comments.

My editor, Susan Arellano, was unstinting in her support and unerring in the clarity of her vision. Herself the mother of a toddler, she knew when refocusing was needed. The book profited greatly from her input.

The vignettes and case examples given in the book involve real-life toddlers and their families. I am grateful to them for allowing me to come close and to work with them. This book could not exist without their cooperation.

Stephanie Berg typed this book's manuscript heroically and was my most immediate editor. Her smile or soberness as she gave me back a newly typed chapter gave me either encouragement or early warning, and she was usually right. Anne Cleary, our administrative assistant, makes me feel that no goal is out of reach and that she is there as a partner in the reaching.

Most of this book was written at home, after hours, in the sustaining company of my husband, David N. Richman, whose depth of thought and feeling enriches my own. He taught me what it means to be accompanied while in solitude, and I thank him for that and for much more.

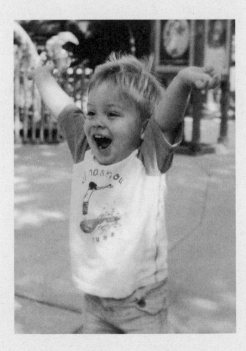

1

The Emotional Importance of Early Relationships

Living with a child between 1 and 3 years of age is an exhilarating experience. Who else could show us so convincingly that a wet, muddy leaf lying on the ground is actually a hidden marvel or that splashing in the bathtub can bring ultimate joy? Toddlers have the gift of living in the moment and finding wonder in the ordinary. They share those gifts by helping the adults they love to reconnect with the simple pleasures of life.

But toddlers have dark moments, too. They are notoriously willful and unpredictable. Their behavior can be difficult to understand and strenuous to handle. At times parents find themselves caught in a contest of wills, vaguely embarrassed at being unable to win more handily at this uneven match. Other times they are simply at a loss. It is hard to fathom what the child is asking for, and the child cannot explain. He or she can only act, repeating the same behavior again and again until the parent finally deciphers the message and comes up with an appropriate response.

Examples of toddler behavior begging for an explanation are many.

- Blair hits his head against the wall if he is angry or frustrated.
- Eddy cries with hunger but rejects every choice his mother offers him for dinner.
- Sandra screams and tries to hide when she sees a picture of an elephant waving his long trunk in a children's book.
- Lenya lets go of her father's hand and runs toward a horse galloping in the field next to her house.

- Mary looks for her mother all over the house only to run out of the room as soon as she finds her.
- Marty goes back and forth between crying to be held and demanding to be put down.

These and many other behaviors defy adult logic. Why would a child seek pain, choose to stay hungry, become terrified of a harmless picture, rush into danger, search for her mother only to run away from her, or want comforting while rejecting it at the same time?

Though inexplicable from the perspective of grown-ups, these reactions make perfect sense from the viewpoint of a child who is 1, 2, or 3 years old. This book tries to explain why this is so. The ideas presented are my personal synthesis of child observation, clinical work with toddlers and their families, theories of development, and current research findings. The organizing themes come from attachment theory, which was developed by psychoanalyst John Bowlby and psychologist Mary Ainsworth to explain the intense need that all children in the first three years of life have for a close relationship with their parents and a small number of cherished adults. The basic premise of attachment theory is that toddlers can grow into happy and competent children if they can rely on at least one adult who makes them feel safe and protected. From this basic feeling of security in relationships grows the impetus to explore how things work in the world and to try out new skills.[1, 2]

The most important emotional accomplishment of the toddler years is reconciling the urge to become competent and self-reliant with the simultaneous and sometimes contradictory longing for parental love and protection. This process is apparent in the behavior of toddlers who have recently mastered walking on their own. The child moves back and forth between staying close to the parent, moving away to do things on her own, and going back to the parent to share discoveries, to be comforted, or simply to "recharge batteries" with a hug or a cuddle before going off yet again for another bout of exploration. They are practicing the balance between their need for autonomy and their need for protection. In order to explore and learn, they need reassurance that the parent will be there to keep them safe while they do things on their own.

Parents serve as the home base for the toddler's explorations. When they respond to the child's experiences with encouragement and understanding, this home base becomes a *secure base*. The child derives a feeling of security from the parent's support, and this security generates the self-confidence to seek larger horizons.

Different toddlers use the secure base provided by the parents in different ways. Some children are shy and retiring by temperament, and they need more time close to the parents before they are ready to explore on their own. Other children can hardly be held back because they are very active and enthralled by novelty. Temperamental tendencies put an individual stamp on how toddlers use their parents and other caregivers as a secure base for their explorations.

Yet most adults are neither fixed in one place nor infinitely available. The secure base is human, and the parent has to attend to aspects of life other than being responsive to the child. Parents have many roles in addition to being parents: they have a work life, a social life, and a private life, in addition to the multiple demands of everyday existence. The separate needs and wishes of parents and toddlers need to be negotiated and balanced in a reasonably mutually satisfactory way. What "satisfactory" means, in turn, differs from family to family and changes in the course of development depending on many factors, including societal opportunities and pressures, the parents' cultural expectations and values, and the individual characteristics and relationship styles of the parents and the child. In striving for family harmony, it helps to remember that satisfaction is often the art of the possible. The English pediatrician and psychoanalyst Donald Winnicott, who was renowned for his deep understanding of the mother-child relationship, coined the term "good-enough mother" to help mothers and society at large relinquish the fantasy that there is such a thing as a perfect mother—or that there should be. Many mothers use "good enough" as a mantra to repeat when they are flooded by guilt and regret that they cannot give their children the ideal life that we all yearn for and that eludes us all.

When the child first begins to walk, parents postpone or adjust many of their own wishes and plans because the new physical and emotional demands of locomotion often call for urgent, immediate attention and quick action. As toddlers get firmer on their feet and acquire greater self-control between about 18 and 24 months, parents are under less pressure to defer to the child. They increasingly expect the toddler to adjust to the adults' plans and wishes rather than the other way around.

The themes of physical and emotional safety must remain a priority throughout the toddler years because parents cannot rely on the child's self-control or ability to judge what is safe and what is dangerous. Toddlers' impetus to move and explore is much more powerful than their capacity to anticipate the consequences of their actions. The areas of the brain that involve logical thinking, abstract reasoning, self-restraint, and long-term planning take a long time to develop and may not be fully mature until early adulthood. As a result, the first years of life have the grim distinction of being also the most risky ones, with the highest likelihood of life-threatening as well as minor accidents such as falls, burns, ingestion of nonfood and sometimes poisonous items, and near drowning. Parents and other caregivers may find themselves taken by surprise, unable to anticipate or keep up with the quick mobility of a single-minded toddler who is intent on exploring how the world works.

Physical safety depends on the caregivers' capacity to identify and respond promptly to sources of danger, which demands ongoing alertness to the child's whereabouts. Emotional safety results from children's consistent experience that parents and other caregivers will be available to protect them and respond to their signals of need. Though physical danger and safety are usually clear-cut, the experience of emotional safety is not monochromatic. Many of the power struggles so prevalent in the second and third years of life stem from parents' and children's disparate perceptions of danger and their often incompatible but nonnegotiable individual agendas. Parents and other caregivers are often exhausted by the extraordinary zest of toddlers for being on the move, their refusal to take naps, and the quick pace of their darting off, climbing, running, and jumping. Two efficient strategies to decrease parent and child mutual frustration are *creating safe spaces* for toddlers that decrease the need for constant parental intervention and *redirect-*

ing their attention by enticing them away from forbidden pursuits. In this sense, physical safety and emotional security can go hand in hand.

This is also the time when many socialization pressures begin. Toddlers are asked to live up to many new parental expectations in a short period of time. We want them to relinquish the satisfactions of being a baby and trade them in for the more ambiguous pleasures of growing up. Most toddlers experience toilet training, giving up the bottle, falling asleep on their own, and complying with the rules of the household as impositions that are more trouble than they are worth. They respond by refusing to do things before they are ready and by throwing a tantrum if all else fails. Yet those protests come at an emotional cost. Toddlers are scared that displeasing their parents will result in losing their love, and this fear finds expression in the common difficulties of toddlerhood, such as separation anxiety, sleep disturbances, and inexplicable fears.

In responding to the needs of toddlers, the caregiving function of parents as protectors undergoes a transformation. They can no longer serve primarily as an external secure base that anchors the child's comings and goings and responds to the child's signals of need. They must now help the child to become a partner in sorting out disagreements and finding solutions that will preserve mutual goodwill.

This partnership is necessarily asymmetrical because the parent and the child are not equal. The parent carries the responsibility for raising the child and must be the one to make the important decisions, although the child may be offered some concrete choices and allowed to take the initiative when appropriate. Young children are reassured by knowing that the parents are confident in their authority. This attitude is conveyed in the recommendations parents receive during a parenting intervention appropriately entitled "Circle of Security," which encourages parents to be "Bigger, Stronger, Wiser, and Kind."[3]

Partnership with the parents is a reliable ally for the child in times of fear, sadness, anger, and frustration because it serves as a protection from despair and emotional collapse. The child learns that she may dislike what is happening in the moment but can tolerate the stress and find pleasure in something else. The parents' supportive attitude in helping the child through difficult moments gradually becomes a part of the child. What at first was an external secure base is gradually transformed through multiple interactions into an internal experience of confidence and safety and becomes an increasingly reliable component of the growing child's sense of self. The child learns to incorporate the parents' care and protectiveness even in their absence. The toddler years are a crucial initial stage in the extended process of consolidating this achievement.

Partnerships are not always harmonious because disagreements cannot be invariably worked out to both partners' satisfaction. This is probably more true of the toddler years than of any other age until adolescence. Temper tantrums, yelling, defiance, striking out, sulking, irritability, and anger are frequent components of family life while raising a toddler. This is an early mirror of the struggles inherent in relating closely to others throughout life. Some degree of ambivalence is an integral component of all human relationships. The more we love and depend on someone, the more intense our disappointment and frustration may become when conflicts are not resolved in the way we wish.

It is neither possible nor desirable to be always attuned and responsive to the moods and wishes of children. Unconditional deference thwarts their capacity to understand that the needs of others are equally legitimate and must sometimes prevail. Parents can lose their sense of self when they turn themselves over to their child, with negative consequences for both the parent and the child. The partnership between parent and child by necessity has to remain unequal for a long time. Testing adult authority and living with the outcome of this testing help children learn about social expectations and enrich their repertoire of social and emotional skills, including frustration tolerance and adjusting to the needs and wishes of others.

It is hard sometimes to keep in mind the growth-promoting potential of the mismatches between parent and child goals because the parents' empathy for the child can make them feel as if it is their fault that they cannot fulfill the child's wishes. Mismatches, however, can be beneficial to the child, even if unpleasant. Many studies show that parents' middle-of-the-road sensitive responsiveness best predicts the child's security of attachment. Such "neither too much nor too little" parental sensitivity in responding to the child is most likely to develop when parents cultivate an attitude of partnership that integrates empathy with reality. This involves an effort to listen, show understanding for the toddler's perspective and feelings, acknowledge that parents and children at times have different goals, look for ways to reconcile differences, and assert parental priorities when needed even if the child does not like this outcome. The child's emotional resilience is built over time and calls for daily practice in problem solving, conflict resolution, and coping with the frustration of not having the last word. Kind firmness also reassures the child that the grown-ups know what they are doing and creates a realistic awareness of and respect for the needs of others through the example of the parents.

Every aspect of the toddler's development is influenced by the presence or absence of a secure base and a partnership between parent and child. Milestones such as toilet training and common anxieties such as fear of separation and sleep disturbances can be understood better from this perspective. Even the child's responses to stressful external events such as beginning child care or parental divorce become clearer and easier to manage in light of these concepts.

A secure base can be established with biological and adoptive mothers and fathers, with a single parent, with each of two same-sex parents, and with other trusted caregivers. In families with a mother and a father, the role of the father often becomes more salient when the baby in arms becomes a toddler. Cultural influences, family circumstances, and individual styles play major roles in shaping the role of fathers in their children's everyday life, but the often observed increased involvement of fathers in the toddler years may be linked to findings that fathers as a group are more likely than mothers to promote the adventurous exploration and challenging play that toddlers are now ready to join.[4] In studies of young children's relationships with their mother and father, a secure relationship with the father is protective of the child's healthy development beginning in infancy. One study, for example, found that children who showed a secure attachment to their fathers by seeking them out for comfort when feeling stressed had fewer behavior problems and showed more competence in school and peer groups than did those who had an insecure relationship with their fathers.[5] In another study, toddlers who showed insecurity with both their fathers and their mothers had more behavioral problems when they were 6.5 years old than toddlers who had a secure relationship with both parents, but having a secure relationship with either parent offset the likelihood of these problems.[6] A growing body of research lends support to the notion that a supportive father presence is beneficial even when the father and the mother are not living together but can create a coparenting partnership on behalf of their child.[7] This is an important message for single parents and divorced parents who are negotiating how to share their access to the child. The experience of toddlers and parents in divorced families is explored in chapter 9.

What are the implications of these findings for children raised in nontraditional family configurations, such as in single-parent households or by same-sex parents? The available evidence consistently shows that the support of friends and family, flexibility of work hours, adequate income and access to social resources, and satisfaction with caregiving arrangements enable single parents to raise children who thrive in all aspects of their development. As with children raised in two-parent childhoods, the emotional quality of the relationship between parent and child is the single most important predictor of the child's healthy development. Similarly, studies of children growing up with same-sex parents consistently show that their well-being—including emotional adjustment, quality of peer and adult relationships, comfort with their gender identity, and academic performance—is influenced by the same kinds of factors that influence the well-being of children raised by two heterosexual parents, including parenting stress, parenting approaches, and couple relationship adjustment. These factors are not associated with parental sexual orientation.[8,9] Same-sex parents often report that when toddlers and preschoolers become aware of different family constellations, they ask, "Do I have a mommy?" "Where is my father?" Even very young children can understand and accept explanations about different family configurations that are offered in clear and simple language by the adults they love. Young children may be the first ones to describe to others what their family structure looks like, as 3-year-old Mary demonstrated when she told the cashier at the grocery store's checkout counter, "My daddy Sam yelled at me, but my daddy Paul told him to stop." The National Association for the Education of Young Children has developed resources that help parents and educators speak openly, comfortably, and inclusively with young children about the diversity of family configurations as a way of promoting cultural understanding and help children from all kinds of families feel that they belong.[10] A book for children, *Who's in My Family: All About Our Families* by Robie Harris,[11] helps parents introduce this topic to their young children.

The parents' beliefs and practices about what is good for the child are shaped by cultural values that carry enormous emotional power even when parents are not consciously aware of them. These values and practices inform every aspect of caregiving, from concrete decisions such as where and with whom the baby sleeps and when to start toilet training to adult expectations about what is right and wrong, including what the child is allowed or not allowed to say and do in different situations. Different cultures have different ideas about the importance of play, the value of talking to babies, gender roles, and what is expected from mothers and fathers—virtually every domain of parenting is affected by culture. Cultural values, in turn, are influenced by many factors that include the family's racial, ethnic, religious, and national identity, immigration history, economic and social circumstances, educational background, sexual orientation, and gender identity. Cultural groups are not homogeneous. For example, people from the same race differ in ethnicity, religion, social and economic conditions, sexual orientation, and gender identity. People often see themselves as having several cultural identities simultaneously because of the different groups to which they belong. One can be a minority within a minority, as when in a particular country the person's religion or sexual orientation is different from the mainstream in the minority ethnic group with which he or she identifies. The parent's acceptance and comfort with the prevailing cultural values of the groups to which he or she belongs adds still more cultural variability to child-rearing values and practices. A deeply religious parent, for example, might have different expectations about what is allowed and what is forbidden in child behavior from those of a secular person from the same ethnic, racial, national, and religious group. As societies all over the world become increasingly culturally diverse, many individuals and their children have mothers, fathers, and other relatives from different identity groups and consider themselves multicultural in a variety of dimensions.

Social change means that cultural values are dynamic, in flux, and enacted through the individuality of each parent and each family. Across cultural groups, parents share the same goal: to help their children grow up to be healthy and productive members of their societies. This goal can be achieved through a large range of specific values and practices. No identity or cultural group holds a monopoly on how to raise children who thrive, and the beauty of cultural diversity enriches the world and all of us. The chapters that follow describe how toddlers think, feel, and respond to the challenges of growing up and how parents can help them meet these challenges with greater self-confidence and joy, but this book also reflects the (often unconscious) cultural influences of its author. Parents can tailor every aspect of the book to their own individual and cultural beliefs in light of what is of value to them.

Parents and children help each other to grow. In raising their children, parents are also raising themselves. They relive emotions from their growing-up years and may find themselves repeating with their children the behaviors and feeling states that they felt toward their own parents. Sometimes the body remembers more than the mind does, through unexpected visceral feelings of tenderness, delight, joy—or, more darkly, sadness, fear, frustration, or rage. Child rearing gives parents the chance to redo their own childhood and to improve on it. Each encounter with their toddler becomes an opportunity either to fall back on old patterns or to create a new response that feels better aligned to the kind of person the parent wants to become. This book will do its job if it helps parents to raise their toddlers in the way they wish they had been raised.

2

Who Is the Toddler?

"The loving mother teaches the child to walk alone. She is far enough from him so that she cannot actually support him, but she holds out her arms to him. She imitates his movements, and if he totters, she swiftly bends as if to seize him, so that the child might believe he is not walking alone. . . . And yet, she does more. Her face beckons like a reward, an encouragement. Thus, the child walks alone with his eyes fixed on his mother's face, not on the difficulties in his way. He supports himself by the arms that do not hold him and constantly strives towards the refuge in his mother's embrace, little suspecting that in the very same moment that he is emphasizing his need for her, he is proving that he can do without her, because he is walking alone."[1]

As if echoing the scene described above, 2½-year-old Linda whispers to her mother, "I am a baby and a big girl." (Her mother, moved almost to tears, thinks, "So am I.")

These two vignettes convey the essence of the second year of life. Toddlers are defined by their capacity to walk without assistance. The ability to walk alone, which develops and consolidates between about 12 and 30 months of age, is a dramatic change, for both parents and child, from the physical closeness of the first year. As little Linda knows, there is continuity as well: as in infancy, the child has an ongoing need to be in frequent contact with the parents; however, with independent movement, the toddler herself can now determine when and where to go, without having to rely on the parent as the necessary (and sometimes unwilling) means of transportation.

This new autonomy brings about a revolution in the toddler's self-concept. Her major emotional task is to integrate the excitement of exploring away from the parents with the feeling of safety that she gets from their ongoing presence. The parents' job (not an easy one) is to protect their child tactfully from the new and unexpected dangers posed by locomotion and to do so again and again while the child gradually becomes more able to protect herself.

In many settings and under many different circumstances, the parents and the toddler need to negotiate a mutually satisfying balance between the safety of closeness and the excitement of exploration and discovery.

In this sense, childhood is an early laboratory for the challenges and dilemmas of adult life. Perhaps more dramatically than any other age, this period brings us face-to-face with two powerful yet contradictory impulses: the longing to feel safe in the protective sphere of intimate relationships and the exhilarating thrust of carefree, unrestricted, uninhibited exploration, where one can soar free without looking back at those who are left behind.

Toddlers feel this duality with passion, and their specific experiences with closeness and exploration have long-term implications. Much of our individual style through life is determined by our unique way of expressing, balancing, and integrating these two impulses. We might experiment with different possibilities at different junctions in our lives, alternating periods of giddy adventure with times of reflective holding back. Ultimately, however, we tend to re-create again and again the unique balance between caution and daring, familiarity and novelty, intimacy and autonomy that in some intangible way feels most like "us."

The question "Who is a toddler?" can be answered briefly by saying that the toddler is a young human being who is emerging from a yearlong initial period of almost total reliance on the parents and is now eager to discover the world and his or her place in it. The impetus to explore propels the toddler forward, but the ability to rely on supportive relationships is still at the core of his or her capacity to learn.

How Does the Brain Shape Development?

Underlying the advances from total dependence on the adults to increasing autonomy, emotional self-regulation, and reciprocity in relationships are the rapid growth and consolidation of brain circuits at a pace that will remain unmatched during the rest of the child's life. Brain development does not occur in a vacuum. It is highly dependent on the child's environmental experiences and most particularly on an expanding circle of relationships that has attachment figures at its core. While the brain develops over time and neuroplasticity (the brain's capacity to change and adapt in response to new experiences) lasts a lifetime, by the end of the first two postnatal years the brain reaches close to 80 percent of its adult weight, marking this period as having the fastest rate of brain growth and creating the foundational structures that scaffold later brain development. The Center on the Developing Child at Harvard University has outlined six core concepts of development and neurobiology that provide a synthesis of the remarkable recent advances in neuroscience and child development research.[2]

- Brains are built over time, with a substantial proportion of brain structure constructed during the early years of life.
- Brain development is shaped by interactions between genes and experience, which depend on environmental input involving sensory stimulation and stable, responsive relationships.
- Brain architecture and developing skills are built "from the bottom up," with basic neural circuits and skills providing the foundation for more advanced circuits and skills over time (for example, babbling precedes the learning of words, which in turn are used to create sentences of increasing length and complexity).
- Emotional, social, and cognitive areas of functioning are inextricably connected and in dynamic reciprocal interaction so that emotional states, social competence, and cognitive capacities influence one another.

- Stress levels that are high, chronic, and unrelieved by protective care burden the body's stress management systems, release persistently high levels of stress hormones that may in time become toxic to brain tissue, and can have adverse effects on brain development, health, behavior, and learning.
- Providing the right conditions for healthy development in early childhood is most effective for long-term well-being because brain plasticity is greatest in the early years and decreases with age.

Brain development, of course, is not an end in itself. It needs to be understood in a "whole child" context in which body and mind are inextricably linked through the mutual influences of biological, social, and cultural factors that interact to create increasingly complex patterns of behavioral and mental organization and integration. Emotional or mental health in infancy and early childhood can be defined as the capacity to regulate emotions and recover from dysregulation; engage in trusting relationships and repair conflict; and explore and learn and cope with frustration—all in the context of the family's social and cultural values and expectations. Each of these facets of early emotional health evolves to become adult emotional health. Each of these facets also involves an effort to integrate harmony and disharmony and the search for repair because dysregulation, mistrust, frustration, and conflict are inescapable components of the human experience. In this lifelong process of growing and learning, brain development is set into motion by genetic programming and given shape by the interaction between genetic and constitutional characteristics and environmental experiences, most particularly by the emotional quality of the child's earliest relationships. In this sense, it is possible to state that relationships become embodied in the child's biology because parental responsiveness shapes the development of the neurological systems involved in the child's responses to stress and social behavior.

Environmental conditions influence not only children's development but also parents' physical and emotional availability and their parenting practices. Poverty, for example, can create stressful circumstances for both the parent and the child. Families in poverty may lack access to adequate nutrition, stable housing, safe neighborhoods, and reliable transportation, creating daily strains that may interfere with time and emotional space for leisure and play between parents and children. Parents in poverty may not be able to buffer their children from these stresses through access to good-quality child care and enriching educational activities, which are as a rule both expensive and difficult to find. These conditions affect millions of children and their families. Young children are the age group most likely to live in poverty: one in five children under the age of 3 in the United States live in families earning less than the federal poverty minimum.[3] The ordeal of young children and families in poverty is not only a private matter because it affects the national fabric through its long-term impact on health, educational attainment, and economic productivity as the toddler becomes an adult.[4,5] As the much-quoted African proverb states, it takes a village to raise a child.

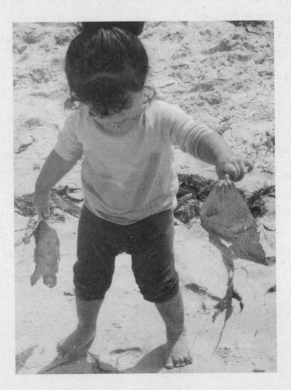

How can we help raise a healthy child? This chapter pays specific attention to the dynamic interplay between the child and caregivers as the main source of developmental nourishment. It focuses on the two major settings of the toddler's explorations: the world outside, where the child exercises the new skills of walking and talking, and the inside world of the body and the mind, which are the sites of new sensations, feelings, and thoughts that provide the substrate for knowing and liking oneself and becoming a member of society. The chapter provides descriptions of how parents and caregivers can equip themselves to respond supportively to the child's need for protection and support in the course of those explorations.

Discovering the World

Toddlerhood brings about a restructuring of the relationship between two basic human motivations: attachment and exploration. Each of these motivations is expressed through specific behaviors that enable parents to understand what the child wants or needs at any given time. Attachment behaviors bring the child close to the parent by approaching, following, searching for the absent parent, reaching for pickup, hugging, cuddling, and clinging. These behaviors indicate that the toddler feels a need for closeness and reassurance. Exploratory behaviors take the child away from the parent in order to walk, climb, run, jump, and inspect the world around. Here, the child's predominant motive is to learn about the world.

As the toddler experiments with attachment and exploration, the parent, in turn, must become comfortable with two complementary sets of caregiving behaviors: protective behaviors that provide the child with nurturance and safety through proximity and closeness, and letting-go behaviors that encourage the child to explore without fear.

Jeannie, 20 months old, is going to her first party. When she and her parents arrive, Jeannie encounters a crowd of strang-

ers in a new house. She holds on to her mother's skirt and hides her face in it, looking out periodically with a worried expression. The hostess tries to entice her with alluring toys, but for the first fifteen minutes Jeannie seems to be glued to her parents. It is clear that she needs close contact with them to feel safe in this unfamiliar situation. Her parents recognize this and do not pressure her. Instead, they point to familiar people and nice features of the room to help her feel at ease. Gradually, as she sees a 9-year-old boy she knows and likes, she relaxes and accepts his offer to play but keeps visual tabs on her parents, who make encouraging comments. Soon Jeannie tags along happily after the other children, although she returns periodically for a cuddle or to show her parents a toy.

Harry, 18 months old, has been asking the whole morning to go to the "pak" (park). It is only nine o'clock, but this Sunday morning, Harry has been awake since 6:30. Cuddling with him in bed, his father keeps him at bay with some toys and short-term promises: "After we finish breakfast, Harry. First I'll get up, and then I'll shower, then we'll go to the park." This litany satisfies Harry for a while. He goes back and forth from the parental bedroom to his own room and brings toys to play with by his father's side. He asks periodically, "Daddy up now? Pak now?" By the time they finally arrive at the playground, Harry lets go of his father's hand and runs joyously ahead to the slide. He is eager to explore, and he knows that his father is following close behind. For a while Harry climbs on the slide by himself, a favorite and well-practiced activity. His father watches him with pleasure, commenting every now and then on his son's feats. After a while Harry decides to move on to the swings. He turns to his father, takes his hand, and starts walking in that direction, saying "Daddy swing." Harry knows that now he needs his father's help and turns to him trustingly with the expectation of getting it.

A Secure Base

These two examples show that the balance between attachment and exploration in the child is mirrored by the balance between protectiveness and encouragement of exploration in the parent. When things go well enough, the parent serves as a secure base from which the child sets forth to explore and to which he can trustingly return for solace before moving off yet again.

Because of this parental role, the balance between attachment and exploratory behaviors in the child has been aptly named "secure base behavior."[6] The toddler, absorbed in the challenges of learning and exploration, uses the parent as a haven of comfort and security when something is scary or when he is tired or in need.

Adults often feel irritated when toddlers become clingy or ask to be held in situations that to grown-up eyes appear perfectly safe. For example, they may feel impatient when their child wants to follow them into the bathroom, cries when a stranger pats his head, clings desperately at the sight of the meekest of dogs, or calls out for company instead of falling asleep at night.

Although these behaviors can be quite trying for parents, it is actually adaptive for a young child to be scared of common situations such as the dark, being left alone or with strangers, and unfamiliar or intense stimuli such as loud noises or sudden movement. In the course of human evolution, such situations became associated with an increased risk of danger in the form, for example, of accidents or predator attacks. Humans (including children) are biologically equipped to recognize cues to danger, and we respond with built-in behavioral mechanisms that maximize safety and enhance survival.[7, 8] These mechanisms include moving closer to people we trust in search of protection—the very behavior that toddlers instinctively rely on when they are upset.

Locomotion is an eloquent preverbal indicator of what the child is feeling. Seeking proximity and contact (attachment behavior) indicates that the child is afraid and needs help to feel more secure. Moving away from the parents (exploratory behavior) suggests that the child feels safe enough and is eager to seek novelty rather than security. The child's development is enhanced when parents are able to recognize the meaning of these behaviors and respond appropriately to them.

Taking Early Fears Seriously: The Biology of Survival

Young children routinely face potentially dangerous situations as part of their everyday life and are often frightened by those situations, making stress and fear an integral although unwelcome presence in development. Stress and fear may range in intensity from expectable, normative, and manageable (e.g., the toddler's distress when first starting child care) to extreme and lasting dysregulations in physiological and emotional balance as the result of traumatic experiences that impair the young child's trust in the parent's capacity to provide protection (e.g., very painful medical procedures, witnessing a violent situation, experiencing maltreatment). Coping with stress and trauma usually involves a three-step process:

1. Recognizing the potential danger
2. Evaluating the situation to choose an effective coping strategy (e.g., fleeing, fighting, freezing in place, turning to others for help)
3. Using the coping strategy identified as most useful

This three-step process usually takes split seconds and is essential to survival. In infants, toddlers, and preschoolers, the most frequent and reliable coping mechanism is to use attachment behavior, turning to the parent for close contact and reassurance. The parents' physical and emotional availability in response to the child's bids for protection is a key element in helping the child return to a state of emotional regulation and a feeling of safety.

Recent research on brain development demonstrates that the areas of the brain involved in detecting, giving meaning, and responding to signals of danger and safety—the limbic system, including the amyg-

dala—are already functional in the first year of life. A 12-year longitudinal study using MRI imaging of amygdala and hippocampus growth
starting at 1 month of age showed peak growth spurts around 2 years
of age and a larger growth rate in brain volume in the first years of
life, leading the researchers to conclude that infancy is a critical period
for neural development.[9] The concept of sensitive periods is used to
refer to developmental stages in which experiences have a particularly
strong influence on the unfolding development of the brain, with the
potential to alter performance in a long-lasting manner. During early,
sensitive periods of brain development, the regions of the brain involved in fear responses may overproduce neural connections in response to intense and chronic stressful or traumatic experiences that
are not alleviated by protective caregiving responses, leaving the child
vulnerable to increased risk of anxiety and other emotional difficulties.
In contrast, young children with secure attachment relationships, who
have consistent experiences of parental responsiveness to their signals
of need, are better able to recover successfully from the stress of frightening experiences.[10] In one study, for example, 24-month-old toddlers
were observed while a stranger approached—a natural cue to danger.
Toddlers who were free to approach their mothers showed fewer signs
of physiological stress (freezing, fear responses) than children who
were physically restrained from approaching their mothers.[11] Far from
becoming "coddled" or "spoiled," young children whose parents respond protectively to their signals of fear become more emotionally
resilient because in learning to trust their parents they also learn to
trust themselves.

The Toddler's Need for Protection

The ability to engage in secure base behavior makes the toddler an active agent in contributing to her own protection. In fact, toddlers seem
to be equipped with an internal monitor system that enables them to
scan the environment and keep track of conditions that make them feel
endangered or secure. Toddlers remain vulnerable to many dangers

they cannot understand or anticipate, and parents must remain vigilant to keep them safe, but it is also important to tailor adult responses in ways that reinforce and expand the child's self-care capacities.

Toddlers take the initiative in taking care of themselves by monitoring their parents' whereabouts and remaining relatively close to them in unfamiliar situations. A British investigator tape-recorded fifteen-minute descriptions of individual toddlers' behavior as they moved about in a London park while the mother remained seated on a bench or on the grass. The results showed that, with a few exceptions, the toddlers seemed to determine their own boundaries and stayed within about two hundred feet from the mother.[12] This happened to coincide with the mother's own judgment of what constituted a safe distance. The mothers did not retrieve their children if they remained within the boundary but did so if the toddlers strayed beyond it. However, nearly 70 percent of the children never went far enough to warrant retrieval. The toddlers had the opportunity to wander off if they wished to, but they managed their exploration in a way that kept them within a safe distance but also blissfully free from the mother's direct physical control.

The exquisite details of secure base behavior are clearly illustrated by different aspects of this study. The toddlers moved in "bouts" that either increased their distance from the mother or brought them closer to her. The bouts accounted for most of the children's locomotion: the mothers served as the center of the children's activities, and they organized their comings and goings in relation to where the mother was. It is particularly telling that the children were most likely to stay in one place when they were close to the mother (within three feet); playing at a distance from the mother tended to be brief. In other words, the children felt most secure where it was actually safest and preferred to spend more time there.

When they were away from the mother, the toddlers kept track of her whereabouts through quick visual checks and pointing at interesting sights. The mothers routinely ignored those behaviors, with one major exception: if the toddler pointed at a potential source of danger, such as a dog on the loose, the mothers called out for their children to come closer and picked them up if they did not comply. This suggests that pointing is an important behavior that helps the child learn what is safe and what is dangerous through the parents' response. When the object the toddler pointed at was safe, the mother paid no attention or expressed mild interest; when it was threatening, she took definite action to protect.

The mothers' behavior in this study illustrates how parents can help their children to be safe and to feel secure. The mothers did not interfere with exploration and did not feel the need to be by their child's side constantly. They took their cues from the child and were available but not intrusive. On the other hand, they moved in instantly when protective action was needed.

Parents' readiness for action is essential because the toddler's ability to cooperate in her own protection is by no means foolproof. The young child's mechanisms for monitoring the environment, though well developed, remain immature for a long time. For example, toddlers do not have fully developed distance vision and cannot appraise accurately whether a somewhat distant object may pose a threat. In addition, the biologically based cues of danger (darkness, sudden loud noises, animals, being alone) are only a subsample of the myriad threats to safety in a modern society. Dangers may lurk in speeding cars, seemingly friendly strangers, stairs, elevators. The list is endless, and the toddler is equipped neither through biology nor through experience to anticipate those dangers. Learning to protect oneself is a long and painstaking process that is never truly complete.

This means that, in spite of their innate competence in seeking protection, children's safety depends largely on adults' better-developed capacity to anticipate danger. Accidents are the leading cause of death in early childhood, a chilling reminder of toddlers' vulnerability. In many circumstances, the adult needs to provide protection quickly and unilaterally, sometimes in spite of the child's energetic protests. Other times, the parent cannot anticipate the potential for hurt in seemingly benign situations. There are also situations where the child has an intense fear reaction that is based on misperception rather than facts. The psychologist and psychotherapist Arietta Slade has written about the inner work of "imagining fear" as a way of putting ourselves into the position of the young child and responding protectively both to external danger and to the internal experience of it.[13]

Secure Base as Metaphor for Inner Balance

Children do not encounter danger only while moving. They may ingest harmful substances, play with matches or sharp objects, or pull heavy objects onto themselves. Every one of the child's encounters with the world may elicit fear or danger and lead to the need for reassurance or protection. In every autonomous action, the toddler comes face-to-face with the paradox of being free to explore yet held hostage to internal limitations (such as fear) as well as external constraints (such as the parents' prohibitions).

The concept of secure base is a useful metaphor for the push and pull of emotions that the toddler experiences in this new stage. Parents help the child to sort out when to explore and when to come near. In this process, toddlers gradually develop an inner trust in the possibility of feeling safe and protected while also becoming outgoing, competent, and increasingly independent. The secure base, initially represented by the parents, becomes internalized as a stable component of the child's personality.

In learning to balance closeness and exploration, the toddler encounters other emotional dualities. Depending on what happens in each situation, coming close to the parent and moving away can represent intimacy versus autonomy; social belonging versus individual fulfillment; being tied down and held captive by others versus soaring free; subservience and humiliation versus personal power; love versus hate and alienation.

Toddlers experience every one of these states because they are constantly facing circumstances that make them feel either powerful and strong or small and helpless. They may dart off and be reckless and minutes later become clingy and whiny and want everything done for them.

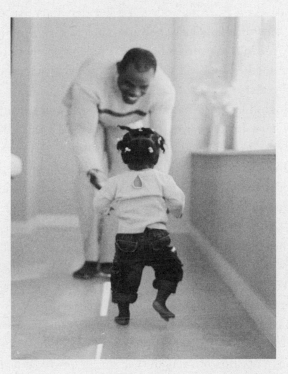

When Johnny can walk from one end of the living room to the other without falling even once, he feels invincible. When his older brother intercepts him and pushes him to the floor, he feels he has collapsed in shame and wants to bite his attacker (if only he could catch up with him!). When Johnny's father rescues him, scolds the brother, and helps Johnny on his way, hope and triumph rise up again in Johnny's heart; everything he wants seems within reach. When exhaustion overwhelms him a few minutes later, he worries that he will never again be able to go that far and bursts into tears.

From the parents' perspective, this is a bewildering state of affairs. If adults experienced and enacted the full range of feelings available to an average toddler in the course of a day, they would collapse from emotional exhaustion (and often do, from the effort to keep up with their child). As it is, living with a toddler demands that parents be ready for anything. Gradually, however, the child will come to an increasingly modulated experience and expression of emotions, and the turmoil of toddlerhood will subside into the relative harmony of the preschool years.

The English language has many expressions that convey the high regard we have for those who can move on their own: "That person will go far"; "She can stand on her own two feet"; "He is an upright person."[14] Though accurate, these accolades play down the hidden liabilities of autonomy. Going far on one's own two feet has its dangers: unprotected aloneness and the possibility of falling and getting hurt. Toddlers' play with blocks, which consists of building towers and then making them fall, is a good symbol of the sudden collapses that often follow new feats of locomotion. By engineering the fall of the tower, the child makes happen what usually happens to him. In other words, he takes control of the situation and acquires mastery over it.

Playing can occur only when the child feels safe. The sequence of building towers and making them fall is a form of remembering hard times from a position of strength (i.e., sitting down). When the child actually falls hard, she does not play. She turns to Mommy or Daddy for help. But this welcome rescue has its own inherent danger because the parents may worry about another fall and forbid further forays. It is no wonder that many toddlers rush off from the parent's arms the moment they can get back on their feet. Children often recover from their mishaps far more quickly than their parents do and are eager to take off again. Being held back is one of the great frustrations of this age.

Developmental Changes in Secure Base Behavior

Toddlers' balance between attachment and exploratory behavior is never static. It fluctuates depending on many factors, including the situation, the parents' mood, and the child's mood. Sometimes the child's impulse to explore predominates for weeks at a time, only to be replaced by a period of intense clinginess that makes the parents worry that their child has seriously regressed. Other times the reverse is true. Weeks of clinginess are superseded by a powerful thrust toward exploration, and the parents find themselves longing for a little more of the very dependence they so recently worried about. In spite of these fluctuations, some broad developmental trends do emerge and are outlined here.[15]

The "Junior Toddler": Walking and Talking

Between about 12 and 18 months of age, most toddlers are elated by their newfound ability to move around in the world. In the upright position, things can be seen from new visual angles and different perspectives, and the child practices his emerging locomotive skills again and again. Returns to the parent are often brief and may consist of no more than a touch; it is the forays into the world that hold the greatest thrill. So absorbed can toddlers become in their new achievements that for a while they may be quite oblivious to knocks and falls. The important thing is to keep on practicing, discovering, mastering.

Exhilaration is a key mood of this period. The toddler loves to run off again and again, only to squeal in delight on being pursued and scooped up by the parent. This game is of great symbolic importance for young toddlers. It reassures them that mobility need not mean alienation or abandonment and that their parents will not leave them to their own (fledgling) devices but will *want* to retrieve the child again and again. For a worn-out parent, this game may seem like an endless tease. For the toddler, it is a crucial reassurance that independence and togetherness can go hand in hand.

The best evidence of the toddler's need to be retrieved when going beyond his limits is what happens when the parent does not do it: the toddler falls down or gets hurt, and the episode ends in tears instead of giggles. In such a situation, the implicit parental message to the child is "You are on your own, and going off in a giddy spree will get you into trouble." The range of experience and feeling the toddler learns to perceive as safe becomes prematurely narrowed down.

Locomotion puts the toddler's body at the center of her experience. Her legs can accomplish wonders: walk, climb, jump, run. The legs, in turn, are in the service of eager little hands. She can now climb onto the dresser to reach that colorful porcelain doll that has always beckoned to her. She can drag all the stuffed animals from her room to join Mom in the kitchen. She can squeeze herself under a cabinet to find a long-lost marble and put it into her mouth. She can be silent and out of sight for a long time, only to be found carefully tearing the pages of a book that she found by climbing on her parents' desk.

The body is the riveting agent of all these pursuits. At this age children first learn to recognize themselves in the mirror and delight in pointing to and naming their own and everybody else's eyes, nose, mouth, ears, hair, hands, feet. They find new interest in their genitals, which they explore attentively and learn a name for. They experience an irresistible urge to bite as new baby teeth erupt in rapid succession. Many moments of intense absorption are spent poking at the belly button, fingering the genitals, looking in the mirror, biting and chewing, examining toes.

Finding names for the important things of the world is as momentous an achievement as walking. There is a marvelous symmetry in the fact that the abilities to name and to walk occur at about the same time. The great myths of creation describe the world as coming into being through the Word. The human child, too, creates meaning through naming the world she is discovering. Some of the names coincide, exactly or approximately, with the labels adopted by the culture at large: "mamma," "daddy," "wow-wow" (for dog), 'ba-ba" (for bottle). Others are totally idiosyncratic, magically created by the child for his own personal use. Language opens new vistas, just as walking does. The joy of creating meaning through words can be as exhilarating as the joy of creating new horizons through motion.

Walking and talking come together in ways that give toddlers a new confidence in their ability to make themselves feel secure.

Ari, 18 months, runs after a kitten, thoroughly intoxicated by the pleasure of the pursuit. As he turns around, he sees that his

mother is not close at hand but has stayed behind, at a greater distance from him than ever before. His face registers momentary shock and disbelief, but he quickly recovers and runs back to her, yelling, "Who coming to me? Who coming to me?" This is the call his mother uses (in the adult version) to entice him back when he strays too far, and he has now made it his own to support himself in a moment of need.

The fear of losing the parent. When the parent or a trusted caregiver is present, toddlers feel elated with their new skills. When the parent leaves, the child often cries and protests by clinging and trying to stop the separation. During the parent's absence, the child's mood can become sober and low key. Activity level often slows down, and interest in exploration diminishes. The toddler seems to turn inward, as if holding on to the reassuring memory of the absent parent. When the external secure base is absent, the young child needs to work hard to evoke it internally through memory and imagination. At this early stage, the toddler has not yet learned that "out of sight" need not mean "out of mind."

The low-key mood comes to an end when the parent returns. The toddler's response to the reunion is an indicator of her personal style and of the way she is experiencing her relationship with the parent.[16] Some children may burst into tears on first seeing the parent as a way of relieving pent-up tension. Others may "pick a fight" by becoming provocative or defiant. Ambivalence may be expressed by simultaneously clambering up on the parent and pushing away from her or giving little kicks against her side. Sometimes the child's low-key mood persists in the form of avoidance after the parent's return: looking away or even moving away from rather than moving toward the parent. Some toddlers continue to play as if nothing has happened, totally ignoring the parent's greeting.

These various responses reflect the child's unique style of showing anger and distress about the parent's absence. The child may worry that the parent is not truly back and may leave soon again, either physically or emotionally. The child's ambivalent greeting is an effort to protect himself from yet another experience of disappointment through renewed separation. Parents can help alleviate this anxiety by being emotionally available when they spend time with the child, by saying good-bye before leaving, by promising to return, and by greeting the child with pleasure and affection even if the child rebuffs them at first. Chapters 7 and 8 focus at length on separation difficulties and what parents can do to help alleviate them.

Most frequently, however, toddlers greet their parents joyfully after a manageable separation. Here, too, the specific responses are quite varied and reflect the child's individual style. One toddler may smile or greet the parents from a distance; another may show them a toy; a third may come close to them and insist on being picked up. All these are attachment-promoting rather than exploratory/distancing behaviors. These unambivalent responses indicate that the child trusts the parent's ongoing availability even during a temporary absence. The child's inner sense of a secure base helps him bridge the gap until the parent returns.

Sometimes there can be too much togetherness, and the child rebels by becoming testy and uncooperative, as the example below illustrates.

Natalia, 14 months, and her mother attend a weekly swimming lesson for toddlers. For forty-five minutes Natalia holds on to her mother as they splash about the swimming pool together. Although she loves these sessions, Natalia invariably becomes angry, moody, and negativistic afterward, when her mother tries to shower and dress her after the swim. Natalia's mother realizes that the child needs a respite from the intense reliance on her that is needed in the swimming pool. She lets Natalia run around on her own after the swimming lesson until the child spontaneously approaches her again. Once Natalia shows that she is ready for more togetherness, the mother tells her that it is time to get showered and dressed. Now Natalia complies happily because, after having a chance to explore on her own, she no longer feels engulfed by her dependency on her mother.

This example shows how a parent can use her toddler's unspoken cues to understand what is needed. Natalia's mother was serving as a secure base by recognizing when it was time to hold back and waiting patiently for her child to return. Parents may feel rejected when their child responds by ignoring them or pushing them away. At such times it can help to remember that the child's relationship with them is in the process of being built and can take different forms depending on how the parent responds to moments of frustration and hurt. Rejecting children for rejecting us prolongs the conflict by making both the parent and the child hold on to their anger. Young children have enormous power to make us feel loved or unloved, important or secondary—and adults have equally enormous power to make children feel that way. Regardless of how they may treat us in the moment, they need our consistent message that we are stronger and wiser than they are and we can tolerate their emotional upheavals and ambivalence without responding in kind. When we do not feel stronger or wiser and when we cannot withstand with grace the intense emotions children arouse in us, we can use the experience to reflect on what happened once we are calmer. These reflections can help us understand our own and the child's experience so we can be better prepared for the next moment of challenge.

This attitude is particularly helpful when the toddler shows shifting preferences between his primary caregivers—a very common occurrence at this age. Babies may adore both their mother and their father, or their two mommies, or their two daddies—adjusting seamlessly to the back-and-forth between primary caregivers while having very individual ways of relating to each of them. By 12 months, there is often a shift in how the child uses each parent figure and there might be a new insistence that only one of the parents will do in situations of stress. Many fathers who share equally in their young children's care find themselves rebuffed when they want to console their toddler, only to find that the child reaches out to the mother while crying to be held by her. Same-sex parents also report that the toddler establishes a preference for one parent in situations of distress even if both parents are equally responded to in stress-free conditions. The preference for one parent over the other may shift again and again at different stages in the child's life, or it may remain stable. It may also be situation-specific, with one parent being preferred for some activities and the other parent being sought for other situations. Single parents often describe the pressure of knowing that their child cannot turn to another parent figure in the household. To alleviate this pressure, many single parents create shared living arrangements with other single parents and their children or cultivate a community of other single-parent families that provides support and relief.

The emotional climate of the family—how parents and other caregivers get along with one another, how they coordinate their values, expectations, and practices toward the child—helps contain the upheavals that the toddler may experience in relation to one or the other adult. When caregivers undermine each other or compete to be the child's favorite parent, the resulting strains are often reflected in child symptoms such as aggression, sleeping problems, or frequent and intense temper tantrums. Conflicts between parents and between parents and children are inevitable, but adults' coordinated efforts at problem solving give a message of emotional availability even in situations of mismatched wishes and needs. This effort at problem solving helps create secure family relationships and safe intimacy in the long run. Everybody wins when parents establish a collaborative partnership with each other as coparents. In striving toward a secure family atmosphere for their child, many parents find that they can heal their own early insecurities and become more confident that the inevitable cycles of emotional disruptions within themselves, with each other, and with their child can be repaired and do not constitute the essence of who they are.

A Transitional Phase: Heightened Insecurity

By about 18 months, locomotion has been perfected and is no longer the driving obsession of the child's life. Instead of being a goal in itself, walking becomes the means to an end. The effort at mastery shifts from locomotion per se to the goals that can be achieved through it.

This evolution contains a psychological paradox. For many children, separation anxiety is at its highest at about 18 months. Longitudinal studies of children's responses to brief separations from the mother show that crying peaks at about this time and declines gradually thereafter.[17] Similarly, the child psychoanalyst Margaret Mahler and her colleagues describe the onset at this age of a behavior they call "shadowing," which refers to the child's incessant monitoring of the mother's every move.[18]

Children also become more demanding of the mother's attention during this period. Dinah, at 22 months, began to yell "Talk only with me!" whenever her mother tried to maintain a conversation with others. Michael, 24 months, agreed to go on family outings only if his mother promised to sit next to him and speak to him alone during the car ride. Some toddlers want to drink from the mother's glass and eat from her plate. They may also offer the mother bits of their food and bring her interesting objects, which they pile on her lap. A combination of escalating demands, screaming, and tears often results when the wishes to have Mommy all to oneself are not granted. The child often becomes very sensitive to minor cuts or hurts and may be unusually distressed when things are broken or disappear.

Why would the toddler become more clingy and needy just when she is also more competent at being on her own? It makes sense to think that following a period of absorption in locomotion and exploration between 12 and 18 months, the toddler needs to rediscover the parent as the ongoing provider of protection and emotional support. Once young children have mastered mobility, they are also more aware of the troubles it can bring. Precisely because the toddler feels better able to stand on her own, she can now indulge the wishes for protective closeness with the parent that were put on the back burner while she was learning to walk.

Again the metaphor of a secure base helps to explain this process. Just as from moment to moment and from day to day the toddler alternates between moving away to explore and then coming back close to the parent, so the growing child goes through extended periods where he is more intensely invested either in exploration or in intimacy. Much of toddlerhood can be understood in terms of the child's gradually coming to grips with the two motives of attachment and exploration, integrating them into a unique individual style that becomes relatively stable through life.

The Senior Toddler: Inner Awareness and Socialization

Around the time of the second birthday, the child's inner life becomes increasingly more accessible to the parent through language and symbolic play. He learns to label feelings as well as physical objects and is quite proud to announce that he is glad, sad, or mad. The words "me" and "mine" become talismans against a world only too ready to take his treasures away. It is not unusual for a 2-year-old to use the word "mine" to greet another child, while a favored toy is clutched firmly in hand. Such a toddler already knows that prevention is the best cure.

Feelings that cannot be talked about often find expression in symbolic play or in reenactment through action. Acting, for the child, can be a form of remembering.

> A little girl, Rhonda, who had lost her mother at age 2, carried socks from the laundry basket and spread them all over the house. Her mother had used old socks to dust the furniture. The nanny asked Rhonda to put the socks back into the basket. The child dutifully obeyed but kept one sock. When the nanny insisted that all the socks be put back, Rhonda retreated to a corner with a sad expression, hugging the sock to her chest. This sequence expressed what she could not articulate: that she missed her mommy and wanted to hold on to her.

The fear of losing the parents' love. The new ability to imagine and fantasize enriches the child's inner life. One consequence is that the older toddler acquires a more sophisticated sense of what to fear. While the younger child worries primarily about the mother's actual whereabouts and is afraid of separation and loss, the older toddler contends with a subtler but equally chilling dread: the parents' disapproval, which he equates (quite understandably) with losing their love. Some of the most meaningful dialogues of this age unfold around the parents' message: "Even when I am angry at you, I still love you." This unbelievably good news is assimilated only gradually by the toddler, who needs to perform a veritable cognitive feat to understand it. He has to counterbalance the immediate and powerfully concrete experience of a parent's angry face and booming voice (or, in the case of more controlled people, an uncharacteristically cold demeanor) with the accumulated memory of past loving exchanges, which at the moment may seem too distant to be relied upon.

It is hard to remember a reassuring past while facing a frightening present. Even adults often lose faith when faced with this ordeal and may ask themselves, "Will things ever feel right again?" Parents often have to remind themselves that they can love and be angry at the same time, and some parents learn this for the first time in the process of reassuring their child.

The toddler's wish to please. The fear of losing a parent's love has a beneficial side: the toddler is willing to do almost anything in order to preserve it. This is a powerful aid in helping the child to develop social awareness and, eventually, a moral conscience. The child's love for the parent is so strong (even when not so visible) that it causes him to change his behavior: to refrain from hitting and biting, to share toys with a peer, to become toilet trained. This wish for approval is the parent's most reliable ally in the process of socializing the child. Appealing to it is far more effective and much more emotionally healthy than threats of punishment.

Emma, 22 months, has acquired an annoying habit of screeching whenever she does not get what she wants. Every time this occurs, her parents say firmly, "Stop it, Emma. It hurts my ears." If she does not stop, they put their hands over their ears and say, "Now I can't hear you." After about a week, the screeching declines markedly, and by the third week it disappears completely.

David, 28 months, has bitten his baby brother. His mother scolds him: "I told you not to do that, David. I am very angry at you." David comes close to his mother and cries his heart out while burying his head in her lap. His mother has her hands full calming down the baby, who is still screaming from the bite. At first she has no patience or resources for David's distress, but then she caresses his head and says, "I don't like it when I'm angry at you, but you can't bite. It's a no-no." David looks at her very seriously, turns his head from side to side, and says, "No-no." His mother repeats "No-no," now in a softer tone, and helps him get back to playing. In the following days, David is seen making pretend biting movements while shaking his head and saying to himself "No-no."

These children are complying with their parents' expectations because they want to please them. Toddlers who are growing well seek approval but are not obsessed with it. They can tolerate reasonable amounts of frustration, and they can go back and forth flexibly between asserting their will and complying with the will of others. Children who are growing well also feel reasonably comfortable with a full range of emotions. Michael, 3 years old, was asked by his solicitous mother if he was happy. His answer: "I am happy *and* sad *and* angry *and* bitey *and* clingy." He refused to be seduced into acknowledging only his happy side.

Parents need to be careful not to squander the gift of their child's innate wish to please them. Toddlers whose parents are too critical may experience difficulties in their emotional development. Such toddlers may be excessively worried about losing love and may become overly compliant. At the other extreme, the child may use defiance as the only way to pursue his agenda, because he anticipates parental opposition and gears himself to fight back. Either reaction—excessive submission or persistent negativism—signals a restriction in the capacity for flexible give-and-take available to the child.

Parents whose children are showing either of those patterns will do well to examine carefully their attitudes of, expectations for, and responses to their child. It is likely that becoming less demanding and more reassuring, supportive, and praising will quickly alleviate their child's difficulties. Chapters 3, 7, and 8 examine common struggles and anxieties of this period and suggest specific steps for coping with them.

The urge to assert one's will. Paradoxically, the toddler wants to please but also needs to risk parental anger and disappointment again and again. This is because being true to oneself becomes a compelling motive at this age. The cycle of disagreement-resolution-reconciliation, occurring with greater or lesser intensity throughout the day, is a cornerstone of the toddler's psychological growth. It allows the child to know that she is not a clone of the parent but has an autonomous will, that disagreements with loved ones are inevitable, and that anger can be experienced and survived. As the great pediatrician T. Berry Brazelton pointed out, toddlerhood is at its essence a (sometimes ambivalent) declaration of independence.[19]

Discovering the Body

The healthy toddler's curiosity knows no bounds. When not in motion, he is deeply absorbed in discovering the mysteries of the body. He touches, pokes, and pulls at himself, learns to recognize himself in the mirror, delights in finding the names for different body parts, and is entranced by the discovery of gender differences. Bodily experiences powerfully shape the child's unfolding sense of who he is and his feelings of security or anxiety.

Self-Recognition

Babies show interest in their mirror reflections early in the first year. At about 4 months, they smile at themselves; between 8 and 12 months, they show active excitement, laughing, babbling, and jiggling with delight. These happy responses are not altered if the mirror is distorted.

The babies seem interested primarily in how their movements change the mirror image, much as if they were squeezing a toy to make noise or shaking a mobile. The question "Who is the baby in the mirror?" does not seem to enter their minds.

These responses change noticeably in the second year. Between 13 and 15 months, toddlers become serious and subdued when looking at themselves in the mirror. If the mirror is distorted, they stare at it intently, as if trying to understand what they are seeing. When someone surreptitiously places a smudge on the child's face, the junior toddler may tentatively touch the smudge *in the mirror*. There is no recognition that the child in the mirror is a reflection of the self.

At about 18 months, toddlers begin to show that they recognize themselves in the mirror. The clearest evidence for this conclusion is an experiment in which toddlers' faces are surreptitiously marked with lipstick. Younger infants point to their image in the mirror rather than to themselves. After 18 months, they touch the mark on their own faces rather than pointing to the mirror.[20] At about the same time, toddlers begin to use the pronouns "I," "me," and "mine," and even proper names, to refer to themselves.

These observations suggest that the toddlers are now able to experience themselves objectively, as people who can be seen from the outside as well as felt from the inside. This important development makes them more self-aware and more interested in their own appearance. Parents report that at about this time the toddler begins to have strong opinions about what to wear and how to look.

> Amy, 2 years old, is being dressed by her mother to go to a party. It is winter, and the mother judiciously chooses warm clothes, including a wool sweater. Amy screams, "Sundress, sundress!" The mother explains that it is too cold for a sundress, but Amy refuses to yield. She twists her arms and her legs to prevent her mother from dressing her, all the while screaming with such determination that the mother gives up going to the party and asks her husband to go by himself.

In its beginnings, the child's ability to see herself from the outside can be easily disrupted by unusual departures from her customary appearance.

> At 22 months, Jessica was bitten in the face by another child and had a swollen lip for a few days afterward. During that period, she repeatedly went to the mirror and looked worriedly at herself, repeating softly, "Jessica?" She seemed to be asking whether she had remained herself in spite of her changed looks.

It is a common observation that toddlers become quite distressed when their parents wear masks, even if the child has watched them putting the masks on. The visual immediacy of the change is so compelling that it overrides the child's emerging ability to identify internal continuity in spite of differences in external appearance. That is why Halloween can be disconcerting and even frightening for some toddlers; the people surrounding them change too radically from the way they look in everyday life. Knowing this can help parents help their child by choosing costumes that do not drastically alter the appearance and by opting for small settings rather than trick-or-treating in the street, which may be too frightening for many toddlers.

After their second birthday, toddlers become more confident and self-assured in their response to the mirror. Now if a smudge of lipstick is placed on their faces, they may wipe it off or look around for the lipstick and try to apply it to themselves. However, distorting mirrors elicit worried looks. The children are still evolving a sense of how they look in the mirror, and any dramatic changes are interpreted as changes in themselves. It does not occur to them that a mirror would play tricks on them. In that sense, they are already partaking of the adult preoccupation with how they look and the relationship between "outer look" and "inner feel."

Gender Awareness and Sexual Curiosity

The interest in how the inside and the outside fit together leads quite naturally to attention to the genitals. Infants of all ages like to touch themselves, but toddlers do so with a new purposefulness. In the second year of life there is an increased capacity for urethral and anal control. As a result, toddlers become more aware of their genitals and more capable of differentiating between anal and genital sensations. Their scrutiny of their bodies helps them find out how they are made. Also, they associate their actions directly with the different kinds of pleasure they feel as a result.

The discovery of the genitals and the pleasure they give is a source of tremendous pride and exuberance. Toddlers love to run around naked, to show off, and to be admired. The body with all its wonders has center stage.

Ira, 30 months, holds his penis while peeing and proclaims, "This is the Empire State." (His father, an architect, had just shown him a picture of that building and told him what a big, beautiful structure it was.)

The future of the toddler's pleasure in herself depends largely on the parents' reaction to it. Responding to pleasure with pleasure puts the child's experience on the firm, reliable base of parental acceptance.

This does not mean that a parent should feel compelled to celebrate and admire all of the child's self-displays. Personal standards and cultural norms are important, and it is up to the individual parents and their social circle to judge which behaviors are publicly appropriate and which are not acceptable in their household and their milieu.

It is the parents' tone and attitude, rather than the specific content of their teaching, that help to socialize the child without squashing pleasure or engendering shame. Giving a toddler something other than his genitals to occupy himself with works smoothly in most situations. When a child is overly self-absorbed in a setting that the parent finds inappropriate, it may help to say something along the lines of "I know it feels good when you touch yourself. You can do that in your room or when you take a bath, because it is something private."

Young children's evolving understanding of the genitals as private is exemplified in an exchange between 4-year-old Matthew and his 2-year-old sister, Elena, who was mesmerized by watching him pee and wanted to touch his penis. He responded firmly, "No, Elena. That is my penis. That is my private part, and nobody touches it." Matthew had learned what his parents had taught him. The following example illustrates a father's response in a similar situation.

Mary, 24 months old, routinely wanders into the bathroom and watches attentively as her father urinates. This happens a few times, with her focusing on the stream of urine. One day, however, she looks at his penis with wide eyes and reaches out to touch it. The father, embarrassed, says, "No, Mary, that's private," and closes his pants. Mary looks very serious and then moves

away. From then on, her father closes the door to the bathroom in an effort to show Mary what he means by "private."

Having a penis or a vagina not only gives pleasure but allows for comparisons with other boys and girls. By about 18 months, children have acquired a deeply ingrained sense of their gender and identify themselves as a boy who belongs with other boys or a girl who belongs with other girls. Mutual comparisons are rampant and go on unabated until the child is 5 or 6 years old. These comparisons can create pleasure in oneself and others but also some anxiety.

Lori, in the bathtub with her friend Nick, tells him, "Yours is gorgeous, Nick." Nick smiles in agreement but does not return the compliment. After a pause, Lori says, "Tell me that mine is gorgeous, too." Children may indeed need reassurance that they are "gorgeous" just the way they are made.

Many older toddlers and young preschoolers can become quite preoccupied with genital differences between the sexes and test out possible explanations.

Oscar tells his mother, "I know why girls don't have a penis. God ran out of them! And for the ones he ran out, he punched a hole in them!"

Matthew comes up with a different theory: "Mom, maybe your penis is in your butt. Where else could it be?"

Knowing that one is a boy or a girl and liking one's gender do not imply that the toddler has given up the notion of being both genders at the same time. Many toddlers who can put their fantasies into words declare emphatically that they have both a penis *and* a vagina. Boys are convinced for the longest time that they can get pregnant, give birth, and be both a mommy and a daddy to their baby. Girls make plans for marrying their mothers as well as their fathers. Boys want to grow breasts and suckle their babies. Everybody wants to have everything. Here again, as in many other settings, toddlers refuse to accept the constraints imposed on them by outside rules—including those of biology.

The emerging awareness that one is a boy or a girl but cannot be both is accompanied by a sense of loss that is often expressed symbolically in children's play. Below is Lori's expression that she is missing something as she plays it out with her mother:

> Lori (as she undresses her doll): Let's see what's happening to this girl.
> Mother: What happened?
> Lori: She has to go to the hospital.
> Mother: Why does she have to go to the hospital?
> Lori: She lost her tail.
> Mother: What is going to happen at the hospital?
> Lori: She'll get an injection.
> Mother: What about the tail? Will she get it back?
> Lori: No. A frog bit my tail. (Pause.)
> Lori: Do you have a tail?
> Mother: No.
> Lori: Get one from a dog. (Laughs and rides off on her play horse, which, by the way, has a very notable tail.)

On another occasion Lori asks her mother to tape a carrot between her legs and then runs all over the house with the dangling carrot, giggling with excitement. Another time her father sees her standing by the toilet, trying to pee like a boy.

It is generally accepted that girls wish they had a penis and express this wish in many overt and covert ways. It is less widely acknowledged that boys wish they had breasts and carried babies. Ari's version of those wishes as they unfold between 28 and 34 months is described below. This period coincides with his mother's second pregnancy.

> **Ari is carrying a doll held tightly in his arms. He says, "Don't cry, baby. I will give you milk." He pretends to breast-feed the doll.**

> Ari stuffs a small pillow under his sweater and parades around the house, saying, "I am having a baby."

> Ari is on the potty, quite constipated. He pushes to evacuate and is in some pain. He says, "Maybe I am having a baby."

> Ari looks at himself in the mirror with a serious expression. He says, "Look at my big stomach. Everybody will think that I am pregnant. Nobody will believe it is because I ate so much."

Perhaps the best approach to a toddler's wish to partake of the gifts of both genders is to sympathize with it and to provide corrective information only when the child asks for it directly. Far from being harmful, wishful thinking and fantasy play such as Lori's and Ari's provide the child with a safe setting to explore reality at her or his own pace. As they experiment, children come up with their own explanations for things. Parents do best not to correct those explanations unless the child asks directly for their input. The child's fanciful ideas will be useful temporarily and will be replaced by increasingly more accurate versions of reality when the child is ready. The parent's role is to be close at hand to provide the facts that the child wants without adding more information than the child is asking for.

> Martin, 36 months, asks his pregnant mother, "Mom, do you love the baby?" Martin's mother tells him she loves the baby very much. Martin now wants to know, "Then why did you eat him?"

A mother could be forgiven for giving her child a long explanation about how babies are made and born. Instead, Martin's mother wisely chooses to answer only what Martin asked. She says, "I didn't eat him, Martin. My tummy is very big because babies grow inside their mommies' tummies." Martin listens wide-eyed but says nothing. Two days later, after having digested this information, Martin asks the next logical question: "Did I grow in your tummy, too?" He smiles with pleasure as his mother tells him how he grew and grew until he was ready to be born. Not until four months later, after his sister is born, does it occur to Martin to ask, "How did she come out?"

Children ask questions piecemeal because they take their time to make sense of the information they receive. They know what they can manage and stop asking when they had enough. It is a good idea to respect this signal and not to worry that the child has not learned as much as we imagine she should.

Learning About Body Products

Just as the toddler loves to experiment with body parts, he is deeply interested in what the body can produce.

> Max, 19 months, sits in his little rocking chair with a far-gone expression on his face. He has his finger in his right nostril and is slowly bringing out a long string of thick mucus, the product of a protracted cold.

> Monica, 20 months, has just begun to use the potty. She sits on it with her legs wide open and lets her warm pee dribble over her hand.

> Andres, 28 months, refuses to have his hair cut. "It's my hair. I made it," he wails. His parents resort to a hair clip to keep it in place. Two months later, Andres no longer objects to having his hair cut after he watches his father getting a haircut and chatting amiably with the barber.

> Sandra, 19 months, is found methodically smearing her feces on the bathroom wall.

> Tobias, 30 months, moves his penis in different directions as he urinates. "I can make drawings with my pee!" he exclaims.

Tina, 18 months, has just emerged from a prolonged tantrum. She slowly touches the tears still on her face and licks her fingers thoughtfully.

Sofia, 15 months, refuses to have her nails clipped. "Mine, mine!" she cries.

Sammy, 28 months, makes careful little mounds of spit on the kitchen table.

Leticia, 30 months, passes gas noisily as she and her mother are in line at the grocery store. "I farted!" she announces gleefully.

These experiences are the building blocks of the child's familiarity with what her body can create. Urine, feces, nails, hair, tears, mucus, saliva, gas—all these are fascinating areas of exploration.

Children do not know that from an adult perspective their behavior is unacceptable. The process of socializing the body is slow and arduous. Toddlers (not unlike adults) would much prefer celebrating the body to disciplining it.

A child can learn about his body and its products with interest and joy or with embarrassment and shame. Much depends on the parents' response. Rejoicing in the body can go hand in hand with learning that some things are private, no matter how pleasurable they are or how natural they seem. When parents can support the child's interest in the body while teaching about private and public domains, they are bringing physical sensations into the sphere of a secure base for exploring oneself.

Discovering How Minds Work

Discovering the body goes hand in hand with discovering the mind because mind and body go together. The toddler years mark the beginning of a "reflective self" that can take into account mental states in oneself and others. This emerging ability to think about oneself and to make inferences about other people's point of view has been called "theory of mind" because it enables the child to make predictions about how other people think, feel, and will behave. The evolution of this achievement in toddlers is rooted in infancy. Even newborns are subtly attuned and emotionally responsive to the facial expressions, voice tone, smell, and behavior of others. For example, a classic experimental design called "Still Face Procedure"[21] helped transform our understanding of young babies' capacities for interpersonal awareness. Mothers and fathers of 2-month-old to 9-month-old babies are asked to engage in playful face-to-face interchanges for a few minutes and then interrupt this joyful interaction by briefly turning away and returning to face the baby with a neutral and unresponsive facial expression. Babies respond to this disruption of their expectations for reciprocal interaction with clear and persistent distress that includes signals of physiological dysregulation such as hiccupping and drooling, averting their eyes from the parent, decreased vocalization, fussing, and making persistent efforts to reengage the parent's attention. When after a couple of minutes the parent becomes responsive again, the baby reengages with the parent, but signs of stress often remain in the form of decreased signals of pleasure and more muted interactions. This and many other experimental studies demonstrate that babies are sensitive to the emotional signals of others from the beginning of life, become upset when their social expectations are not met, and participate in repairing the interpersonal disruption when offered the opportunity, although repair is not necessarily instantaneous.

The capacity to read, interpret, and respond contingently to the signals of others becomes increasingly more sophisticated in the first five years of life. "Self-conscious" emotions emerge at around 18 months, when toddlers become more self-aware and display embarrassment, shame, guilt, and pride.[22] Individual differences in response to perceived social mistakes are clearly apparent at this age. In one study, 2-year-olds showed different responses after they believed that they had broken the researcher's "favorite doll." Some children tried to fix the doll, a behavior interpreted by the experimenters as a possible manifestation of guilt and efforts to make amends. Another group averted their faces away from the researcher, as if ashamed.[23] This is also a time of increased empathy for others, including efforts to find out what caused another person's distress and efforts to help.

> Sammy, 20 months old, watches with a sober expression as another child cries after hitting her head on a table. He then approaches her and offers her his teddy bear.

> Linda, 24 months old, accidentally breaks a cup and reacts by covering her head with her arms with her eyes closed. When her mother expresses displeasure at the broken cup, she offers the mother her own plastic cup.

These young toddlers are showing that they understand how other people feel and want to make them feel better, even if they themselves don't feel the same way. In the case of Linda, she also knows that it is her action of breaking the cup that has made her mother upset, and she is able to experience her own feelings of embarrassment or guilt (and engage in an effort to fend off this distressing state of affairs by closing her eyes to it) while also making an effort to repair her mistake and make her mother feel better by offering a substitute: her own cup.

The capacity to pretend is an early manifestation of the child's emerging ability to understand internal states in the self and others, including experimenting with the difference between appearance and reality. In pretending, the child needs to know both the literal and the make-believe aspects of a situation. In effect, the toddler acts "as if" the pretend situation is real, but in the process of experimenting with play and reality she learns a clear differentiation between the two. By the time toddlers become preschoolers at about 3 and 4 years of age, this ability to pretend is increasingly translated into their capacity to put themselves into the position of another person, when they understand that what they see from their specific physical location is not necessarily what other people see from their own different location, and what the child knows is not necessarily what the other person knows.

Children need their parents and other trusted adults to learn about their feelings and the feelings of others as an integral component of their theory of mind. "Being felt with" is an expression developed by the psychologist Erna Furman to describe the sense of emotional discovery that even very young toddlers experience when their feelings are recognized and given expression by their parents, as in the example below.

At thirteen months, Mary was one day running around discontentedly, kicking at her toys, and ignoring [her] mother's requests to join her for a snack. Mother watched for a while and then said, "Mary, you are angry at Mommy." Mary stopped, looked at Mother bewildered, and questioning. "Yes, when you kick and run around and won't come with me and nothing feels right, that's when you are angry. It's okay. Everyone gets angry." Mary's face lit up with relief as if something suddenly made sense and fit together. She came to a halt, drew herself up tall, and repeated, "angry," "angry." "Yes, you can tell me you are angry," said her mother. The experience of understanding herself through being understood and having it all contained in a word, a symbol, provided so much pleasurable ego mastery that Mary even forgot her anger. It returned later and could then be linked to its cause, mother going out and leaving her with her sitter.[24]

Mary's mother was helping her child to know and accept herself through the mother's understanding and acceptance. Toddlers also need adults to learn about the point of view of others, a capacity that becomes the substrate of a moral conscience. The example below illustrates a common scene where parental support enables the child to learn simultaneously about self-regulation, the feelings of others, and the difference between right and wrong.

Andrew, 22 months old, wants the truck that his friend is playing with. His friend refuses to give it to him, and Andrew bites him hard on the arm. His friend's mother, furious, roughly yanks An-

drew away and tells him he is a "bad boy." Andrew starts to wail.
Andrew's mother, containing her own fury at the other mother,
says, "He is not a bad boy. He is learning not to bite." She picks
Andrew up and holds him until he calms down. Then she says
to him with much feeling and in a stern voice, "You cannot bite
even if you want to. It's a no-no. It hurts. See? Your friend is also
crying because you hurt him." Andrew looks at her quietly, averts
his eyes, and squirms to get down. He looks quiet and subdued
for about fifteen minutes. Later in the day, the mother sees him
pretending to bite his own arm gently, staring at it, and then
shaking his head in a mute "no."

This example has many layers of meaning. Andrew's mother was
able to keep her attention on her son's experience, containing her own
feelings of anger toward the other mother and preventing the situation from moving from a squabble between the two toddlers to a fight
between the two adults. She also responded empathically to Andrew's
distress after he was scolded by his friend's mother, but this empathy
did not make her lose track of the fact that he had expressed aggression
in a hurtful and socially unacceptable way and needed to be taught
differently. By responding first to Andrew's most salient emotion—his
own distress—the mother calmed him and restored his capacity to
turn his attention outward, building the scaffolding needed to teach
him about not biting once his attention could move from his own intense feelings to what the mother had to teach him. This simultaneous attention to emotional regulation and socialization enabled him
to practice feeling what his friend might have felt when he bit him. As
this example illustrates, learning about one's own mind and the mind
of others begins in the toddler years and involves emotional, social,
and cognitive aspects of development working in synchrony with each
other through the vehicle of relationships.

Understanding about minds and the ability to pretend has a dark
but useful side: the enormously useful although much-disapproved-of
capacity to engage in deception and lying. It is an unsettling reality
that the human proclivity to alter the truth to suit one's purposes is a

skill that evolved in the course of evolution in the context of a dangerous and highly competitive environment where being more cunning than one's enemies was often the key to survival. In young children, the emergence of self-conscious emotions such as shame and guilt goes hand in hand with the wish for approval and the desire to disguise ignorance. The poet Kornei Chukovsky offers this touching illustration and commentary on the toddler's creativity when feeling the need to camouflage ignorance:

> While taking a walk with his aunt, a two-year-old boy stopped by a book stall. The vendor asked him: "Can you read?" "Yes, I can." The vendor gave him a book and invited him to read. Imitating his aunt, the boy felt in his pocket and said, "I forgot my glasses at home." The child would not resort to such tricks of diplomacy if his awareness of his incompetence did not cause him so much distress. No matter what, he wants to consider himself capable and informed. Evidently such deception is, for the time being, necessary for the child. . . . The instinct of self-assertion is usually quite strong at this age.[25]

When the self-assertion is harmless and inconsequential, it is most often best not to call the child's bluff. We all need our defenses, and we all depend on the benevolence of those we love to protect us at times from unpalatable vulnerabilities. Toddlers are no exception.

3

The Challenges of Being (and Raising) a Toddler

There is a widespread belief that it is the very essence of toddlers to be stubborn, defiant, and negativistic. In some ways, this is a useful belief. When an exhausted parent emerges from a seemingly endless battle with her toddler, she may worry that she's raising an irredeemable monster who will go through life antagonizing friend and foe alike. At such times, one consoles oneself by thinking that the real culprit is the child's age rather than the child's nature. We know that age changes; we are not so sure that nature does.

It is true that raising young children is a stressful activity. Home observations of mothers and their preschoolers show that mild to moderate conflicts take place once every three minutes and major conflicts occur at the rate of three per hour.[1,2,3,4] The younger the child, the more frequent these disturbances. Conflicts between 2- and 3-year-olds and their mothers occur twice as often as for 4- and 5-year-olds.[5] As a result, mothers of toddlers often experience such tension and fatigue that one author was moved to describe them as "the unacknowledged victims."[6] This view is more pessimistic than it needs to be. In a study of toddlers between 14 and 27 months old, the findings showed that toddlers' defiant behavior went hand in hand with willingly compliant behavior and was associated with measures of maternal competence such as showing supportiveness, promoting autonomy, and having low depressive symptoms. Toddlers who defied their mothers more often also initiated interaction with their mothers more often and smiled at them more often. In addition, defiance tended to decline with age and was increasingly replaced by problem-solving strategies such as negotiation.

Findings such as these support the idea that toddlers' defiance and resistance to parental demands often reflect an age-appropriate wish to control events rather than problems in development or in the parent-child relationship.[7] The pediatrician T. Barry Brazelton calls the toddler years "a declaration of independence." The strains and stresses of raising a toddler can feel less burdensome when toddlers' defiance is seen from a developmental perspective and with a touch of humor. As one sympathetic aunt told a harried mother whose daughter finally relented and agreed to share a toy after repeated refusals, "Lina is showing us that 'no' is not her last word." Little Lina had adamantly refused to give her mother a toy car but complied promptly when the aunt said sweetly, "But Mommy wants so much to play with you. Can you please give her your car, and then she'll show you how it can go really fast?" Once Lina understood the context of her mother's request and no longer saw it as a threat of deprivation, she engaged in happy play, sharing the toy car with her mother and aunt.

Not all conflicts end so smoothly. This chapter is based on the premise that not every problem of this age has a clear and immediate solution. There are conflicts that will be revisited again and again. There are areas of irritation, dissatisfaction, or regret that will resurface at different times with more or less intensity.

The goal of this chapter is not to provide quick fixes but to describe the emotional experiences of toddlers and parents, offering an attitude for understanding the trials and tribulations of this age. The challenges of toddlerhood—negativism, defiance, temper tantrums, no-win situations, and parental frustration, anger, and fatigue—are necessary, inevitable, and indeed valuable hurdles as toddlers learn to become individuals aware of their own needs and wishes but also mindful of the needs and wishes of others. To help the child in this process, a parental attitude of give-and-take partnership with the child needs to be guided by the parent's awareness of the age-appropriate rights and responsibilities of each partner. How a secure base evolves into a partnership, how this partnership develops, and the upheavals that accompany its formation are the main topics of this chapter.

The Parents' Experiences

What makes child rearing so emotionally charged? For one, it can often be lonely. Without the support provided in the past by extended families, stay-at-home parents may find themselves having to run a household *and* be attentive to their children without the assistance and companionship of other adults. Lack of recognition and appreciation adds to the burden, since stay-at-home parents are traditionally considered "nonworking," although depending on their circumstances they may clean, mend, cook, wash clothes, iron, shop, do errands, manage money, pay bills, drive, coordinate the family's activities, and find time and energy to nurture, stimulate, and socialize the children.

Depending on the number and age of the children in a family, time spent doing unpaid work can be up to six and a half hours a day higher in families with children than in childless households.[8] A larger proportion of this extra time is filled by mothers, who tend to divert to their young children the time previously spent in personal care (including sleep) and leisure activities, according to a time-diary analysis in which mothers and fathers recorded how they spent their time in the course of the day in five-minute intervals.[9]

When we introduce into this picture the figures indicating a high frequency of parent-child conflicts, all of which need to be negotiated and resolved, it becomes clear that parents—and particularly mothers in a large proportion of households—have a lot to do. When stressed and overburdened, parents are less likely to muster the patience and resilience that would help them cope with the boundless determination of a healthy toddler. The very energy of the child may seem at times like an assault on their frazzled nerves and weary bones. The child's resolute defiance may look every bit like a personal attack. Advocating an attitude of partnership then seems like the invention of an ivory-tower moralist. At such times, it might be useful to withdraw from the conflict, take a little time out, and reflect on one's own experience and that of the child. The child psychiatrist Dan Siegel and early childhood educator Mary Hartzell coined the term "parenting from the inside out" to describe how understanding emotions—one's own as well as the child's—is essential to negotiating the challenges of parenting and provides a blueprint for building trusting family relationships.[10]

Obstacles to a Secure Base

The previous chapter described toddlers' use of the parent as a secure base from which to learn about themselves and about the world. This works well when parent and child are relaxed and getting along. In the midst of conflict, finding a rewarding balance between closeness and exploration can be a taxing process for all involved.

Four different factors contribute to the upheavals between parents and toddlers: disagreements about what is safe and what is not; the toddler's desire to "have it all"; the opposition and negativism that accompany this new sense of a personal will; and the temper tantrums that may follow when the parent says no. Each of these factors becomes easier to handle when parents understand the cognitive and emotional challenges facing the child in the second and third years of life.

Discrepancies in Toddlers' and Parents' Perceptions

Toddlers and parents often have sharply opposing views of what is safe. These disagreements often result from different understandings of what constitutes danger.

> At 22 months, David refuses to hold his mother's hand while crossing the street. Cars and busy roads are a familiar feature of this urban child's life, and he sees adults using them with equanimity. He cannot understand that they pose a threat to his well-being. Why can't *he* cross the street on his own like everybody else?

> Lateesha, 24 months, cannot fall asleep at night. "The monster will come," she says. Her parents know that monsters will not

come in the dark, but they cannot persuade her of this fact. They make a big show of looking under the bed and behind doors for monsters, saying loudly, "No monster here!" after each search. They show her that the front door is locked so no monster can come in. Leaving a night-light on also reassures her.

Nathaniel, aged 30 months, is found playing with matches. His father scolds him roundly. Nathaniel replies indignantly, "But you do it!" The father responds, "When you are tall like me, you can do it." From then on, matches are carefully kept out of the child's reach.

Seth, 15 months, is mesmerized by the glowing embers in his family's fireplace. He lurches forward, and his mother barely manages to retrieve him in time. He screams, "Shiny! Shiny!"

Amy, 28 months old, screams and insists on leaving when the lights go off during her first visit to a movie theater. All efforts at reassurance are useless.

Kamil, 30 months old, cries every time he sees an African mask in his uncle's house. "Bad man," he says. Reassurances that the mask is not real are only marginally helpful in calming him down.

These examples illustrate toddlers' often puzzling fear reactions to situations adults find commonplace and their breezy confidence in tackling their own enterprises that make their parents tremble with fear.

Clearly, toddlers and adults do not see the world in the same way. Selma Fraiberg, in her classic description of early childhood, speaks about the magical quality of young children's thinking.[11] They reach their own conclusions about the relationship between cause and effect, they have their own ideas about the magnitude and limitations of their own and their parents' power, and they develop unique theories about what is real and what is pretend, what is safe and what is scary, what is alive and what is inanimate.

Toddlers are always trying to make sense of what happens to them and around them. When their theories seem to work, they derive a strong feeling of pride in their emerging reasoning powers.

> **Marc, 30 months old, wakes up with conjunctivitis. His mother tells him, "You have a red eye." Marc looks at himself in the mirror and says pensively, "Because I looked at too many red things." That day, he carefully avoids looking at red objects, seeming quite confident of his approach to treatment. (In fact, it seems to work. The red eye is gone a day later.)**

Sometimes things are not resolved so smoothly. Toddlers can become quite unsettled by their fantasies of how the world works. Many of the seemingly bizarre fears of this age are based on faulty causal reasoning that goes undetected because the child does not yet have the language skills to explain what she is thinking.

> **Cynthia, 18 months old, has been screaming loudly for a week every time she needs to take a bath. She loves the swimming pool, so her parents know that she is not afraid of the water. On close observation it emerges that Cynthia eventually relaxes when she can hold on to her mother while in the bathtub but screams and clings to her mother when the water bubbles down the drain at the end of the bath. Cynthia's mother suddenly remembers that a small toy animal went down the drain the week before. The child's fear then becomes clear: If her toy could disappear with the water, what would stop her from disappearing, too?**

Adults often laugh at these irrational terrors or feel impatience at the inconvenience they cause. Yet the simplest way of relieving them is to take them seriously. Listening attentively, asking questions to clarify what the child believes, and providing a reassuring explanation as well as the promise of protection ("I am here"; "I will take care of you"; "I won't let you get hurt") are good ways of letting toddlers know that their perceptions are being respected and that the parent will make sure they are safe.

The Toddler's Wish to Have It All

The mastery of locomotion develops hand in hand with a new sense of personal will. The toddler desires things with a passion that the more jaded adults might well envy. "I wannit, I needit," says Jessica, fearful that her merely wanting something may not fully convey the urgency of her inner state. For a while, this formula is applied to everything she wants: her mother's new necklace, a doll in her aunt's house, toys in a store window, the cookies carefully set aside for after dinner. Her "I want it, (ergo) I need it" equation is not manipulative; it is her best effort at expressing the longing to own whatever it is she likes, to enhance herself through her possessions.

Fulfilled desire brings the toddler ecstatic pleasure and an inner experience of fullness and completion. We are all familiar with the sublime expression of joy in the face of a toddler who just got what he wanted (such as a balloon). However, the child is often faced with the need to choose between mutually exclusive sources of pleasure. He wants everything, but he usually cannot have everything at once. He cannot be close to Mommy while running free. He cannot stay at Grandma's house but also go somewhere with Mom and Dad. He cannot go down the slide and be on the swing at the same time. But he wants to, because everything is so full of wonder and possibility.

Choosing means having something but also giving something up. The toddler's puzzled expression as he learns this bitter truth is the best barometer of his confusion. The world he discovers is not made quite the way he would have it, and its rules fly in the face of the way things ought to be.

The toddler responds to this displeasing state of affairs with characteristic bluntness: she refuses to accept it and learns to say no. Sometimes the "no" is said primarily for the sweet pleasure of savoring its possibilities. "No," says Lucy quite placidly when her mother announces that they will go to the park, then cheerfully takes her mother's hand and trots along. Other times the refusal is fiercely, deeply felt: "No, no, no, no!" clamors the same easygoing Lucy as her mother makes one suggestion after another regarding her outfit for the day. Exhausted, the mother narrows the list to two choices: the red or green sundress? "The green," answers Lucy, proud of having the power to decide.

Opposition and Negativism

The toddler encounters a world full of nos, and for better or for worse, it falls on the parent to be the primary naysayer. "No, you can't climb on the record player. No, you can't put your fingers in the electric outlets. No, not in the cat's mouth, either. No, you can't eat the dirt from the plants, no matter how yummy it tastes. You can't bite your sister, and you can't pull the dog's tail. And you can't hit me when I tell you no."

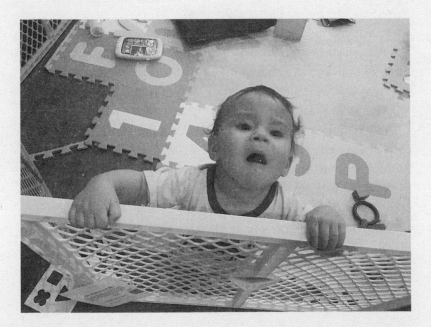

The list of prohibitions is nobody's fault. It is part of the long and often tedious process of converting a toddler into a person who will gradually learn to live according to the values and rules of his culture. No matter how thoughtfully parents childproof the house or how tactfully they divert a child to acceptable pursuits, there are still many no's that need to be said fair and square. It is small wonder that the toddler (being a fast learner) also feels compelled to announce his personal list of no's, for the sake of fairness if nothing else. The underlying theme of the child's negativism is "No, I am not your clone, and I will not relinquish my sense of myself to do what you want me to do and be who you want me to be." From this self-oriented perspective, toddlers can be quite easy to understand and not so terrible after all.

Still, the child's passion in enforcing her message can make parenting challenging at best. Some parents feel angry and discouraged in the face of the relentless opposition. They miss the earlier months when their baby was cuddly, complacent, and compliant and they knew how to read and respond to her signals in a way that brought mutual solace. As the toddler becomes assertively independent, even imperiously demanding, many parents long for the lost intimacy of babyhood, with its shared agendas and its physical closeness.

Parent and toddler often stare at each other across a gulf of mutually opposing expectations, and hugs alone can no longer restore the pleasure of the bond. Nothing will do but learning to accept, respect, and even love their differences. Only then can the old intimacy of the first year survive and be weaved into the new order of things.

Toddlerhood is also a fertile ground for the emergence of negativism because the child's immature language skills leave much room for miscommunication with the adults. Toddlers' curiosity about the world, their intense feelings about themselves and their body and their increasing autonomy and willpower would best be served by the ability to talk well. But language is slow in coming and painstaking in evolving. As a result, toddlers encounter many frustrating situations. They want to express something but do not have the words to say it. They do not know, want to learn, but are unable to ask. They find that they cannot understand what others say, and others cannot understand them.

They become embarrassed, upset, or angry when they are corrected because they say or do things wrong from the perspective of adults.

When toddlers are unable to speak about urgent matters, they must resort to crying or screaming. This happens even with adults. The voice is the carrier of emotion, and when speech fails us, we need to cry out in whatever form we can to convey our meaning. Often, what passes for negativism is really the toddler's desperate effort to make herself understood.

Temper Tantrums

When the "no" does not do its job and the child finds his will thwarted by higher powers, he may have little choice other than to throw a temper tantrum. What else can a toddler do? His language skills are not developed enough to articulate his case persuasively. His access to the family resources is minimal, so he cannot get his way by threatening to withhold an allowance or take the car keys away. Offended emotional withdrawal requires too much self-control for such a passionate creature. A temper tantrum—throwing oneself on the floor with a mixture of heart-rending crying and angry screaming—is a wonderfully eloquent if seldom appreciated expression of the toddler's inner experience. It represents his inner collapse as well as his proud protest at finding out that his will does not reign supreme.

Much of the emotional turmoil in the second year revolves around the difficult task of integrating the child's will into the family constellation. The child learns that her personal wishes (so cherished, seemingly so right) need to fit reasonably well with what others want. The useful term "no-nonsense parenting" reflects the idea that parents, particularly those living in stressful or dangerous circumstances, do not need to be subservient to their children. They provide effective caregiving when they protect their children from danger, promote their self-regulation, respect their safe autonomy, and give them clear guidelines for behavior—even stringent directives when necessary to support their adaptation to demanding circumstances.[12] These are the

ABC's of solid parenting. The parents learn that they, too, have to say no with firmness and conviction but hopefully without harshness.

This is why temper tantrums are so important for healthy development. Tantrums take a child to the very bottom of his being, helping him learn that anger and despair are part of the human experience and need not lead to lasting emotional collapse. If the parents can remain emotionally centered while firm in their position of denying something, tantrums also teach the child that his anger is not dangerous, that the parents will not abandon him, and that he will not be left alone in his "dark night of the soul."

Helena, 13 months, likes to career down the hall pushing a toy chicken that moves smoothly on wheels. On this particular day she wants to expand her horizons and pushes the toy through the door to her father's study. One wheel gets stuck, and the chicken won't budge. Helena throws herself on the floor, sobbing and hitting the floor with her head. Her father is not happy to be interrupted, but he picks her up and says, "I'll help you." Helena continues sobbing. The father repeats, "I'll help you," and puts Helena's hand on the stuck wheel. He then guides her hand until the toy gets unstuck. Giddy with pleasure, Helena pushes her chicken into the study.

Tommy, 18 months, wants his older brother's shiny new tricycle. He cries and screams. His mother talks to him soothingly, saying "You can have one when you are big like Daniel." She takes him outside to look for bugs, an activity he loves.

Sandra, 24 months, has a tantrum when her mother tells her she cannot have cookies until after dinner. She throws herself on the floor, screaming and banging her fist on the floor. Her mother says firmly, "I am sorry, Sandra, but dinner first, then cookies." Sandra cries for a while, lying on the floor. Her mother continues cooking, saying "It is not too long to wait, and dinner is yummy." While Sandra screams, the mother keeps an eye on her to make sure she does not hurt herself but does not intervene. When Sandra stops crying and seems calmer, the mother asks, "Are you ready to watch how I cook?" Sandra complies.

Jerry, 28 months old, hits his mother when she tells him that they cannot go to the park at night. She holds his hand and says sternly, "I know you don't like it, but you cannot hit me." Jerry pushes her hand away and kicks her. She puts her hand on his leg and says angrily, "You cannot kick me, either!" Jerry becomes a veritable motion machine, throwing himself against the mother and pummeling her. Mom picks Jerry up and carries the child to his room while he screams loudly. She says, "You have to stay here until you are ready to be with me again." She closes the door behind her and waits outside until Jerry stops crying. She then opens the door and asks, "Ready to be friends again?"

Managing a tantrum involves nothing less than the formation of character. Even the parent's capacity to cope well with conflict can improve with this experience. When a parent knows he is right and does not give in for the sake of temporary peace, everybody wins. The par-

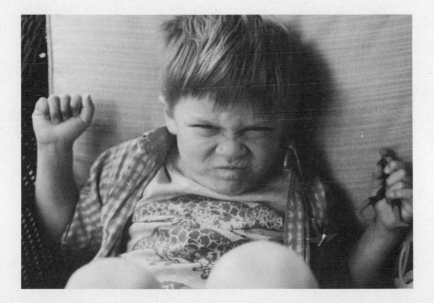

ent learns that denying some pleasure does not create a neurotic child, and the child learns that she can survive momentary frustration.

The child's insistence on having his way confronts the family with important issues in communal living. Both parents and child must at some time or another delay gratification and tolerate the resulting frustration with some grace. We all need to channel anger and even flashes of temporary hatred in acceptable ways, and we also have to maintain a tolerable balance between exercising power and yielding it. The lessons derived from managing tantrums are valuable not only within the family but in other social situations as well.

When anger and frustration prevail over closeness and reconciliation, a child may become precociously hopeless about the fate of human relations. Gabriel, 3½ years old, whose parents had recently separated, observed, "Grown-ups live together, then they fight, then they can't live together anymore." His comment related only to adults and reflected an unconscious assumption, based on the good parenting he continued to receive, that this did not happen to children. However, it was clear that his experience of his parents' separation had led him to conclude that adult anger is conducive to alienation rather than to repair.

Gabriel, of course, expressed a profound truth. Anger is difficult to manage, and expressing it in inappropriate ways can spell disaster. In the raising of every toddler, society recapitulates its own development. When a child is caught between the impulse to strike out (bite, hit, kick) and the fear of its consequences, conscience begins to be formed and civilization begins. Under the best circumstances, physical aggression is gradually replaced by the ability to verbalize anger and find a negotiated solution to intense disagreements.

For the child, parents represent a secure base to explore not only the external environment but also the wide range of feelings that emerge in the course of growing up. The parents' ability to guide the child through episodes of anger and despair helps toddlers learn that parents are reliable allies in time of need. The sections that follow discuss how the experience of a secure base can be transformed into a rewarding partnership between parents and child.

From Secure Base to Partnership

Ari's mother is 8 months pregnant and feeling it. Faced with a living room strewn with toys just before Ari's bedtime, she says, "Ari, you need to put the toys away." Ari answers, "You do it, Mommy. I'm too tired." The mother replies, "I am tired, too, Ari. Let's do it together." Ari responds, "Okay, together. You pick them up, and I watch you."

It is hard to know how Ari arrived at his definition of "together." Did he really believe that watching his mother pick up the toys was a legitimate part of the task? (This is possible. After all, he had done precisely that many times before.) Or did he pretend to believe that watching was a form of helping, hoping to fool his mother into agreeing with him?

No matter how he arrived at his suggestion, Ari was engaged in an active negotiation with his mother. He knew that she had a goal (getting him to put the toys away) that differed from his own (not doing it). He first invoked a reason for his goal—being tired—that had served him well in the past. When his mother not only dismissed that defense but also took it over for herself, he had to think fast for another avenue to reach his aim. His mother provided the perfect entry by suggesting that they do the dreaded task together. Instantly, Ari allocated to himself the only part of the job that was to his liking: watching it be done. The fact that his offer was not accepted does not detract from his brilliant if somewhat transparent negotiating skills.

In this exchange, Ari was practicing the nuts and bolts of *goal-corrected partnership*,[13] a concept awkwardly named but useful for understanding how children become social partners with their parents. When toddlers insist on carrying out their personal agendas, they come to realize that their mothers and fathers have their own plans and that those plans may be quite different from what the child had in mind. When the competing goals of parents and child can be accommodated or reconciled through negotiation, their relationship is characterized by flexible give-and-take, and it becomes a partnership in which the parties work together to readjust their goals in order to arrive at a mutually agreeable course of action. In goal-corrected partnerships, caring for the relationship takes precedence over the urge to achieve each partner's individual goal. Respect for the feelings and point of view of the other makes it possible to take the time to solve problems instead of moving ahead unilaterally to achieve what one wants.

Children begin to learn about partnerships from their parents' example, and it can take a long time (sometimes a lifetime) to become adept at being a true partner. Toddlers are like other people at trying first and foremost to further their own goals, which can remain quite stable over time. Three months after the incident just described, in almost identical circumstances, Ari came up with yet another compelling reason for not picking up his toys: "I can't now, Mommy. I only have two hands, and I am doing something else." Children's resourcefulness in furthering their interests calls for ever-increasing creativity on the parents' part to protect *their* goals. In this case, Ari's mother more than lived up to the challenge. She said, "Your hands have been doing the same thing for too long, Ari. They need to learn something new right now."

Upheavals in the Road to Partnership

In secure base behavior the child finds a comfortable balance between two opposing goals: proximity to the parent and exploration away from her. When the parent is physically and emotionally available, the toddler can decide freely when to leave and when to return to her side. This is when we see toddlers at their happiest and most charming. To move away and discover new vistas when one wants to and to be welcomed back warmly by the loved one whenever one chooses to return—that is the definition of happiness for an active young child.

When the child can come and go at will and the parent is always present and receptive, the parent's goals coincide with those of the toddler and there is no clash between the parent's and the child's plans. Harmony prevails because the parent is willing and able to be totally available, just as the child wants her to be.

Many factors interfere with this ideal state of affairs. Most poignantly, the child often wants to be close to the parent when the parent cannot be available, be it physically or emotionally. She may need to go to work, or she may wish to have time for herself or for other important people in her life. The toddler may not be able to simply let her go. The mother is the center of his universe, and he feels the need for her too strongly to be capable of such equanimity. The child clamors for her and clings to her, and she needs to peel him off and remove herself from his reach. Sometimes she does so with anguish and guilt; other times she feels irritation or annoyance. When a parent and child cannot meet each other emotionally at a time of strong need, the result is often mutual estrangement, anger, and frustration.

Other times the child is eager to move away, and the parents cannot let him do it. They may want to protect him from a realistic source of danger, they may disapprove of what he is about to do, or they may simply want to keep him by their side to enjoy his company. At such times it is the child who pushes away, feeling engulfed by the parents' presence and constricted by the parents' demands. The parents, in turn, may feel rejected, unneeded, and unloved.

It is in these situations of strong competing needs that a goal-corrected partnership becomes most critical to a resolution of the conflict. Parent and child have to find a way of moving away from a confrontation where one rigid "no" is pitted against another, with escalating anger and impotence on both sides.

The Value of Distraction

Toddlers' eclectic interest in the world and their relatively short attention span are great allies in preventing and resolving conflicts. A wonderfully effective way of redirecting young children's attention away from a forbidden object or activity is to give them something else to do. Distraction might seem straightforward, but it has long-term benefits for the child's social competence. In one longitudinal study of limit-setting with mothers and their toddlers at 12, 24, and 36 months of age, for example, mothers were asked to engage with their child in a variety of activities that included a three-minute limit-setting exchange. Mothers and children were seen again when the child was 5 years old. Mothers who actively distracted their toddlers from a forbidden activity by actively redirecting the child's attention, joining in with the child's interests, and using reasoning and explanations as early as 12 months of age had children with more developed self-concepts at age 3 and greater delay of gratification at age 5.[14] Giving directions or commands without active engagement with the child did not seem an effective teaching and socializing maternal strategy. Toddlers find it difficult to translate their mothers' directives into the desired action when their own wishes and impulses propel them in a different direction. When the mother models an alternative to the forbidden activity through her own active engagement with the child, the child learns socialization through the mother's example.

Distraction is often effective for young toddlers because it meets them where they are in their cognitive and social development. Between 12 and 24 months, children are enthralled by the enthusiasms of the moment, but their attention span is short enough that they can become equally excited about another opportunity for exploration that is presented to them with conviction and enthusiasm. Young children get their cues from adults, and if the caregiver shows interest in an object or activity, the child is most likely to become interested as well. "Social referencing" is the human tendency to become influenced by other people's emotional expressions and it is already observable in the first year of life. For toddlers, who are experiencing a veritable explosion of interest in and understanding of their own minds and the minds of others, social referencing becomes a central guidepost for behavior. A sense of theater on the part of caregivers can do wonders to entice children to engage in the ways we hope they will: using somewhat amplified emotional expressions helps persuade the child of the legitimacy of what we are asking him or her to do.

Distraction works to a certain extent. As the child's attention span and intentionality increase, parents need to increase their repertoire of strategies to repair mismatches and to socialize. For some very intense toddlers who have very high levels of persistence, efforts to divert the child's attention to different activities may take a lot of time, patience, and energy, and sometimes there are no simple interventions that work easily.

Negotiating Disagreements

What are some of the obstacles to a negotiated solution? Sometimes the parents fear that giving way will spoil the child. They believe that once having said no, they need to stick to it in order to be consistent.

> Mary, 18 months, starts playing with a golf ball that is reserved for playing "catch" with the family dog. She throws it and then runs to retrieve it, in almost perfect imitation of the dog. She giggles with excitement and delight. Her father tells her that the ball is dirty and she can't play with it. Mary cries bitterly as her father takes the ball away. Mary's loyal 5-year-old brother sticks up for his sister, saying "But we all play with the ball, and she's not putting it in her mouth." The father feels a little foolish, but he must stay the course in order to be effective. He announces, "I said no, and that's that."

> Stefan, 3 years old, is splashing with his bare feet in the puddles left by the garden hose as his mother waters the plants. It is a hot summer day, and the mother is tired and irritable. "Stop it, Stefan," she says. Stefan replies, "But I like it." "No!" says his mother. "Why?" asks Stefan. "Because I said so," replies his mother, unwilling to reverse herself.

Many parents are haunted by inner and outer demands to respond always in the same way and not give in to the child. They cling to every

inch of their wavering willpower in confrontations with the child because for them being "consistent" has acquired the aura of a transcen-
dental virtue.

All of us make decisions in the spur of the moment that seem silly
or unnecessary on further reflection. Insisting on that course of action
against our better judgment smacks of rigidity rather than consistency.
If another adult pointed this out to us, we would agree with relief and
change our minds. Why not do the same when it is our child who protests one of our less inspired edicts?

Toddlers can be remarkably perceptive when it comes to parental
shortcomings. At 34 months, little Josh said to his screaming mother,
tears streaming down his cheeks, "That is not fair, Mommy. You should
do better than that." His mother heard him and did do better. She
stopped screaming, pulled herself together, and explained, "Let me tell
you why I got so mad, Josh. I don't like it when you don't do what I say."
This mother's willingness to change her behavior led to a very fruitful
conversation with her child about what each of them was supposed to
do to get along with the other.

Willingness to change our minds in the face of persuasive evidence
teaches the child a higher form of consistency: the readiness to engage in dialogue about differing points of view. The child's and the parent's "theory of mind" becomes more sophisticated when it is open to
change as the result of new evidence.

There are many times, of course, when the parent's goals need to
take precedence over the child's and when the adult's "no" has to prevail.

Let's think of a common occurrence: parents who are getting ready
to go out for the evening, leaving their toddler with a babysitter. The
child clings to the mother's neck, screaming "Don't leave me!" The
mother feels torn between empathy for her child's distress and irritation, between the lure of a night out and the impulse to stay home. No
compromise seems possible in such a situation. Is there any room for
partnership?

To do justice to the situation, we need to look first at its background.
What are the child's motives? Has she had some satisfying times with
the parents during the day, or does this outing add insult to injury

because the child had no opportunity to fulfill her attachment needs? Does she know and like the babysitter, or is this a new person who cannot yet inspire trust as a temporary replacement for the parents? The child's protest may serve as useful incentive to evaluate whether perhaps we are expecting too much from her and not giving her enough support to cope with our absences.

"Well," the parent may answer, "it is true that the day was harried, and our regular babysitter canceled at the last minute, and we had to find a replacement our child barely knows. What are we supposed to do now? Don't our needs also count?" Of course parents' needs count! The question is how to assert those needs without losing track of the child's experience.

Paying Attention to Feelings

Understanding how the child may be feeling and how we may have contributed to it need not change our actual decision (in this case, going out). It does change the tone with which we explain the decision to the child. Toddlers find it very reassuring to hear a sympathetic description of what they are feeling but cannot put into words. The toddler is relieved to hear us say that we know he is upset, that Mommy and Daddy were busy today and had no time to play, that here they are going out yet again, and that is not fair. We can tell him that we know he doesn't like to stay with this new lady because he doesn't know her but that *we* know her and chose her because she is nice with children. We can assure him that we will come back and kiss him on his cheek while he is asleep and make sure he is all cuddled up and warm under his blanket. We can promise him that tomorrow we will make a special time to be together to make up for the little time we had today. We can say all this, a little at a time, or focus only on what seems most relevant for the child. Then we can say that now we need to go and perhaps solemnly give the child a small transitional object (a shell, a toy, a safe object that belongs to the parent and that the child likes) and tell him that the object will keep him company until we return.

Sometimes, of course, our children cling to us before we leave even if we spent the whole day with them and their favorite babysitter is available. Here, too, there is room to talk. We can tell them that it was wonderful to do all the things we did together during the day and that it is hard to stop. We can say that their babysitter will help them have a good time even while we are gone. Then we tell them that we need to go now. As the child psychiatrist Stanley Greenspan has pointed out, "setting firm limits" (that magic formula handed down from generation to generation as a panacea to the complexities of child rearing) need not preclude appropriate empathy for the child's feelings about the experience.[15]

Putting Feelings into Words

Children understand language much earlier than they can speak it. When the parent is able to translate the toddler's experience into words of understanding, this helps contain the child's negative feelings and make them bearable. In this sense, talking can represent relief from amorphous feelings because it puts some order into chaos.

The preverbal child is at the mercy of rages and anxieties centered in the body and experienced viscerally: hunger pangs, teething pains, the abdominal urges of defecation, the sudden shocks of falling, the stabs of ear infections. (It is said that Martin Luther first understood the devil during a bout with constipation.) Loneliness, too, although not originating in the body, is experienced through it. Longing for the mother takes the form of inner emptiness and of undefined hungers and thirsts. All these can be expressed at first only through sounds of anger and distress: whining, crying, and screaming.

A parent tries to find meaning in those noises, searches for their origins, and ministers to their causes. When she is successful and can make a difference, the child is soothed. When she is not successful, the child remains in the clutches of unnameable pain. This is why the mother and father are at the center of the young child's sense of well-being or despair: they are the ones in charge of understanding the child's experience and attending to it, and they are also the ones who find a substitute caregiver to act for them when they are not there.

With the acquisition of language, toddlers acquire a new tool for communicating with the parents and other important people in their world. They can now describe experiences that could not be talked about before. Even before this happens, toddlers learn from listening to their parents that language is a vehicle for sharing emotions.

> Reggie, 14 months, has been moved to an adoptive family from the home of loving but temporary foster parents with whom he has lived since birth. He has not yet started to talk. During the first two weeks in his new home, he screams almost continuously, hardly sleeps, and throws himself on the floor, sobbing hopelessly at the slightest frustration. His adoptive mother begins to have serious doubts about keeping him; she worries that he is not a normal child. In consultation, she is advised to respond to every episode of screaming by holding him very tightly and saying repeatedly, "You are staying here with me. No more bye-byes. I am your mommy now." This incantation serves to contain her own fear and distress as well as the child's. The message is received. Reggie's tantrums soon decline and eventually disappear. However, he remains quite worried about his new mother's comings and goings, monitors her closely, and cries when she is out of sight. His parents help him by playing games of disappearing-and-reappearing with him, "peek-a-boo" and "hide-and-seek." Reggie also spends long periods of time with "Jack in the Box"–type toys, making the toy hide and then pop up again. The repeated reappearances have a visibly comforting effect on the child.

Reggie's new mother's empathy and her ability to name his fear enabled him to transform his lonely rage and despair into a trust that someone heard him and understood. In time this trust will help him use words to express what he feels. Reggie's experience, although painful, is more hopeful than that of a child who has nobody to translate his feelings into words of caring and support. At the same time, Reggie remains vulnerable to separation anxiety, a realistic and adaptive fear in light of his losing the only parent figures he knew at a time when fear of loss is a salient feature of the toddler's emotional landscape.

Using language enables toddlers to become more equal partners in their interpersonal relations. They now have a richer behavioral repertoire to which they can resort in their negotiations with others. Language provides the child with a practical set of symbols that can be used as a concise way of representing complex experiences. The word "Mommy," for example, can evoke major portions of the child's experience with the mother, such as the loving looks, the comforting smell, the soothing voice, the warm touch, the cherished games. One word captures the emotional flavor of thousands of exchanges. As a result, each word is an economic way of encoding meaning and helping the child remember. Words enhance the child's memory, the capacity to understand how things work, and the understanding of cause and effect. Words also allow the child to think about different alternatives and decide what course of action to take.

Because of all this, toddlers can use language to put into words feelings that previously could be expressed only through action. They can say "Go away" instead of pushing someone off or "Mine" instead of grabbing another child's toy or "Me mad" instead of hitting. The ability to use words can serve as a protection against being overwhelmed by anxiety, rage, and fear.

When Words Are Not Enough

Language opens new vistas for communication, but it also has its limitations. Precisely because of the conciseness of language, subjective experiences are seldom captured completely, in all their multiple and subtle nuances. Words can address aspects of an experience but not the whole experience in its global multisensory texture. The word "Mommy" may evoke only the positive feelings the child has for the mother. The struggle, ambivalence, anger, and fear that form a part of the relationship may remain outside the realm of speech.

In this sense, putting things into words has an inherent alienating effect because the part of the experience that remains unnamed is cut off and fragmented from the portion that is given official existence through language.[16]

This applies also to the child's emotional life. Because the young child feels with such intensity, he experiences sorrows that seem inconsolable and losses that feel unbearable. A precious toy is broken or a good-bye cannot be endured. When this happens, words such as "sad" or "disappointed" seem a travesty because they cannot possibly capture the enormity of the child's loss. He needs a loving adult presence to support him in his pain, but he does not want to be talked out of it. As Kevin Frank put it:

> The impulse is to calm the child, to make things better. But the scream comes back, "Don't even try to calm me down!" whether in words or equivalent. Why is this so unnerving? Doesn't it evoke all the fear, resentment, frustration, which hasn't really changed at all since our own childhood? And isn't the impulse to get the child calmed down, by any means possible, an impulse to stifle this Pandora's box? It's an enormous challenge to really be with the child in its inconsolable state.[17]

At such times, only staying near wordlessly does honor to the child's experience. Hugging and holding if the child allows it can convey feeling much better than words. In fact, to use language in such conditions as an effort to explain away intense feeling may be to misuse it. There will be time enough for words later, when the parent is helping the child to reflect on what she just went through. Coaxing children to express their feelings in words before they are ready alienates them from access to the unspeakable realms of experience and teaches them wrongly that talking is equivalent to feeling.

Collapses in the Sense of Partnership

There are times when the parents cannot be emotionally available or helpful because the child's anger and pain trigger their own buried emotions. Instead of staying near, offering support, or putting feelings into words, they may find themselves screaming or withdrawing into an icy silence. Whatever sense of partnership has been built between parent and child comes tumbling down and seems irretrievably lost. Hatred replaces love. Neither the relationship nor one's inner space offers a secure base for immediate retreat.

Without necessarily advocating such loss of control, we can take some consolation in its being only too human. It may even have some advantages. If not overdone, it may help the child to appreciate that his parents, not only himself, have (sometimes unwanted) access to a full range of feeling.

Parents are under much societal pressure to be unfailingly empathic and supportive. They are asked to cultivate conscientiously their children's optimal mental health, cognitive development, creativity. This is a tall order and may actually have some serious costs. In an atmosphere where parents are always trying to be attuned to the child, the toddler is deprived of important opportunities to learn about deep, spontaneous emotion. When a parent is overly solicitous, the toddler gets the unspoken message that she should reciprocate in kind. In order to deserve such well-behaving parents, she had better be very well behaved herself. This pressure can be very constricting for a young child.

Sometimes toddlers' behavior is truly annoying and unacceptable, and it goes on and on in spite of the parents' best efforts to be firm but civil in stopping it. The parents' eventual anger (whether perfectly modulated or quite out of proportion) carries an important message for the child: *your inappropriate behavior has consequences that you will not like.*

Toddlerhood is the time to begin understanding this. Toddlers learn best through feelings—their own and others'. A parent's outburst can actually be helpful for toddlers because it teaches them that they do not need to control themselves all the time.

Making Up After a Fight

The important question is what to do after the parent has lost her temper. Here, language can be of enormous help because it enables parent and child to discuss together what happened "when Mommy and Daddy got so angry."

No matter how righteous a parent's anger, it is always frightening to the child. This fear can be made more manageable by explaining how Mommy or Daddy felt, asking the child how he felt, and reassuring him that he is loved even when the parent is angry at him. When children can find meaning in difficult experiences, their sense of security is temporarily shaken but not permanently impaired. In fact, repairing lapses in partnership again and again gradually inoculates them against hopelessness and despair when the usually loving parent suddenly turns into a frighteningly angry one. They learn that closeness is restored after tempers calm down.

What about those times when the parent "loses it" because of personal reasons and the toddler's behavior becomes a pretext for an angry outburst? Here again, talking helps. Telling the child "I am sorry" can spare her undeserved shame, reassure her that she is not to blame, and shore up her self-esteem. Of course, this happens only when parents mean what they say. Talk becomes cheap when it turns into a formula to alleviate adults' guilt. Children are very perceptive in sensing when their parents are really trying to do better and when they are saying "I'm sorry" simply to put the episode behind them until the next blowup.

Repairing episodes of conflict with the parent helps the child develop inner controls. The long-term goal of making up is to help the child build an internal model of the secure base that the parents represent on the outside. When this is successful, the child acquires a profound sense of centeredness and self-respect that can help through difficult times.

At age 4, Josh told his father after he yelled at him, "Dad, I am a small boy, and adults should not yell at small children. You should be able to stop yourself." The father, still in the midst of his anger, replied, "Sometimes I need to yell at you when you don't listen to me!"

Josh's words are a summary of the truths he has learned since he was a toddler from many exchanges in which he felt heard and met emotionally by his father even in the midst of the emotional turmoil between them. The father, for his part, upheld the legitimacy of his own emotional experience in expressing his frustration at Josh's disobedience. The father's compelling statement conveyed to Josh the message that accountability goes both ways—a manageable lesson for a child his age.

The Emotional Value of Disappointment

Partnership often involves modifying our plans to accommodate our partner's. Just as often, it means accepting that we will disappoint our partner because we cannot do what he or she wants. This is as true of toddlers as of adults. Disappointment is a very early experience, and toddlers need to learn that they can feel it without falling apart forever.

Nevertheless, parents often feel guilty for disappointing their children. Guilt can be a powerful obstacle to forming a partnership if the parents consistently give in to the child's wishes at the expense of their own. This automatic yielding conveys to the child that her wishes are the natural order of things, and she learns to experience frustration and disappointment as dangerous emotions that should be avoided at all costs.

Guilt can also lead parents to over-negotiate. They plead with their child to agree to their requests and to accept a situation with a pleasant demeanor. I remember a very loving and sensitive mother who wanted to go home with her toddler at the end of a wonderful birthday party. Sophie, naturally, did not want to leave. The mother cajoled her child in the most persuasive terms: "Let's go, Sophie. I know you want to stay, but you are tired. All the children are gone. Tommy needs to go to bed. You need to go to bed. Please let's go." Sophie's answer: to run away and continue playing. When the mother finally picked her up to leave, Sophie threw herself on the floor and screamed. The mother again pleaded and cajoled, "You are too tired, Sophie. That is why you are crying. Please let's go." This lasted for the next forty minutes, with escalating frustration for mother and child, not to mention the hosts.

Paradoxically, this mother's effort to get the toddler's permission to leave actually robbed the child of her right to dislike something and protest it. She was deprived of the freedom to express negative feelings and was instead coopted by the pressure to please. Nobody, not even a toddler, should need to renounce the right to negative feelings. To give up anger, sadness, and disappointment is to give up the right to a part of oneself.

Toddlers who don't learn gradually about disappointment lose their resilience through lack of practice in exercising give-and-take with other people's needs. They can become self-centered, demanding, and difficult to like or to be with. Sophie's mother would have done her daughter and everybody else a favor by overriding her protests, picking her up, and taking her home.

When the Past Intrudes:
Ghosts and Angels in the Nursery

Raising a child inevitably takes us back to our own childhoods. Feelings from long ago make an uninvited comeback as parents find themselves experiencing a multitude of emotions that often seem to come out of nowhere and to be beyond their capacity to control. Where do these feelings originate? How do they become expressed through behaviors that may often remind parents of their own parents, even when they promised themselves that they would never repeat with their children what their parents did with them?

William Faulkner wrote, "The past is never dead. It's not even past." This is because we carry early memories in our bodily sensations, perceptions of ourselves and others, assumptions about relationships, and spontaneous responses to emotional and social situations. This form of nonverbal early memory is called "implicit memory." It does not require conscious attention to become encoded in the brain, and for that reason it exists outside of consciousness. Implicit memories inform much of our emotional life but are not accompanied by a conscious sense of recollection. This is because those memories began to form before we could talk and before the neural circuits that connect the nonverbal parts of the brain—the brain structures that register signals of danger and safety, pain and comfort—formed sturdy connections with the later-developing parts of the brain associated with verbalization, logical understanding, and conscious awareness. Early memories are relived in the form of sensations, perceptions, and reflexive, spontaneous responses that are not connected with the explicit recall of factual experiences that can be verbalized. These implicit memories seem to lead an autonomous existence independent of willful control because they have not become integrated into the conscious organization of the sense of self. Implicit memory begins at birth but continues to accrue experiences throughout the lifetime. Our bodies absorb much more experience than we can consciously process and recall, and the imprint of those ongoing nonverbal experiences may emerge again at any time.

The later-maturing form of memory is called explicit memory. It involves conscious recall, the ability to put experiences into words, and an autobiographical component that begins to develop in the third year of life. It starts to develop in the second year and includes a sense of recollection when retrieved. The autobiographical aspect of explicit memory requires self-awareness and conscious attention to become encoded in the brain and for that reason is associated with the child's emerging capacity to develop a theory of mind starting in the toddler years.

All memory is strongly shaped by interpersonal experiences. Relationships guide what the child is given permission to feel, process, put into words, and remember. Children enlarge and enrich their emotional repertory when parents accept their emotion of the moment and help channel the emotion into safe emotional expression. They learn that they are feeling glad, sad, mad, or all three at the same time. Parents help a child create connections between feeling and knowing when they understand how the child might feel in response to stress, name feelings acceptingly, and help the child manage and channel overwhelming emotions safely. These bridges between feeling and knowing create internal coherence and an organized sense of oneself.

When adults forbid the knowledge and expression of feeling, children encounter an untenable emotional dilemma that John Bowlby, the creator of attachment theory, labeled "knowing what you are not supposed to know and feeling what you are not supposed to feel."[18] Distressing real-life events and the intense negative feelings that they evoke are then shut off from conscious awareness but continue to have a powerful influence on thoughts, feelings, and behavior. These life events can be classified into two main categories:

1. Family situations that carry great emotional weight but that the parents wish their children not to know about (e.g., a sibling's death; a parent's suicide; shame-inducing circumstances such as a parent or close relative being in prison; domestic violence).
2. Parental treatment of the child that the parent denies or misrepresents ("I will give you something to cry about"; "I hit you for your own good"; "You are lying"; "It's all in your mind").

Being pressured not to know and not to feel can lead children not to trust their own senses, to feel mistrustful of intimacy, and to negate the feelings of others. Once they become parents, they may find themselves having difficulty understanding and giving legitimacy to their own children's feelings and may in turn pressure their children to know and feel only what they know and feel. This process was described by Selma Fraiberg with the metaphor of "ghosts in the nursery"—emotional experiences that were suppressed in childhood and are now reenacted in the parents' present experience with their child. Parents struggling with these experiences have difficulty seeing things from their child's point of view because their own "theory of mind" was not validated by the acknowledgment of their own early emotional experiences.

> The father of Oscar, age 2, finds himself flooded with anger when the child pushes him away as a way of saying "no," for example when the father wants to wipe the child's mouth after eating ice cream or to change his diaper while he is playing. The father is ashamed of wanting to hit the child but can barely suppress the impulse to do so. In a conversation with friends who are sharing parenting moments, he reveals his struggle with a mixture of self-deprecating humor, embarrassment, and bravado. His oldest friend, who knows him from elementary school, asks, "What do you expect after all the beatings your father gave you?" The father, taken by surprise, blurts out, "But I deserved it!" He had incorporated a view of himself as "bad" that helped him exonerate his father for the fear inflicted on him while growing up, but he was now viscerally experiencing his own toddler as "bad" and deserving of being hit.

Reflecting on their past enables parents to retrieve early experiences and feeling memories that help give meaning to their emotional responses to their children. This happens not only with difficult experiences but with memories of feeling accepted, loved, and protected as well. The two examples that follow illustrate how nurturing these memories remain decades later.[19]

One mother recalls, "When my son was born, I immediately took to singing to him. One day, as I was rocking him to sleep and trying to remember the lyrics to favorite songs from my childhood, I found myself singing the 'I found a peanut' song while I cuddled him, gently rubbing his back and smelling his sweet scent. Instantly, I remembered sitting in my mother's lap in the rocking chair in our small den as a young child, hearing my mother sing the lyrics to this song as I snuggled against her, feeling tired but comforted and soothed in my sickness at the time. I then remembered several gentle, loving moments with her comforting me when I was sick, holding me, loving me."

Another one says, "Everything about my dad was warmth. I mean, you just walked into his presence and you felt like smiling. He used to like to sit on the couch when he'd get home and read the newspaper, put his feet up . . . he always had his arm like this, like arched around, and it was like that was your spot, and he'd just wait for you to come."

These "angel memories" serve as antidotes to fear, anger, and pain and can be used as "guardian angels" to guide parents' search toward becoming the kind of parent they want to be.

Encouraging a Partnership

How can one get toddlers to comply in healthy ways? Let us count the ways.

- Give them a likable alternative. This works most painlessly for all concerned ("We'll go home now, and then we can watch *Sesame Street*."). Of course, this is not always possible or effective.
- Use a tone that conveys your conviction that your request is important and meaningful. Then the child will also find meaning in it because toddlers are strongly disposed to believe and want to please the parent. ("You need to come in from the rain. Children get sick if they are out in the rain for too long.")

- The toddler's natural sense of fairness is the parent's ally in many circumstances. Explaining that a particular behavior bothers other people helps the child to learn that other people have different needs. ("Please stop banging the table with your spoon. It hurts my ears"; or "I don't want you to call me 'stupid.' It hurts my feelings.")

- In many situations, the parent needs to explain that she is the one in charge of deciding what to do. Many toddlers have been cured of uncontrollable tantrums by their parents' newly found confidence in saying "I am the one who decides that." There is nothing more reassuring to toddlers in conflict than the parent's benevolent authority, even if their strong protests make this hard to believe.

- If all else fails, humor sometimes works. If a parent can make a game out of a toddler's outrageous request, for example, saying in mock disbelief "You really want to eat your dessert before dinner? I just can't believe it!" and go on playing with this theme, the toddler may join in the spirit of the game and learn in a playful way what is permitted and what is not.

- Taking action is sometimes the only sane thing to do. This is particularly the case with toddlers between 12 and 18 months, who are still not very verbal. With older toddlers, taking action is best done as a last resort, when nothing else works or when it is important to react fast for the child's safety. Picking a child up to take him somewhere sometimes works better than cajoling, pleading, or explaining because it teaches the child that the parent is doing his or her job in taking charge of raising him.

What are counterproductive ways of encouraging compliance? Inducing fear or guilt is the most obvious culprit. At a more subtle level, admonishments such as "You need to cooperate" or "You have to share" make the child feel confused and hopeless at the enormity of the task. How is one to comply with such all-encompassing, abstract commands? (In the same vein, can one really obey the injunction to "be good"? Even the Ten Commandments are more simple and concrete.)

If we replace the oppressively big word "cooperate" with the simple statement "I need you to help me," we appeal directly to the child's innate wish to please. If we say, "It's time to let Johnny have a turn now," we address the toddler's sense of fair play. Toddler-size words speak to the child's feelings. This helps toddlers learn directly about the values of reciprocity, fairness, and empathy that are the bases of good human relationships.

Parents sometimes worry that telling a toddler about their own needs and wishes will make them feel guilty or dampen their natural exuberance. This is unlikely to happen for very long. Ira overheard his mother saying that she was feeling much better after a bout of flu. He immediately perked up and asked, "That means I can bother you again?" Children's own needs and wishes reassert themselves spontaneously if the parents do not stifle them. In fact, toddlers and parents are quite well balanced in their ability to get what they want: only about 50 percent of parental requests are initially complied with by toddlers in the second year of life.

Opposition, negativism, and temper tantrums are challenging for both parent and child. Their virtues, however, should not be overlooked: they force us to learn the complex but rewarding art of reconciling competing goals and building a lifelong partnership.

4

The Question of Temperament

Babies are unique individuals from the time they are born. Some are cuddly, others do not relax into the parent's arms; some cry lustily, others barely whimper; some seem to be in constant motion, others hardly stir; some seem unaffected by changes in routine, others collapse in tears when their feeding or sleeping schedule is altered.

Observations such as these indicate that infants come into the world already equipped with very personal ways of responding to their own body processes and to what happens around them.[1, 2] Sometimes these responses become a stable part of the baby's personality, but in other instances the behavior may change or vanish as the child develops. Only time will tell.

Where do these individual differences come from? How do they evolve? What determines whether they persist or disappear? Can we find ways of categorizing the different patterns of behavior, or are they totally random and unpredictable? These and many other questions have long puzzled those who try to understand human development.

The concept of temperament is a useful tool for trying to answer some of these questions. Temperament is defined as the "how" of behavior: in looking at children's temperament, we try to describe how intense, moody, adaptable, and predictable they tend to be. The focus is behavioral style, not ability (the content or "what" of behavior) or motivation (its reason or "why").[3]

In describing temperament, we often find ourselves using adjectives that involve nonverbal, kinetic experience: high strung, low key, bursting with energy, slow to warm up. These terms overlap with what the child psychoanalyst Daniel Stern calls "vitality affects"[4]—qualities of feeling that accompany the basic or vital processes of life, such as hunger and satiation, falling asleep and waking up, breathing in and out, moving around, experiencing different emotions surge and fade away. In this sense, emotionality and activity level are the hallmarks of temperament.[5]

For a long time, temperament was seen as immutable, a personal gift or burden one was born with and could use and endure more or less wisely but never quite shake off. Mark Twain, writing in 1909, had Satan proclaim, "Temperament is the *law of God*, written in the heart of every creature by God's own hand, and *must* be obeyed, and *will* be obeyed, in spite of all restricting or forbidding statutes, let them emanate whence they may." (*Letters from the Earth.*)

This notion of temperament as a form of predestination is currently out of favor. Current views of temperament minimize the notion of fate and emphasize that the child's development is shaped by the interacting influences among genetics, constitution, and environment. Temperament alone is not destiny. This view of development emerged from the realization that temperament is not a single, unchanging trait but a set of relatively stable tendencies a person has to react in particular ways. These propensities may be magnified, downplayed, or changed in quality in the course of development, depending on the nature of the child's encounters with the environment.[6]

Just what are these propensities? How exactly do young children differ from one another? Not surprisingly, different experts have different ideas about which tendencies are based on temperament and which tendencies are learned from the environment. Different experts also have their own favorite dimensions to classify and study temperamental traits, but there is remarkable overlap among the different dimensions proposed even when they have different labels. The pioneers in the study of temperament—Alexander Thomas and Stella Chess— identified as many as nine dimensions of temperament as they followed 136 children from toddlerhood to adult life. These dimensions involved *activity level, regularity of biological rhythms, tendency to approach or withdraw* as the first response to new situations, *adaptability* to change, *intensity* of response, *sensitivity* to stimulation, *predominant mood* (positive or negative), *distractibility*, and *persistence* in pursuing a goal.[7,8,9,10] Children could be high, medium, or low in any of these categories, giving rise to many subtleties in each child's temperamental makeup.

A child who rates consistently high or low in any one of these categories is not predestined to always react that way. She may surprise everybody by behaving quite contrary to expectations in a particular situation, or she may change dramatically on one dimension or another at a given age. Many parents comment that their children were very active and intense as toddlers but became quiet and mild during their school years. Even more common is the complaint that their friendly, outgoing, perennially happy school-age children became unrecognizably withdrawn and irritable as adolescents. At different ages, children's experiences and the way they perceive themselves and their world may mobilize new coping mechanisms or may elicit unsuspected vulnerabilities. The temperamental dimensions outlined here are not rigid categories of functioning but rather useful guidelines to recognizing recurrent patterns of response in a child.

Temperament Types

Nine categories are a large number to keep track of, no matter how useful each one may be. To make things less cumbersome, Thomas and Chess looked for recurrent combinations of traits in the children they studied. They found three constellations that were particularly common in their sample. The children showing these constellations of traits were called *easy, slow to warm up,* and *difficult.* The "difficult" label in itself is difficult to accept, although it carries a strong intuitive appeal when one is faced with a child who consistently challenges one's patience and best intentions. Every toddler (like every adult) can be exceedingly difficult for days or even months at a time, depending on what he or she is going through and depending just as much on the parents' level of acceptance and flexibility—which is often affected by what the parents themselves are going through. Efforts to find a less pejorative label for a challenging temperamental style have led to descriptions such as "fussy," "feisty," and "inflexible." In this book, the "difficult" category is called "intense." A fourth category, the *active toddler*, was not identified by those authors but has emerged from many observations of young children.[11,12,13]

Not everybody agrees with these labels, but the temperamental types they refer to are certainly worth considering because they have been extensively researched and seem to show continuity from early childhood to early adulthood. The sections that follow describe every one of these types, providing specific examples of how the child's temperament influences the relationship with the parents and the styles of secure base behavior and partnership that may develop. At the same time, it is worth noting that many leading researchers of personality are moving away from thinking in terms of categories to thinking in terms of dimensions because people—including children—do not fit neatly into global categories. For this reason, the following categories are offered as useful ways to think about temperament rather than as a way of classifying children.

Easy Temperament

This type of temperament has flexibility as its core modality. Biological cycles are regular and predictable; mood is predominantly pleasant; there is receptiveness to new situations and relatively easy adaptability to change; and emotional reactions are for the most part of mild to moderate intensity.

Because of these features, children with predominantly easy temperament are integrated relatively seamlessly into the rhythms of the household. Parents can plan their activities around the child's mealtimes or naps because these occur at about the same time every day. The toddler can be taken shopping, to visit friends, or even to work (if feasible or necessary) because he can be counted on a substantial portion of the time to be in a good mood, show interest in the new

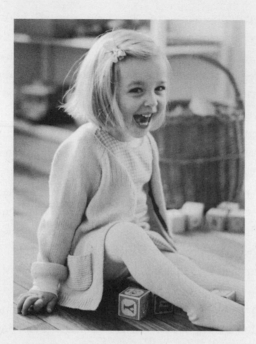

situation, and adapt quickly if at first things are not particularly to his liking. Parental spontaneity is possible: plans can be made or changed at the spur of the moment without fears of eliciting a minor catastrophe in the baby's rhythms. Whether pleased or disgusted, the child will show his feelings in a thoughtfully mellow tone. These characteristics make children with predominantly flexible temperamental dimensions a pleasure to care for. As a result, their parents tend to feel effective and skillful in their caregiving. This is not surprising, since they are rewarded with a positive response to almost everything they do.

> Joey is usually in a good mood. He tends to wake up with a smile and ready to play. This attitude prevails during the day. He accepts changes of routine with equanimity. For him, things easily become a source of pleasure and interest. His responses are usually moderate in intensity, whether he is showing pleasure or pain. He greets his parents and other people he likes with a

happy expression but without exuberance. New toys elicit laughter but not shrieks of pleasure. By the same token, he complains only quietly during medical exams. Even his reaction to vaccinations consists only of a moderate cry rather than intense wailing.

One possible problem with children who have flexible temperaments is that they are easy to take for granted. They may be so agreeable that parents may push them beyond what in fairness they can be expected to tolerate. But even easygoing children become sad, scared, and angry, and parents may need to remind themselves of this in order to remain attuned to the emotional needs of their easygoing toddlers.

Slow-to-Warm-Up Temperament

When faced with a new experience, children who are slow to warm up may first withdraw, and they take a long time to adapt. Slow-to-warm-up temperament often goes with subdued activity level and mild emotional reactions, which escalate into an intense response only when children are pushed beyond their endurance into new situations. Children with slow-to-warm-up temperament need some time to observe from the sidelines before they are ready to join in. Once they feel ready to participate, they can show just as much zest as their less tentative peers. Children who are slow to warm up are often considered shy or timid because of their reluctance to enter new situations readily.

Erin is low key in new settings. She observes new objects and new people for a long time before engaging with them. She cries if pressured to approach more quickly than she is ready for. In physical activities, she has slow and measured movements. She prefers sedentary activities such as reading books and solving puzzles. She tires easily when playing active games, although she enjoys them for short periods of time. She asks to be carried after walking just a short while in spite of her ability to walk, run, and jump very well for her age.

One possible risk facing children with the slow-to-warm-up temperamental style is that people looking for psychological motives for their behavior may label them "anxious" or "insecure."

There is no evidence that slowness to warm up and insecurity go together. A child may be quite confident of her parents' physical and emotional availability, she may trust her own abilities to cope well with different situations, and she may still prefer to first observe from the sidelines and only later join in. Of course, insecurity may result if others criticize, ridicule, or try to change this tendency instead of accepting it as the child's personal and normal way of adjusting to new situations.

This raises the question of how the parents feel about their toddler's shyness. There is some evidence that shyness may be biologically based: in studies of adopted and biological infants, there is a higher correlation of shyness between infants and their biological mothers than between infants and their adopted mothers. There is also evidence that a tendency to respond to novelty with wariness and inhibition is a temperamental trait that can be observed by 4 months of age and can remain relatively stable across development in a subset of children who initially demonstrate this tendency.[14] Young children who have a stable tendency to respond to novel stimulation as if it were a threat may also be more prone to be socially anxious later in life, as if their tendency toward cautiousness generalized to social situations.[15]

Parents with a shy toddler may respond to the child's slowness to warm up in different ways. Some parents empathize with their children and allow them to get into situations at their own pace. Other parents wish to protect the child by minimizing exposure to new and challenging situations. Still others try to help their children "outgrow" their shyness by encouraging them to join in before they are ready. There are a few parents who feel personally indicted by the child's behavior and respond with impatience or embarrassment, as though the child is shaming them.

These responses may reflect in part the parents' experience with their own temperament. Some shy parents feel mortified that their child shares this trait with them. Others understand instinctively what their child is feeling. Some outgoing parents feel slowed down and constricted by their child's reserve; others find their child's shyness re-freshing because it relieves them of the expectation to be more socially available than they want to be. Parents who feel ashamed of their child's shyness may be reexperiencing with their child memories of feeling misunderstood, not accepted, pushed, or bullied when they were grow-ing up. Recalling those experiences and processing them emotionally from an adult perspective can help parents differentiate between times when they are responding viscerally to their own "ghost" memories and times when they are responding to the child's individual develop-mental and emotional needs. Toddlers use their parents as reference points that guide their own responses. When their parents feel threat-ened, they feel threatened—a perpetuation of a cycle of wariness and fear from one generation to the next. This cycle can be interrupted and repaired if parents cultivate the practice of taking some "internal time out" to become self-aware, contain their own emotions, and clear their minds so they can restore their attention to the present moment in sup-porting their child's ability to cope with a challenging social situation.

Intense Temperament

Children with the constellation of temperamental dimensions that make up this category are often irregular in their biological functions, have difficulty adapting to change, get into a bad mood easily, and have intense emotional reactions. In short, their responses are difficult to predict and modulate, and one cannot pursue one's plans without tak-ing their reactions into account.

> Jenine is often on the verge of a bad mood. Her parents feel as if they are "walking on eggs" because she gets upset so easily. She wakes up crying in the morning, and it takes her a long time to be ready to play. She dislikes novelty, and her parents must hold her for a long time before she is ready to explore. Jenine has a hard time adapting to change. She cries when her babysitter first arrives, although she has a good time after a while. Similarly,

she often screams on first climbing the slide at the neighborhood playground, although she also likes it very much and does
not want to get off. Jenine responds to most situations intensely.
When she is in a good mood, she greets the arrival of her favorite
aunt with peals of laughter and a dizzying run toward her. When
she is in a bad mood, she refuses to look at her for a long time.
When she goes to her doctor, whom she knows and likes, she gets
into a fistfight with him when he tries to examine her ear. When
he offers her a toy after it is all over, she gives him a tight hug.

Not all toddlers with challenging temperaments are exactly like Jenine. Toddlers with difficult features express their difficulties in their
own personal ways. Some have frequent and prolonged tantrums.
Others cry easily. Still others have problems with eating, sleeping, and
elimination.

Parents often find it reassuring to learn that such trials and tribulations may result from their child's difficult temperament and not necessarily from some fault in their child-rearing methods.

All toddlers need their parents to provide a secure base that can become the building block for a rewarding partnership. All toddlers also
need adult help to find words for their feelings, to regulate their emotions, and to become aware of the needs of others. Toddlers with intense temperaments need these adult responses even more because their
moodiness and readiness to withdraw work against them in many situations. People often respond to the difficulties of toddlers with moodiness
and withdrawal of their own. This is a pity. Sometimes the most challenging toddlers are also the most interesting to be with because their
intense emotions and sensitivity help them notice things other toddlers
are not aware of. When they feel criticized or rejected, these children may
internalize a view of themselves as "bad" or "unlovable" that can perpetu-
ate their temperamental tendencies into becoming personality features.

The prescription that most parents of children with intense temperament find useful for managing everyday life has five major ingredients:
not taking the child's behavior personally; having a sense of humor;
being patiently available when one is with the child; setting clear guide-

lines for behavior; and establishing a support system that allows the parent "time-out" and breathing space from the child. This recipe is crucial to keeping one's perspective at the most trying times. Throughout this book, parents whose toddlers have temperamental challenges should pay particular attention to the suggestions offered to help children through taxing situations such as separations and reunions, sleeping difficulties, discipline problems, sibling rivalry, toilet training, and so on. All toddlers deserve sensitive handling of these challenging situations, but toddlers with intense temperaments need it more than most.

High-Activity Temperament

The impact of a high activity level on the child's behavior is particularly apparent in the toddler years, when the child's judgment about what is permissible and what is not is still very rudimentary. Children with high activity levels tend to have a different, more expanded definition of the perimeter for secure base behavior. Rather than staying within a radius of proximity considered safe by their parents, high-activity toddlers may take off and move on without looking back.

> Adam is constantly on the move. As a baby, he crawled very early and seldom sat in one place. In his second year, he runs rather than walks, climbs on tables and cabinets, and loves high-energy games such as chase and playing ball. He does not hesitate to run into new situations and barely takes the time to look at a new object before grabbing it. He becomes restless and irritable when forced to be still, for example, during long car rides or while being dressed.

Adam illustrates the fundamental temperamental features of a high activity level. When they also have a high propensity to approach novel stimuli, high-activity toddlers can seem unstoppable because they not only crave movement for its own sake but are also irresistibly attracted to the many objects that surround them.

High activity level does not necessarily go with high sociability. Some toddlers are so absorbed in physical pursuits that people do not hold a special interest for them. Even other children may serve primarily as partners in physical pursuits. Sedate social exchanges are not up to their speed.

These toddlers and their parents often encounter many obstacles in their daily lives. People are frequently bothered by their high vitality level and resent the constant motion these children engage in. Parents report that they often feel subtly or overtly criticized for not "setting limits," as if the child's need for physical activity were completely under the parents' control. "House proofing," a necessary method for keeping the peace in any home with a young child, becomes essential for safety. One problem is that many people resent having to childproof their house when the high-activity toddler is visiting for a few hours, and the parents then feel additional pressure to keep their child within acceptable bounds. This situation can set up many conflicts between the child and the adults because constraints are so aversive that the child can become cranky and testy in response. Many a social visit ends with a feeling of failure as a result.

The Socialization of Temperament

Temperament is nobody's fault. What one does with one's temperament, how one builds on it and tames it when necessary, are what education and character building are all about.

This is where parenting as an acquired art comes in. The way parents and caregivers respond to a toddler's temperament will help determine whether the vulnerabilities of the child become magnified and entrenched in his sense of himself or whether, hopefully, those difficulties are framed by the more competent aspects of the child and do not become a dominant part of his personality.

The temperamental styles of children tend to be outside their control in the early years. A toddler is not likely to wake up crying on purpose in order to spite the parent. She is also unlikely to hide behind her mother at a birthday party because she is trying to manipulate the situation to get people's attention. Yet toddlers are often unfairly blamed for behavior they cannot control.

When a child's behavior irritates or embarrasses us, we often respond by seeing murky motives behind it. In a way, we are trying to justify our negative reaction by looking for equally negative motives in the child. This is very human, but it is neither fair nor helpful to the parent-child relationship or to the child's emotional development. As mentioned earlier, temperament describes *how* the child responds, not *why* he is responding that way.

Keeping in mind that these tendencies are part of the child's innate makeup will help parents empathize with the child's experience and find ways of responding to behavior they do not like in ways that preserve the child's self-esteem. For example, it will help to comfort rather than scold a toddler who wakes up crying and to give time to a child who needs to stay near her parent at a party before being ready to move off on her own.

The Child's Temperament and Secure Base Behavior

The toddler's temperament influences the ebb and flow of secure base behavior. As described in chapter 2, secure base refers to the balance between moving away from the parent in order to explore and then returning to restore the emotional connection or to seek comfort and reassurance.

Children's temperamental propensities tend to color the style of their secure base behavior. In general, toddlers who are active and love novelty leave their mother's side readily. Children who are slow to warm up and withdraw from novelty tend to stay longer by the parent's side.

Toddlers with long attention spans and high persistence often stay away from the parent for long periods because they like to spend much time manipulating and sorting out things. Conversely, these same children may also spend more time close to their parents once they decide to approach them because they become quite engaged in whatever they are doing with them.

Highly adaptable children are likely to move away from the parent to explore a wide range of novel surroundings; less adaptable children need a long time to get comfortable with change and may explore freely only in familiar settings.

Even the child's mood quality and intensity of reaction may affect secure base behavior. Children with strong negative reactions to new stimuli are likely to stay close to their parents and may need encouragement and reassurance before they can move off and explore on their own. The following examples describe how their very different temperamental features influence the secure base behavior of four different toddlers: Joey, Erin, Jenine, and Adam.

Joey is a very curious, precocious, exuberant 22-month-old. He seems to be perpetually in a good mood. His episodes of distress are usually short-lived: his mother describes him as "the image of resilience." Joey can entertain himself for a long time with activities that range from pretend play, such as putting his turtle to sleep

and building a block "house," to talking to himself, looking at his books, or using the climbing equipment just outside his room in the backyard. At those times, Joey's mother needs to keep an eye on him every once in a while to make sure he is all right. At other times, Joey shows no interest in playing by himself and wants to be near his mother for long periods of time, singing to her, asking to cook with her, or asking her to join him in play. If his mother is not available on demand, Joey becomes distressed and is not easily redirected. He then shows none of his exceptional ability to entertain himself when he takes the initiative to do so. However, he accepts speaking with his mother and singing together as substitutes for close physical contact. This child's secure base behavior shows a clear dichotomy between "time on his own" and "time with Mother."

Erin is a quiet, mild-mannered 2-year-old. She is somewhat shy and tends to be watchful at first, but she easily becomes interested in novel surroundings. Her expressions of pleasure as well as distress tend to be low key. She neither ventures too far from her mother nor clambers up or clings to her. Her movements away from her mother and back to her are subtle. She may move away a little bit at a time, and her approaches may also be gradual, as if they were a side effect of pursuing a rolling ball or becoming interested in a toy that happens to be near her mother. Erin's secure base behavior, like her overall personality, seems to have no dramatic swings: a well-modulated balance between attachment and exploration behaviors predominates.

Jenine is a bright 22-month-old who has much difficulty managing her mood. When she is at home and in her mother's presence, she can delight in playing with her toys and chatter happily in an animated description of what she is doing. However, she easily becomes angry and despondent when things do not go exactly as she wants. Should her mother leave the room, for example, she becomes alarmed, cries, asks where her mother is going, and often follows her while wailing. She often rejects comfort from one parent when she wants to be with the other parent: "No, Mommy!" or "No, Daddy!" she screams when one parent is not available and the other wants to help her. When Jenine and her parents visit friends' houses, Jenine stays close to both her father and mother but turns preferentially to her mother. An older child may persuade her to play for a little while, but she soon becomes distressed and seeks her mother again.

In unfamiliar situations, Jenine refuses to move away from her mother and often screams in distress if her mother tries to get her off her lap and interested in nearby toys.

Jenine's secure base behavior can be characterized as including short bouts of exploration away from her mother and prolonged periods of proximity and contact with her. Because the child has a low threshold of sensitivity to stimuli, she is easily alarmed even by routine events such as her mother's comings and goings about the house and periodic visits to friends' houses. Her high intensity of response means that she responds with marked distress to those situations and needs prolonged contact with her parents—particularly her mother in unfamiliar situations—in order to feel safe again.

Adam is a rambunctious 2-year-old who seems to be always in motion. Even while he sleeps, he thrashes about in all directions. He walked at 10 months, and locomotion is his favorite mode of expression. He approaches novelty with glee, reaching out to dogs on the street, stopping to pick up little pieces of paper, plastic, or any object that he encounters as he moves about. He is seldom wary and rarely frightened by unfamiliar situations. When not held firmly by the hand, he races ahead without looking back, making little noises of excitement or delight as he marches on. Although quite affectionate when he chooses to be, he has little patience for extended cuddling and scrambles off his mother's lap after a few minutes. He occasionally approaches her in the course of his explorations to touch her knee or give her a toy, but he more often looks, smiles, or speaks to her from a distance, often showing her the toy he is involved with. He accepts his mother's overtures to play together with pleasure but is equally contented to play on his own. His secure base behavior can be described in terms of sustained periods of exploration interspersed with brief but satisfying episodes of proximity to and contact with his mother.

All four of these children are developing in normative ways and have distinctive patterns of attachment and exploration. Each of them has a very personal style. Their different uses of the parent as a secure base helps us understand whether they are introverted or extroverted; whether they are needy or self-reliant; whether they feel protected or endangered and alone; whether the world is a source of joy or a reason for fear. More subtly, secure base behavior carries the stamp of the child's individuality in her sense of herself, her way of interacting with those closest to her, and how she negotiates familiar as well as unexpected situations.

Parental Style and Secure Base Behavior

Parents have unique styles of encouraging or dampening exploration and attachment in their toddlers. Two distinctive parental patterns are holding on and letting go. When things are unfolding well for both parent and child, these two patterns complement each other in response to the child's developmental needs to go away and then come back. When the parents' own emotional needs distort their perception of the child, there is often a tendency to overemphasize one pattern or the other, holding on too tightly or letting go too readily.

Parents' and toddlers' patterns influence each other. An overprotective parent may increase a shy toddler's tendency to hold back by giving the message that the world is a dangerous place and the child can be safe only by staying near. Alternatively, parental overprotectiveness may trigger a very different response of rebelliousness and even reckless testing of the limits in an active, feisty child.

The toddler's style may also influence the parent's patterns. A daring, adventuresome child may delight shy parents by acquainting them with new horizons or may terrify a parent who is not so ready for such feats. A cautious toddler may trigger impatient urgings to explore in one parent, while another parent may find this behavior very compatible with his or her own style.

Temperament, Partnership, and Goodness of Fit

Not only children have temperaments; parents do, too. When the temperaments of parents and child are compatible, parents find it easier to work with the harder edges of the child's behavior. This compatibility contributes to the pride and satisfaction that the parents derive from who their child is. At the same time, parents do not have omnipotent control over their children's development. The famed child psychologist Erik Erikson expressed this simple but often overlooked truth most eloquently when he wrote:

> We distort the situation if . . . we consider the parent as "having" such and such a personality . . . and then . . . impinging upon a poor little thing. For this weak and changing little being moves the whole family along. Babies control and bring up their families as much as they are controlled by them; in fact . . . the family brings up a baby by being brought up by him.[16]

This brings us back to the question of partnership explored in the previous chapter. When the parent and child are well matched in their temperament styles, it is easier to establish a partnership because each of them feels comfortable with the other's pace and emotional tone. On the other hand, mismatches of temperament can interfere with finding mutually acceptable solutions when the parent and child have competing agendas and conflicting expectations.

Compatibility does not mean sameness. It means that the parent and child fit well with each other. "Goodness of fit" exists when the parents' expectations and demands of their child can be met by the child's motivations, capacities, and behavioral style.[17,18,19,20] A poor fit occurs when there is a mismatch between the parents' expectations and the child's ability to fulfill them.

Goodness of fit can be observed in the course of the moment-to-moment transactions that take place between parents and toddler. At the end of the day, a methodical observer may emerge with a score. For example, "good fit: 50 percent of all interactions; medium fit: 30 percent; poor fit: 20 percent." These particular scores would probably reflect a daily routine in which parents and child manage to be reasonably well attuned to each other's needs and wishes for a good portion of the day. We can imagine some of the sequences that contribute to the final tally:

> At 5 a.m., when his parents are still badly in need of their sleep, Andy demands breakfast. Mother groans and buries herself under the blanket. Father musters his most authoritative voice to say it is still sleeping time. Andy (a persistent sort by temperament as well as emerging habit) insists that he is hungry. Father remembers that the child fell asleep before supper the previous night; by this reckoning, he hasn't eaten for about twelve hours. Convinced that the child might indeed be hungry, Father gets up, prepares a bottle, and tells the child firmly that he will need to drink it in his crib and let Mommy and Daddy continue to sleep. Andy complies grudgingly. He calls a few more times from his crib but gives up when his father replies that he needs to sleep now. Soon father and son are fast asleep. (Score: High goodness of fit between parent and child's mutual expectations and abilities.)

> It is 7:30 a.m., and parents and toddler are up. Mother needs to take Andy to a regular pediatric checkup by 9 a.m. She discovers that he is badly soiled and that only a bath will remedy the situation. Rushed, she overlooks the fact that the child is used to long, leisurely play with her in the morning. She gives him a bath, which he (being a basically adaptable child with predominantly positive mood) accepts with pleasure. But he protests intensely when Mother tries to make the bath short and businesslike. He is

an active child who is well rested and naturally wants to splash, play with his duckie, and roll around the tub. Mother impatiently says there is no time for play today and abruptly takes him out. He screams. Mother realizes she is pushing him too hard, hugs him, and uses a corner of the towel in which he is wrapped to play "Where is the baby?" This is all he needs to get back into a cooperative spirit. Grateful for his resiliency, Mother begins telling him step by step what they will do during the day, distracting him with this story as she quickly dresses him. Andy likes the idea of a car ride, which Mother highlights because she knows he will be receptive to it. The process of getting ready is completed without further disagreement. (Score: High goodness of fit. Both mother and child are able to experience conflict with each other through different expectations and plans and to negotiate a way out of the conflict that satisfies both of them.)

It is 8:40 a.m. On the way to the doctor's, Mother is feeling pleased that she managed things on schedule that morning, but she is also apprehensive about the pediatric checkup. She knows that her child has an excellent memory and that he will remember the medical exam and the shots he received in the previous visit as soon as they enter the medical building. At that time Andy cried and fought the doctor off for a long time. She decides not to say anything about going to the doctor in order not to spoil the child's good mood prematurely. Her forebodings are confirmed as soon as they park in the back of the building. Andy cries, "No doctor, no shot!" and refuses to get out of the child seat. Mother is mortified. She is rather shy and hates public scenes that make her the center of attention. She is now keenly aware of people looking at them as she tries unsuccessfully to reason with her child. Mother decides that Andy is too upset to go through the pediatric appointment and decides to cancel it. She tells him so, and he calms down immediately. She drives away and calls the doctor's office from a public telephone in order to reschedule. (Score: Poor goodness of fit. In her embarrassment about the child's tantrum, the mother mistook her own difficulty in withstanding a public scene as Andy's inability to cope with the pediatric visit. Occasional stress, by itself, need not be damaging to children. They have the ability to experience and tolerate strong emotion provided they have access to a trusted and supportive adult and provided also that the situation is developmentally appropriate by cultural standards. Withdrawing children protectively from situations that they need to go through undermines their confidence in their own ability to cope with anxiety.)

It is 6:30 p.m., dinnertime. Andy's father, who is very concerned about good nutrition, heaps the child's plate with chicken, mashed potatoes, and vegetables. After eating his fill, Andy starts experimenting with the mashed potatoes while his parents finish their dinner. He kneads the potatoes between his fingers and eventually, bored by the lack of attention, begins to alternatively smear it onto his hair and drop it onto the floor. The father tells him to stop and cleans him up with a napkin, but he wants Andy to remain in his high chair until the parents finish dinner. Andy becomes increasingly restless. His mother and father allow him to get off the high chair and play on the floor next to them. (Score: Medium goodness of fit. It is hard for a toddler to be good company at the table when he is no longer hungry. After a bout of somewhat unrealistic expectations, the parents realize this and change their demands to a more age-appropriate approach.)

It is 8:10 p.m., and bedtime is nearing. Father and child are playing hide-and-seek. Father announces that after two more times, it will be time to go to bed. Andy protests, and Father reassures him that he will still "find" Andy two more times. After the time is up, Father tells the toddler that now it is time to get into his pajamas and brush his teeth. As the child complies with the routine, he asks for more play. Father says, "We'll have more play tomorrow." The child is reassured by this promise, and the bedtime rituals of reading a book and singing a song with the lights out proceed smoothly. (Score: High goodness of fit. The father gives the child some time to adjust to the transition from play to bed and is appropriately firm but sympathetic as the child expresses his understandable reluctance to give up the game.)

These examples were selected to emphasize that goodness of fit does not imply absence of conflict. Rather, it involves the ability to keep conflict within manageable emotional levels. This is possible when the parents can perceive accurately the child's capacities in a particular situation and when the child is receptive to reasonable parental wishes and demands.

Persistent Conflicts Between Parent and Child

There are times when the conflicts between a parent and a child are a predominant component of their relationship and are not simply a reflection of the regular ups and downs of daily life. In these cases, the parent feels chronically frustrated and irritated with the child. Moments of spontaneous pleasure between them are rare and short lived. There seems to be a fundamental discrepancy between who the child is and who the parent wishes him to be.

The child's temperament may play an important part in this situation. He may indeed have a difficult set of temperamental characteristics, such as unpredictable mood swings, intense reactions to mild frustration, signals that are difficult to read. More often than not, however, it is not only the child's temperament but how the parent perceives it and responds to it that leads to a poor fit between parent and child. For example, one parent may see a crying child as manipulative and slap him to "give him something real to cry about." Another parent may interpret the crying as a sign of distress and try to find out the reasons for it.

A study by the researcher Susan Crockenberg illustrates this point.[21] She found that very fussy, irritable newborns tended to have an anxious relationship with their mothers at 12 months, but only when the mother consistently ignored their crying and had little social support herself. In other words, when their mothers feel supported in their daily lives and are responsive to the child's cries, even irritable babies can become secure in their attachment relationships.

Why do some parents respond appropriately while others get tangled in conflicts with their toddlers? The section "When the Past Intrudes: Ghosts and Angels in the Nursery" in chapter 3 provides a possible explanation, but in general it is easier to ask this question than to answer it because the answer has many layers and individual variations. As Leo Tolstoy observed, happy families resemble one another; unhappy families are unhappy in their own particular ways. A comprehensive answer needs to encompass the biological, psychological, and social levels of family life. A sketch of these levels is offered below.

1. The parents have a difficult time accepting themselves and their child. There may be various reasons for this difficulty. Sometimes the temperamental makeup of the parent is at odds with the child's temperament. For example, the parent may be active, extroverted, sociable, intense; the child may be slow, introverted, shy. When the parent cannot find pleasure in these differences, a mismatch may occur: what a parent considers fun, her toddler may find painfully overstimulating. Conversely, the activities that enthrall a toddler may be excruciatingly boring to the parent.

> Mrs. Barker is an outgoing, energetic, athletic woman who takes pride in "working hard and playing hard." She talks loudly, laughs uproariously, and moves fast. Her child Ashley is the antithesis of her mother: retiring, low key, easily scared. Mrs. Barker feels impatient trying to tone down her behavior to match her daughter's slower rhythms. Ashley, on the other hand, seems to quiver in her mother's presence, as if overstimulated by her.

Alternatively, the toddler may be active, sociable, intense, and the parent may be slow, quiet, and shy. In such a pair, the child is constantly searching for more stimulation, and the parent feels always on the verge of exhaustion by the child's demands.

> Mr. Preston is a bookish man who would stay home all day read-ing if he had the choice. His son Kevin, in contrast, can best be described as "hell on wheels": adventurous, unstoppable. Kevin tries to entice his father to play ball, climb playground struc-tures, run after him. Mr. Preston tries to get Kevin to read quietly with him. The two seem always at odds with each other, because they cannot open themselves to the activities that give pleasure to the other.

These examples show the discomfort that can result from mis-matches between parent and child. On the other hand, parents do not need to have the same temperament as their children for their relation-ship to go well.

Building a partnership often involves compromises. Mrs. Barker found a much wanted area of compatibility with Ashley when she dis-covered that they both loved the water and could go swimming together. This commonality made her more willing to go slow when her daughter needed her to. Mr. Preston and Kevin found a different solution. They "traded" times together by agreeing to go to the playground after read-ing a book together or vice versa. In other words, each of them was willing to do something for the sake of spending time with the other.

In one study, toddlers with high activity levels played more com-petently when their mothers did not intervene very much. Conversely, toddlers with lower activity levels were able to play better when their mothers were highly stimulating.[22] These findings suggest that high-activity children probably need their autonomy and feel cramped by an equally active parent when they are interested in playing alone. Chil-dren with a lower activity level may feel supported by the parent's help. The match between parent and child at any given time affects what the child is able to achieve on his or her own.

Sometimes the difficulties in accepting oneself and the child go beyond temperamental mismatches. Some parents feel at ease with who they are and what they have become. Others feel divided inside themselves, guilty about their imperfections, dissatisfied with their achievements. Parents who are struggling with themselves often find it difficult to cooperate with their child.

It is difficult to be an accepting and contented parent if one is displeased with oneself. We often project our deepest longings and most secret fears on our children, and when this happens we tend to see in them what we suppress in ourselves. The young child can become for the parents a mirror of their own most shame-producing attributes, a reflection of their hopelessness and their frustrations. Conversely, the child can give the parents new hope and stimulate them to find more fulfilling ways to live.

2. *The parent's subjective experience of the child.* Each child makes his own unique imprint on the parents' psyche. The parents may feel delighted, irritated, threatened, enraged, or conflicted by the child's existence at a visceral level. This may have to do with many factors (for example, the circumstances of the child's conception; who the child resembles; the child's birth order; the child's temperament and emerging personality; each parent's sense of self). Ultimately, however, the parents' visceral reactions have much to do with how they recognize themselves in the child.

Parents sometimes believe that they are able to detect the very essence of their child. How this essence is perceived may be fateful in shaping who the child can become.

One mother was convinced that her 14-month-old son would become a juvenile delinquent when he grew up. This mother perceived her husband as controlling and insensitive. She had been physically abused by her father when she was a child, and she feared her husband would eventually become physically abusive as well. Her toddler was enmeshed in the harshness of the mother's experience. He was, in fact, an active child with a sunny disposition. However, he had become the carrier of his mother's anger at her husband and at her life in general, and she inter-

preted his mildest protests or expressions of displeasure as a por-
tent of his future as a "good-for-nothing."

This mother had relatively unconflicted relationships with
her other three children, all daughters. She could not entertain
the notion that her perception of her son was an extension of her
own anger at her abusive father and her controlling husband.
Instead, she thought that her feelings for her child showed that
she knew him better than anybody else. Her behavior toward
him was shaped by this conviction. She spoke openly to him
about his disobedient nature and treated him with a mixture of
punitiveness and rejection. Only as she was able to get in touch
with her own pain and anger at her abuse by her father was this
mother able to become more aware of her son's need for her. She
gradually began to perceive his protests and signs of displeasure
as the normal responses of a toddler in need of firm but affectionate guidelines rather than as the signs of a delinquent in the
making.

This example shows a distortion of the normal parental experience
of attributing a variety of virtues and defects to the young child. These
parental attributions often say more about the parents' wishes, fears,
and expectations than about the child's true nature. Attributions may
be flexible or rigid, and they may be more or less influenced by the
child's actual characteristics. Most often the attributions are positive,
benign, and largely attuned to the child's own emerging individuality ("She will be such a tomboy, you can see it from the glint in her
eye"; "He sure will be a success with the ladies"). In these cases, the
parent-child relationship unfolds on a basis of mutual trust and hopeful expectations. When the attributions are negative or malevolent
and cannot yield to disconfirming evidence, the parent and child are
headed for a relationship filled with conflict and mistrust. In such situations, the parental attributions may have their origin in painful and
frightening experiences in a parent's childhood—"ghosts in the nursery" that continue to exert their power on the parent's perceptions and
attitudes as an adult.

3. Difficulties in coordinating coparenting values, expectations, and practices. The symbolic role the child acquires in each parent's life can have pervasive negative effects on the parents' relationship as partners and coparents. The child's objective characteristics may become virtues or defects depending on how each parent perceives them, creating strains about how to respond. For example, a child's assertiveness may be seen as aggressive by a parent who feels uneasy about this trait, whereas the other parent may take great pleasure in the child's ability to speak up for herself.

> Mr. and Mrs. DeCarlo have a child, Anthony, who is very clear in stating his likes and dislikes. Anthony does not give in when he wants something and protests loudly when he does not get his way. Mr. DeCarlo, who thinks of himself as too stubborn and has problems yielding to other people, believes that Anthony's "willfulness" should be curbed. His wife, who sees herself as overpowered by her husband, is delighted by her son's feistiness and thinks it would be damaging to set firmer limits. Each of these parents is perceiving Anthony from the perspective of his or her own psychological needs. The father consciously wants to spare the child the problems he himself has, but he also wants to control Anthony and bring him in line with his own wishes. The mother relishes Anthony's outspokenness because it compensates for her own feelings that her husband always has the last word. The parents cannot agree on a coordinated response when Anthony is being willful and defiant, and the child's behavior escalates out of control when the parents argue with each other about allowing it or restraining it.

4. The quality of the parents' support system. It is difficult to establish and maintain a good relationship with a child when parents are stressed out and isolated, with few supports to help them feel secure. They are sometimes so absorbed in coping with difficult circumstances that there is little time and energy left for the child.

We usually think of support systems in human terms: a spouse, a parent, a sibling, a friend. This is understandable because human relationships are essential to a sense of personal well-being. However, support systems also consist of community networks that provide supplies and services: adequate housing, sufficient food, efficient transportation, safe streets, good schools, accessible medical care.

When these services are readily available, they are "psychologically silent": we do not notice the enormous contribution that they make to our personal well-being, to our ability to have harmonious human relationships, and to our capacity to be adequate parents. It is only when one or more of these supports are lacking that their importance can be appreciated because of the stress that the family experiences in their absence.

How is this related to temperament? As the following examples suggest, parents' responsiveness to their child's individual needs can be severely tested when the parents are struggling to secure basic needs and services for themselves and their children.

Mrs. Fisher needs to work full-time and can afford only a mediocre day care center with too few caregivers for too many children and a high staff turnover. This setting makes it impossible to accommodate her child's unusually strong, temperamentally based needs for predictability and consistency in his daily routine. As a result, since beginning to attend day care 2-year-old Dave has become prone to severe and prolonged temper tantrums. He is constantly anxious, sucks his thumb, and follows his mother around the house.

Mr. Morgan became unemployed when the high-tech firm he worked for went bankrupt. His unemployment benefits have run out, and the family has no medical insurance. He and his wife worry about the present and fret about the future. Mrs. Morgan, who left her teaching job to raise their daughter, is trying unsuccessfully to find another position. The parents are so intent on the daily effort to make ends meet that they have less time and patience for their daughter, Annie, 30 months old. Always a sensitive, easily frightened child, she has begun refusing to eat in order to save food. She has also started biting her nails and has regressed in her toilet training. She constantly asks her mother, "Are you okay?"

Mrs. Compton and her family live in a deteriorating inner-city neighborhood. Their small apartment has deficient plumbing in the kitchen and bathroom and is often infested by cockroaches and mice. The manager of the building has promised repairs for six months, but nothing has been done. "It's the same in every apartment," he says. Because of concerns about crime, the family is afraid to go out at night. The parents would like to move to better conditions but cannot afford it. There is frequent quarreling as a result of frayed nerves and hopelessness. This situation is affecting little Ricky, an intense child who responds strongly to even minor stimulation and who would optimally need a calm, predictable environment to help him organize and modulate his behavior. At 30 months, he has frequent nightmares and cries easily at minor frustrations. His attention span is very short, and in spite of good intelligence he is unable to persist at trying to solve an age-appropriate task. He often seems worried and distracted.

In such situations the strain on the parents, the child, and the parent-child relationship originates in society's failure to provide an adequate safety net for families in need. Though all children suffer from exposure to inadequate conditions, some children are more temperamentally resilient and able to cope, with fewer emotional costs, while other children are more vulnerable.

5. Cultural matches and mismatches in the family and social system. In our increasingly diverse societies, the pace of social change means that patterns of child rearing are changing rapidly in response to changing conditions. Well-established child-rearing expectations that were traditionally handed down from grandparents to parents

and from parents to children are being disrupted as their legitimacy is questioned by the younger generations. Different members of the family may have different opinions about the importance of children's obedience to elders, self-expression and self-assertion, the relationship between the sexes, the structure of family relationships, the primacy of individual wishes and pursuits versus deference to the needs of the family, and many other areas of family and social life. Parents may find themselves criticized by their own parents about the way they are raising their children, and grandparents may feel marginalized by their inability to influence how their grandchildren are raised. Families from minority groups may value child characteristics that are not valued in the broader society. For example, a preschool director was quoted as saying "Asian kids are very quiet in the classroom setting. I think their parents are very pushy at home, and also they have very high expectations for their preschoolers, which I do not think does any good, but we help them to be themselves here."[23] One may ask: What does it mean to "be oneself," and who defines it? How might a toddler or preschooler feel trying to navigate conflicting family and school expectations about who they should be and how they should behave?

Misunderstanding of cultural values can lead to stereotyping. These automatic negative attributions strain communications among adults who have different caregiving functions in relation to the child and detract from social cohesion. However, different cultural groups may value different temperamental characteristics and different personality styles, and these differences can expand the perspectives of everyone involved. Respect for different points of view and active dialogue to find common ground and to solve disagreements hold the key to adult partnerships on behalf of the child. Toddlers are capable of learning what is appropriate behavior in different contexts when adults support the child and one another in holding developmentally and contextually appropriate expectations, even if the expectations differ from one setting to another.

Upholding the importance and the challenges of giving respectful space to different perspectives and the contexts that shape them, the psychologist Chandra Ghosh Ippen wrote, "The last word comes from my *Obaachama*, my Japanese grandmother, a small woman whose voice rang through the house as she watched sumo wrestling: *ganbatte!* It is a battle cry, an encouraging call to act that says that we are together as we tackle the challenge of integrating context into all aspects of the work. It means, 'Go for it!' 'Do your best,' 'Work hard,' 'Good luck,' 'Keep at it.' *Ganbatte.*"[24]

The preceding examples illustrate the concentric circles of influence on a child's well-being. The child's temperament and personality are shaped by the family environment, which in turn exists within a larger social, cultural, and political context. Each context has its own complexities, but no individual—no matter how strong, talented, and resourceful—exists on her or his own. Children differ in their sensitivity to context. The physiological makeup of some children makes them more susceptible to variations in their environment, so that they may show exceptional achievement in response to optimal conditions and greater vulnerability in response to deprivation and stress. Other children tend to have an inner biological compass that makes them relatively steady in their developmental trajectory regardless of the characteristics of the environment.[25] Across individual differences, however, each one of us is helped or hindered in innumerable, often invisible ways by how our temperamental propensities are supported or undermined by the conditions in which we live.

The next two chapters will focus on two temperamental styles that are quite common among toddlers: shyness and its counterpart, bold activity. The chapters will describe the specific patterns of behavior that characterize these styles and the pleasures and special difficulties that they might bring.

Though temperamental differences are very real, most toddlers are shy sometimes and boldly adventurous at other times. Because of this, parents may recognize familiar aspects of their child in both chapters, even if they do not usually think of their toddlers as either particularly active or particularly shy.

5

High-Activity Toddlers: Racing Ahead

Toddlers are by nature tireless explorers. Exactly what they like to explore varies with the child and with the developmental stage. Some children resemble miniature scientists, bent on laboriously pulling apart every object they can get their hands on to see how it is made. Others experiment with language: they mix and match, make up words, engage in feats of linguistic construction. Still others build elaborate structures that seem to defy the imagination as well as physical gravity. Some do all of this and more, while others focus on different activities at different stages in their development.

Among these explorers, there are toddlers who are mesmerized by movement and by the pursuit of a far-off goal. They career through the world with their eyes set on whatever is just out of reach, with little regard for what stands in their way. They seem undaunted by obstacles, bumps, or falls.

Exploration from a Secure Base

In the balance between the exploration and attachment behaviors that define secure base behavior, toddlers who have high levels of activity and low levels of fear in response to novelty show a clear preference for exploration. Parents learn to cherish the brief moments when the child is so tired that she needs to cuddle for a while. This does not mean that these tiny adventurers have no feelings of love or wish for closeness. It is simply that, at least for the time being, action and novelty exercise an irresistible pull. For them, a secure relationship consists of the willingness to take risks away from the parent. It is as if the parents' love for the child fuels the child's love of the world.

This is not fanciful thinking. Toddlers raised in sterile institutions show little energy or interest in taking off because they have no loving base to take off from.[1] Secure, actively exploring toddlers can risk leaving the parents' side because they rely on their ongoing availability. Rather than needing to stay close for protection, they take off fully expecting that the parent will be there when needed.

Movement and Language in High-Activity Toddlers

High-activity toddlers are not always overly active as babies, but they often walk early following a relatively brief crawling stage. Their first steps may be at 8 to 10 months (instead of the more usual 11 to 13 months), with autonomous walking following about a month later.

Some toddlers begin to walk months before they say their first words. Many infants say their first words by about 12 months, but there are very marked individual fluctuations in the timing of this achievement. Toddlers also differ in the rate of acquiring new words and in how quickly they move from single words to two- and three-word sentences.

There is also great variability in the importance that language has for different toddlers and in the pleasure that they derive from using it. Some 2-year-olds are very attuned to language; others are not. Toddlers who thrive on activity and experimenting with movement are often not too interested in talking or listening until they get older and their motor skills become better integrated with their overall sense of themselves. Until this happens, they pay little attention to the "no's" and "stop's" of the adults. This makes language an ineffective tool for trying to restrain them. Caregivers often need to join action to their words in order to redirect the very active child.

Toddlers with a strong motivation to race ahead and be on the move show a combination of at least three traits: a high activity level, a high intensity of response, and a short attention span when it comes to sedentary activities. Such a child is unlikely to spend much time looking at books or trying to assemble puzzles. On the other hand, if she has access to a climbing structure, she may practice going up and down and in every other possible direction until she (and her parents) collapse from fatigue.

Particularly in the 12-to-24-month period, movement is so central to the active toddler's sense of well-being that enforced immobility, cramped spaces, or simply being indoors for too long can set off irritability, restlessness, and finally temper tantrums. These are the child's ways of indicating that the urge to move and explore needs to find an avenue for discharge.

In the section that follows, a little boy named Adam will be described to illustrate some typical features of a well-developing, unusually active, seemingly fearless toddler. The description also highlights some of the adaptations his parents had to make to cope with his high energy level and tireless urge to explore.

A Tireless Explorer: Adam

Most toddlers carry a measure of bold initiative inside them, and in this sense Adam illustrates vividly the normal state of affairs at this stage. He just did it more often, more intensely, and for longer periods of time. Here are some highlights of Adam's life between 10 and 30 months.

Adam's First Year

Adam began walking at 9 months. From then on it seemed as though he could never stop. His mother described herself as feeling like a Seeing-Eye dog, because she was always vigilant to Adam's whereabouts and ready to rescue him from danger. (She was a veterinarian, so the analogy came easily to her.)

10 months. Adam is walking by himself and refuses to be carried anywhere. His parents observe that he is so enthralled by attractive distant objects that he fails to notice obstacles in his way, such as steps or pieces of furniture. He trips over objects, falls down, bumps himself. He is often covered with bruises in spite of the family's concerted efforts to move faster than he. The house becomes thoroughly child proofed, with gates everywhere. This proves only somewhat helpful.

Diapering time is "a nightmare," in his mother's words. For Adam, a dirty diaper is a minor nuisance compared with the indignity of lying down and staying put while being changed. He kicks vigorously, protests, cries. His mother decides to switch from cloth diapers to disposable ones to minimize the hassle for both of them. She is constantly exhausted, but there is some respite. He sleeps soundly at night and takes two naps, for a blessed total of about fourteen hours of sleep a day.

Adam's mother feels as if her little boy grew overnight. She longs for the tender moments of quiet cuddling they had in earlier months, and her arms feel painfully empty at times. On the other hand, her own legs never stop now because she is always having to catch up with Adam. She says laughingly that their way of being together moved down from the torso to the feet.

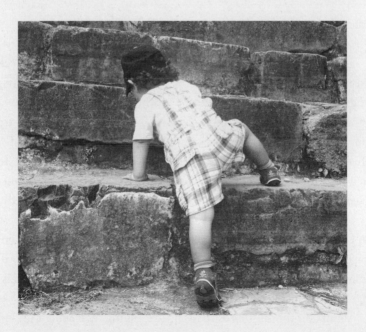

12 months. Adam says his first word, "cat." This word choice may not be a coincidence and may be related to Adam's fascination with movement. The family cat is an important member of the household, the center of much conversation, and an agile presence that jumps easily from the floor to the kitchen counter, flees swiftly when pursued by Adam's eager hands, and moves gracefully and at will throughout the house. Maybe the cat represents Adam's fledgling version of an "ideal self," seemingly free to move everywhere and happily unconstrained by cumbersome realities such as gravity, loss of balance, and parental efforts at holding him back.

The word "ousside" appears soon afterward. When expected to stay indoors, Adam stands by the door, banging at it and repeating this magic word again and again. If he is not taken "ousside," he becomes increasingly agitated and distressed. Adam's mother finds herself spending a lot of time in the yard and following him as he insists on going farther and walking up and down the block. She reports, "I got to know all my neighbors really well during that time."

Adam from 14 to 30 Months

14 months. Adam begins hitting his head when he cannot succeed at doing something he wants to. How can we understand this behavior? Adam is a precocious child, and he has high expectations of himself. He wants to climb on his high chair all by himself or open the front door to go "ousside." When he cannot live up to his own standards, he refuses adult help and instead deliberately punishes himself: he stops what he is trying to do, looks for a good hard surface such as an uncarpeted portion of the floor, and bangs his head loudly and repeatedly.

This dramatic behavior looks worrisome and is very scary to watch but is actually common among toddlers with a high intensity of emotional response. This does not mean that parents should ignore it. Doing nothing gives the child the message that punishing oneself is an appropriate reaction to feelings of failure and frustration.

Adam's mother responds to his head banging by placing him in his crib while telling him that she cannot let him hurt himself. At first she feels guilty and worries that putting him in the crib is punishing Adam for punishing himself. However, Adam responds well to this maneuver. He bangs his head softly on the mattress, as if rehearsing a discharge of motor tension in a safe setting. His mother stays near, sometimes talking soothingly to him, sometimes letting him be on his own. Adam eventually calms down. This positive response convinces his mother that she has intuitively found the right way to soothe her child.

The crib serves as a comforting container for Adam's unruly emotions. It is noteworthy that this very athletic child does not begin climbing out of his crib until 30 months, in spite of being physically able to do so much earlier. He clearly likes his crib and regards it as a safe place to be in.

Some children respond best to being held and cuddled while having a tantrum. Adam's mother found that this did not work well for him. When Adam was upset, he refused to be held and responded by arching his back, squirming, and pushing away. At those times he did not experience being held as a loving act but as a physical restraint that was extremely unpleasant to him.

The rejection of being held is a common response at his age when the toddler is experiencing a conflict of ambivalence: he simultaneously wants to be comforted by the parent and to assert his own autonomy. This conflict may be expressed by turning against the mother or father and hitting them or pushing them away. The parents are serving here as the recipient of the child's inner conflict.

It is better not to leave toddlers alone when they are having a tantrum. They need their parents as a secure base that will not leave them in the lurch when they are feeling alone, angry, and scared by the intensity of their emotions. If the parents can respond calmly rather than with anger or emotional withdrawal, the child's ambivalence will resolve itself in the course of development as he becomes better able to negotiate being close versus being separate and autonomous.

15 months. Adam learns to kick a ball, and a beach ball becomes his favorite toy. His parents put a basketball hoop in the kitchen at his height level, and he delights in putting the ball through the hoop again and again. He loves watching sports on TV, although neither parent relishes this activity. He cries when they try to change the channel, saying "Fooball, fooball."

16 months. Adam and his mother take a five-hour plane ride to visit his grandparents. He is miserable unless he is going up and down the aisle. He climbs on the few empty seats and tries to talk on the flight attendants' telephone. Adam's mother does her best to catch up and keep up, but the frowns of the crew are hard to bear. She mumbles to herself, "I bet they've never been around a kid."

Before this visit, Adam's mother looked forward to staying at her parents' house and sharing Adam's care with two other adults. Images of going for a walk by herself or even reading a book in the middle of the day floated dreamily through her mind. These fantasies fail to materialize. Her parents—Adam's grandparents—are clearly unable to match Adam's speed and energy level. Much as they enjoy him, they are unsettled and exhausted after a two-hour stint as his sole caregivers and worried about his safety if they cannot respond quickly enough to his forays. Adam's mother realizes with sadness that she needs to revise her expectations of her parents and adjust to the limitations imposed by their becoming older.

18 months. Adam begins to cry bitterly when his mother leaves, even when his much loved father is there to stay with him. She has to peel him off as he clings to her. This continues until he is 30 months old. The distress upon separation indicates that Adam is very conscious of his mother's role in making him feel secure. His distress is short lived, and he accepts substitutes well. He develops a warm relationship with two babysitters who care for him while his mother works a few hours a day. He greets his mother warmly when she returns home.

19 months. Adam begins attending a toddler group for two hours a day, twice a week, with five other children. His mother stays with him during this time. The teacher is experienced, cheerful, energetic. All the signs seem to indicate that this will be a good experience for Adam and his mother, but events prove otherwise.

The first day of the group, Adam climbs to the highest rung of the climbing structure and falls down, luckily without hurting himself. The teacher proceeds to unscrew the two upper rungs, commenting that no toddler has ever tried to go beyond the first three levels. Adam's mother is grateful for the teacher's flexibility.

The second day, Adam upturns a heavy wooden bench and uses it as a climbing structure. The teacher removes the bench from the area, saying cheerfully "Adam is teaching me about possible dangers I never knew about."

The third day, Adam cries continuously because it is raining and the children can't play "ousside." He does not mingle with the other children. He climbs on the furniture and invents games based on movement that the other children find fascinating and try to imitate. Mostly, however, he is very unhappy about being there.

The fourth day, after watching Adam's preference for moving on his own rather than playing with the other children, the teacher says to the mother, "I think Adam is not ready for this." His mother is devastated. She thinks, "If only I were more creative and energetic and could come up with novel ways of channeling his energy, he would fit better." Adam's father is philosophical. He consoles her by saying, "He is just fine. I was just like him. Actually, I still am."

20 months. Adam and his father go for an outing and come back radiant. They have spent the whole day riding buses and finding exciting things to do between bus and bus. On the bus rides, Adam gleefully climbs on the mostly empty seats and goes up and down the aisle in the back of the bus.

Adam's mother wishes such outings could happen more often. His father works very long hours and often comes home just before Adam goes to sleep. Everybody in the family regrets this situation. When singing a homemade version of "Old MacDonald Had a Farm," Mother asks, "What does the daddy say?" Adam replies, "Bye bye." He is only too aware that much of his daily experience of Daddy consists of seeing him leave.

It becomes clear that Adam has an internal motor map that allows him to navigate the world with an inner sense of competence. He
is like his father in this regard; his mother has no sense of direction.
When driving through the neighborhood where his best friend lives,
he points in the right direction, yelling, "Tony, Tony!"

22 months. Mother's best friend comments that she doesn't feel she
has a relationship with Adam. "He never lets me do anything for him,
and he doesn't like to do things like solve puzzles or read books with
me," she laments. Adam's mother worries that maybe he is not sociable
enough to be liked by other people.

Adam says his first two-word combination. Not surprisingly, it is
"No, myself."

23 months. Adam balances himself on a swing, refusing help by
using his handy new utterance, "No, myself." But there is a new twist:
his mother hears him muttering to himself "Be careful" as he eases
himself down.

Adam begins to say "Be careful" whenever he embarks on a new
feat. He also begins to ask for help: "Mommy help." This marks a transformation in his mother's perception of him. She begins to trust that
he can take care of himself. She is right: his reality testing regarding
danger has become more accurate. He has internalized his mother's
protective role, and he can now use her help as well as his own coping
devices to make himself feel secure.

24 months. On Adam's second birthday, his mother reflects, "It's
a miracle we never had to end up in the emergency room." In spite of
his bold behavior and his many falls, Adam has never been badly hurt.
This is probably a combination of his innate sense of his own capabilities and of his mother's and caregivers' readiness to spring into action.

As she thinks of herself during the past year, Adam's mother reflects, "I feel like a hypervigilant, overprotective mother." Is she accurate in her self-assessment? Truly overprotective mothers do not
generally know this about themselves. They believe they are protecting

their children from very real and immediate dangers, but in fact they tend to overestimate the risk of a situation. Adam's mother, on the contrary, was clearly responding to her child's need for protection before he could reliably take over this function by anticipating danger and protecting himself. She learned to accept and admire his boundless determination to explore as a personal trait that she needed to monitor but could not change. Because of his mother's availability, both physical and emotional, Adam was free to be himself without conflict or shame.

On the other hand, it is worth noting that Adam's father felt less compelled than his mother to retrieve and rescue him. Adam did not get hurt more often in his father's care, although he did get banged up more. Adam's mother worried more about physical safety than his father did, but that was all right with them. Individual differences between the parents can be very useful in giving children alternative but equally valid perspectives on how to negotiate the world.

30 months. Adam continues to be very active, but now his activities are modulated in a way that conveys new skills of self-control. During a trip to the beach, he makes a beeline for the water but stops right at the edge; he then runs all the way back to a line of trees but does not venture into the woods.

After an initial moment of panic as she watches him running between the water and the woods, Adam's mother realizes that he knows when to stop and gives up trying to run after him. She positions herself by the edge of the water, where she can keep an eye on him as he covers this exciting new territory. She is ready to spring into action, but she has a new confidence that she will not need to.

Adam spends long periods of time building with blocks and solving puzzles. His attention span has been redirected to quieter pursuits now that movement has been mastered. This has a good effect on his ability to relate to adults, who prefer sitting with Adam rather than running after him.

Language has become a major avenue for partnership between Adam and other people. At the doctor's, he follows the nurse's instructions to the letter. At home, his parents can now tell him what to do and he does it without physical coaxing. He also reports to his parents what his day was like. Conversations have become based on taking turns, and he listens while others talk. He puts feelings into words, describing himself and others quite accurately. He shows awareness of and empathy for his parents' and his little friends' experiences.

Adam is happy in his preschool. He has friendly relations with all ten children in his class. He fits in just fine. He loves being naked. He discovers his penis and is enamored of it. He notices and comments when he has an erection: "Mommy, my penis is big. Touch it, right here." He is also interested in differences between boys and girls. He plays with a little girl, saying "This is my eye. Where is your eye? . . . This is my nose. Where is your nose? . . . This is my penis. Where is your penis?" These developments indicate that Adam's interest in the body is switching from an unwavering focus on movement to a growing fascination with how he is made, how he is similar to other boys, and how he differs from little girls.

Adam's second year shows the trajectory covered by a little child with a boundless craving for movement as he or she learns to modulate a high activity level. The key to developmental progress is the child's ability to gradually integrate physical movement with cognitive and social milestones in development, such as the ability to interact with peers and adults, the use of language, and the evolution of fantasy play.

A Time-Limited Period

Parents who do not share the child's level of activity (and very few do) may have a difficult time during this period. Mothers of very active toddlers often comment that they feel at times like social pariahs because of their children. Family friends fret over their belongings when the child comes over. There is a covert or overt social message that the parents should do more to keep the child "under control." One mother commented, "People did not understand that for Danny a coffee table was not a coffee table; it was something made to climb on." She went on to explain that her own self-esteem suffered because she was ashamed of her child's wild behavior. This mother believes that her child's early self-esteem might have suffered as well because he was constantly experiencing the disapproval of the adults. (She might have been right, but her son did not seem to carry this early hurt into his preschool years. He was a happy, talented, and much liked child.)

The good news is that the period of unbridled motor exploration is generally time limited and begins to wane at about 30 months. By 3 years of age, children are generally much more in control of themselves, and life in the household becomes quieter and more pleasant.

The next two sections describe what happens when the child's high activity level becomes a source of friction between parents and child. The last section offers some suggestions that may help to defuse conflict and build islands of quiet activity to promote partnership between parents and child.

Conflict in Motion: Melinda

When a toddler does not feel emotionally supported in her search for a satisfying balance between closeness and exploration, movement may become the carrier of conflict in the parent-child relationship.

That was the case with Melinda, the youngest of four children and the only girl. Melinda's parents had longed for a girl for many years, and they were overjoyed when she was born eight years after their youngest son. Mrs. Powell experienced a resurgence of youth and hope as she cuddled her little girl, dressed her in frilly outfits, and daydreamed about playing with her daughter the way she herself had played as a child. She had saved a beautiful dollhouse from those happy days, and she began collecting miniature furniture to outfit it in style by the time Melinda could play with it.

But Melinda's emerging personality did not fit in with Mrs. Powell's dreams. She was a smiley, sturdy little girl who loved her mother but was totally mesmerized by her boisterous and playful older brothers. As soon as she could walk, she ran after them when they played outside, trying to catch a Frisbee or kick a ball. The boys sometimes welcomed her and other times resented her intrusions. As a result, they alternated between including her and shoving her away. Melinda was giddily happy when her brothers played with her and screamed in rage when they did not.

Mrs. Powell went along with Melinda's interest in her brothers' games until she was 2 years old. The mother believed that a 2-year-old should start learning to play like a girl rather than a boy. Melinda's second birthday present was her mother's childhood dollhouse, fully equipped with doll-size furniture and dolls to match. Melinda played with it briefly, broke the leg of a little table, pulled out the stuffing of a tiny armchair, and then trotted off to see what her brothers were doing. She played "tag" with them, running wildly around the yard.

Mrs. Powell was hurt, but she would not allow herself to admit it. Instead, she became more firmly convinced that Melinda was now a little girl and must not be allowed to be so wild. She became curt and critical whenever Melinda was exuberantly active, which was often. When Melinda came close to her mother after falling down or getting hurt in the course of her play, Mrs. Powell said harshly, "That is what happens to you for being so wild." If Melinda was sweaty and covered with dirt after playing in the yard, she snapped. "Don't come near me when you are dirty like that."

Melinda soon learned to associate physical excitement in active play with rejection by her mother. She also began to acquire a dim sense that little girls should not "run free." Instead of finding a receptive mother when she returned from her forays, she found emotional distance and disapproval.

Melinda continued to have happy moments with her mother, but only when she was quiet and controlled. By 28 months, she became aware that playing with dolls and having tea parties made for moments of rewarding intimacy together. She began to purposely seek out her mother for this kind of play, bringing her a doll or saying, "Let's have tea, Mommy." Mrs. Powell's heart seemed to melt at those times, and she would stop whatever she was doing to play with her daughter.

In spite of those times of closeness, some incidents suggest that

Melinda's relationship with her mother had become emotionally constricted. When she got very excited, she often stopped herself abruptly and looked worriedly in her mother's direction. When she fell as a result of daring activities, she sometimes said to herself "Bad girl" and did not seek out comfort from her mother. At those moments, it seemed as if Mrs. Powell's disapproving demeanor had become part of Melinda's sense of herself.

If everyone in this child's world had adopted her mother's attitude and frowned on her activity level, it is possible that Melinda might have internalized the adults' disapproval and begun to feel bad about herself for not living up to the ideal of a properly feminine little girl.

Fortunately, this conflict about activity did not become pervasive because Melinda's father and brothers continued to play rough-and-tumble games with her and to enjoy her liveliness. At those times Melinda seemed to be truly happy, particularly if her mother was not present. If she got hurt during those activities, she readily went to her father or one of her brothers for a cuddle. This is a reflection of young children's sensitivity to how different adults respond to them and their ability to tailor their behavior accordingly. The emotional tone of relationships can be very different between the child and every one of the important adults in her life.

If Mrs. Powell had been less wounded by her daughter's failure to be the sedate little girl she wanted, she might have been more accepting of Melinda's boisterous behavior and more able to help the child learn that enjoying tea parties and climbing trees, far from being mutually exclusive, could be two integral parts of herself and her world.

What is Melinda's long-term outlook? If the family continues to function as it does now, it is possible that she will learn to associate physical and emotional freedom with being a boy and self-constraint in the physical and affective spheres with being a girl. As she grows up, this could perhaps contribute to unnecessary conflicts over being a woman.

On the other hand, a turn for the better could well occur. After all, mothers and fathers grow and learn from their mistakes. It is possible that Melinda's mother might become less uptight about what she sees as Melinda's "tomboyishness." There were signs that her family and friends were working to make this happen. Mrs. Powell was good-naturedly ribbed by her family for what they called her "prissiness" toward Melinda. Her husband often spoke up in private, telling her she was being "too hard" on the child. A close friend made a helpful comment when the mother poured her heart out about her worries and wishes about Melinda: she pointed out that Mrs. Powell had often felt lonesome at home among "all the boys" and was relying too much on Melinda to provide some female companionship, which was beyond the capacities of a 2-year-old.

Those reactions might help Mrs. Powell become more aware of how her own needs are affecting her attitude toward her daughter. If she becomes more accepting, Melinda could in turn feel more secure about being good and lovable just as she is, tomboyishness and all.

Reckless Accident Proneness: Paul

Some children express their conflicts over their parents' lack of availability as a secure base in the form of an uncontrollable urge to explore recklessly that often ends up in accidental injuries. These reckless toddlers may wander away from the house, dart across the street, get lost in supermarkets and shopping malls, pull the contents of shelves onto themselves, and in general constantly get into trouble. It is not the occurrence of a couple of incidents that defines a reckless toddler; it is the frequency of fairly serious accidents or enough close calls to warrant ongoing concern for the child's welfare.[2]

Sometimes it is difficult to know when a toddler is reckless as a result of inner conflict or relationship problems with the parents; when he or she is simply still too young and too active to be able to anticipate danger; and when he or she might have difficulties with sensorimotor coordination that interfere with motor planning. One clue that something might be wrong is that reckless children remain uncontrollable long after outgrowing toddlerhood. Unlike Adam, they do not become more aware of danger and more careful and attentive as they enter their third year.

Another sign of trouble is that, paradoxically, reckless toddlers tend to show numerous symptoms of anxiety in a variety of areas. Although all toddlers show age-appropriate fears, reckless toddlers are often overwhelmed by them. They might be excessively afraid of the dark, of animals, of strangers, or of unusual noises. They might have frequent and intractable tantrums; be afraid of going to sleep or wake up screaming several times during the night; suffer from acute separation anxiety interspersed with episodes of darting away. Their apparent fearlessness in exploring seems to be counterbalanced by their excessive fear in other realms. Sometimes their anxiety emerges in the form of anger and aggression: hitting, biting, and kicking.

At 28 months, Paul showed all these behaviors, making him a very difficult child to live with. His parents and pediatrician were so worried that they undertook an extensive medical evaluation to determine whether he was hyperactive. When the results were negative, Mr. and Mrs. Donahue were actually a little disappointed. They wanted a concrete medical reason for Paul's behavior, something that could be cured by taking pills. They did not want to get into the amorphous realm of psychological difficulties. Nevertheless, they were concerned enough about Paul to agree readily when their pediatrician recommended a psychological evaluation.

The best place to observe a toddler's psychological functioning is at home, where he feels least restrained by the demands of an unfamiliar situation. In the course of a two-hour home visit, Paul was quite ready to show me what his parents were worried about. While they spoke about his uncontrollable behavior, he climbed precariously onto a windowsill and jumped down noisily, twisting his ankle; he pulled down a portrait of himself and his family by climbing on a piece of furniture; he got into a fight with the cat by pulling its tail, getting scratched as a result; and he hit his mother when she tried to look at the scratch.

In spite of all this turmoil, Paul quieted down and looked at me with wide, sad eyes when I spoke with him. I told him that he was showing me that he and his parents were having a hard time together and that I had come to help things feel better for them. Those words had the effect of calming him down. He clearly understood what I was talking about.

In the sessions that followed, a curious pattern emerged. Mr. and Mrs. Donahue were so convinced that their son was an aggressive, powerful, uncontrollable "little demon" (as they called him) that they could not see the ways in which he was also a fearful little boy. They were frightened of him and perceived his night terrors, difficulty in going to sleep, and fitful crying on separation as cunning efforts to keep them under his control. "He is just pretending," they would say. "He is afraid of nothing. He is just trying to fool us into doing what he wants." The Donahues had become so angry at their son that they had no empathy with his plight. Their own suffering blinded them to Paul's desperate bids for help.

How had all this come about? Observations of Paul with his parents showed that Mrs. Donahue had little patience for any behavior that might be construed as dependent or needy. When Paul became alarmed by a fire truck and clung to her skirt, she laughed and told him he was being silly. When he cried as she left him in a toddler group, she said, "You have no right to cry. You are always running away from me. See if you like it when I do it to you." When he cut himself on a piece of glass he had broken, she told him, "It is your own fault for being so destructive."

Mr. Donahue, although less active than his wife in Paul's life, followed a similar pattern. He encouraged Paul to be "strong" and was critical of him when he was frightened or hurt. In addition, he tended to spank Paul quite hard to keep him in line. Paul had begun to hit him back, which alternately amused and enraged his father. When he was amused, Mr. Donahue would laugh appreciatively at his son's feistiness and say, "You are tough like your old man." This reinforced Paul's readiness to use aggression to fight back. But when his father was not in the mood for such feistiness, he became enraged and hit the child even harder to "show Paul who is the boss." At such times Paul would collapse in tears and then be sent to his room, where he would scream in protest for as long as forty minutes at a time.

Such exchanges with his parents gave Paul the message that he was on his own. He had no secure base to which he could turn when he felt fearful or needy. His father could not help Paul modulate his anger because he could not control his own. His mother disliked any show of weakness and encouraged him to be independent, but she also scolded him for the often disastrous results of his efforts to "stand on his own."

Mr. and Mrs. Donahue misinterpreted Paul's high activity level as a sign of defiance that needed to be punished. They also mistook Paul's efforts to establish physical closeness or proximity as symptoms of dependence, and dependence was not acceptable to them. They rejected Paul's efforts to establish a secure base with them because they did not understand that that was age-appropriate behavior.

Thoughts and feelings that are unacceptable to the parents can easily become unacceptable to their child. From this perspective, we can understand Paul's recklessness and darting away as an effort to counteract his wish to approach his parents, which he knew would be rebuffed. The more he fought off the desire to approach his parents for comfort and reassurance, the more scared he became of succumbing to that wish. The sleeping problems and the separation anxiety were efforts to engage his parents' help and to ensure that he would not be left alone with his fears. This high-activity child was using motion as a defense against anxiety, but the fears surfaced at night and when his parents were leaving—that is, in situations where he could not run away.

Children like Paul are asking "How far do I need to go before Mom will bring me back? How much danger is too much so that Dad will protect me? How scared do I need to be for Mom and Dad to help me feel safe?" Mr. and Mrs. Donahue had to struggle long and hard before they could understand the urgent reality of Paul's fears and before they could respond to his recklessness as a cry for help. In the process of learning to know their child, they had to remember their own fears and longings as little children who had been punished too harshly and expected to do too much too soon.

The repetition of a painful past in a painful present is often at work when parents are at a loss as to how to protect their child. The Donahues were helped in child-parent psychotherapy to reexperience their own early, unheeded wishes to feel protected and secure. This helped them understand their child's fears better, and they could then begin responding to Paul's call for help. For example, they held their son when he clung to them and said, "You are okay. I will take care of you," instead of pushing him away. They retrieved him when he darted off in unfamiliar places and told him, "I get scared when you run away. I don't want you to get hurt." They helped him when he asked for help. As the child began to heal from his anxieties through those loving ministrations, the parents found that through experiencing empathy with their child they were also beginning to heal themselves of the wounds left by their own harsh childhoods.

Some General Reflections on Temperament and Partnership

The cases of Adam, Melinda, and Paul show how the child's temperamental style and the parents' acceptance of it can have a powerful influence on the kind of partnership they are able to develop. When parents accept the child's style and adapt to it, their partnership promotes successful development. When the parents are rejecting or critical of the child's style, conflict and alienation may result.

Adam's mother did not have the same temperamental style as her son and often longed for a less active child. However, she managed to remain emotionally available and attuned to his whereabouts by reminding herself that he was not an extension of herself but a little individual with very strong predispositions of his own—that he was, in fact, more like his father than like her.

Melinda's mother, in contrast, could not accept her daughter's active style. She was too disappointed by the child's inability to fulfill her dream of quiet mother-daughter intimacy.

Paul's parents went one step further in their inability to be receptive to their child. They became punitive in response to his difficult behavior and rejected him when he came close. Those were the only responses they had learned from their own parents as they were growing up.

Adam, Melinda, and Paul showed distinctive adaptations to their parents' treatment of them. In response to his mother's acceptance, Adam explored in a manner that was self-assured and free of conflict and was progressively able to internalize his mother's protection to modulate himself. Melinda, aware of her mother's disapproval, learned to inhibit her exuberance in order to please her but indulged in the pleasure of bold activity with her father and brothers. Paul internalized his parents' harshness and punished them as well as himself through his aggression and proneness to accidents. We see through these three children how one developmentally dominant behavior—an exceptionally high activity level—may lead to three very different early personality configurations as a result of differences in parental response.

The other side of this process is the extent to which children educate receptive parents to adapt to their style. Adam's mother, after much daydreaming about how peaceful life would be with a less active child, had the chance to babysit for just such a toddler. She spent the day with a quiet, docile, companionable little boy. Much to her surprise, she found herself bored and restless and had to suppress the impulse to push the child to become more active.

Living with a High-Activity Toddler

How can one try to cope productively with an exasperatingly energetic child? The first step is to remember that such toddlers are just as eager to please their parents and to form a partnership with them as are more sedate children. They are simply unable to stop themselves even when they want to because the urge to explore is so strong. The parents' strategy needs to involve an effort to instill gradual self-control around specific unacceptable behaviors.

One way of doing this is to address the situation at hand rather than the child's essence. It is not helpful to a toddler to be told that he is being a nuisance, because he would not know what to do to change and because such a global statement would only make him feel bad about himself. The child can cooperate with the parents when he is told the specific behaviors that he needs to stop, including a simple explanation so that the child can start to learn about the connection between his behavior and its effects. For example:

- "I am very angry because you ran away."
- "I got so scared that you would get hurt. I love you, and I don't want anything to happen to you."
- "I don't like it when you don't do what I tell you."
- "You need to stop when I tell you to stop."
- "You need to be in your room until you are ready to be with people again."

If words are not enough, take firm action to stop the child and then tell her why you did it. Young toddlers in particular learn better from parents' protective actions than from their words alone.

Intense children often need an intense parental response to match their inner experience. A mild "Don't do that" is not likely to persuade such a child that the parent means it. If a parent says "I am angry" with the conviction of his emotions, the child will hear it as a statement that must be taken seriously. No threats will be needed to encourage compliance, because the parent's approval is incentive enough.[3]

There are also other ways of helping very active children remain true to their nature while minimizing parental burnout and family conflicts. The following suggestions may help.

- Set up areas inside and outside the house where vigorous play is possible and permitted. This helps the child discharge energy and increases the likelihood of quiet moments following high-energy play.[4]

- Make the most of quiet moments. Enjoy the brief moments of cuddling to the fullest. When the child rests, try to take a rest as well.

- High-activity toddlers crave novelty. Try to come up with new ideas that will keep you and your child from getting bored. While you cook, give him scraps of vegetables and ask him to make a salad or mix some flour and water to make "bread." Hide toys that he has tired of, and make them reappear some weeks later. Schedule outings and arrange times together with other parents and their children. Try to get to know your neighbors so that they can become part of a neighborhood network of social support.

- Keep an eye out for subtle cues of wariness or fear, and be receptive to calls for help. Sometimes it is easy to typecast children as "fearless" and assume that they are self-sufficient all the time. This is not accurate. Even the most intrepid of toddlers gets needy and scared.

- Try to share the care of your child. Children between 8 and 13 can be great babysitters at this age if you stay around. As a rule, they are too young to leave alone with an unruly toddler, but they can match your child's energy level and help to bring some organization and good judgment to physical feats. Responsible adolescents are generally able to care for toddlers on their own. They can provide the parent with a welcome relief from the ever-vigilant stance that high-activity toddlers demand.

- Relax your standards for as many things as you can get away with: meals, household chores, entertainment, even your work standards if you can afford to. You can catch up later, when your toddler is no longer an obstacle to other pursuits.

- Pick your battles with your child carefully, and do not be afraid to give in if the issue at stake is a relatively trivial one. As one very wise mother put it, "His capacity to passionately insist on wanting something outlasted my capacity to say no." After all,

negotiating and giving in are part and parcel of building a partnership. In the middle of a struggle, learn to ask yourself: What
is the point here? If your answer is that you are doing something
important, hold on to your position. If, on the other hand, you
are trying to be "consistent" or to save face, do yourself a favor
and find a graceful way to give in. Occasional yielding will not
spoil your child, unless it becomes such a habit that you no longer have the will to enforce basic rules about safety, regard for
others, or care of property. On the contrary, your flexibility can
help teach your child the value of persistence and give her confidence in her ability to make her point well. It will also save
you precious energy that you need for the here and now and for
more important battles in the long run.

Your child is your best partner in working out conflicts over keeping close and moving away. Games of hide-and-seek, mutual chasing,
and "tag" enact these conflicts about secure base behavior in the language children understand best: the language of play. Fantasy play also
contributes to the gradual mastery of these conflicts. The child psychiatrist Henri Parens described a little girl, Cindy, who at 14 months
showed inexplicably increased irritability and testiness toward her
mother. She started moving away from her only to stop abruptly, go
closer to the mother, and have a tantrum. After a week of repeating
this sequence again and again, Cindy found a symbolic way of trying
to master her dilemma: she sat close to her mother and engaged in a
game of throwing her doll off the sofa and then lovingly retrieving it.
Six weeks after playing this game again and again, Cindy was able to
move away from her mother for increasingly broader perimeters.[5] She
had found a way of coming to grips with an inner impasse about her
use of her mother as a secure base, and she moved on to a new integration of daring and intimacy.

Slow-to-Warm-Up Toddlers: Taking One's Time

Buoyant and irrepressible as toddlers can be, they are also capable of a mood of quiet reserve. This state of mind is most likely to occur when the child encounters an unfamiliar situation. At such times, activity level subsides, the facial expression becomes sober or worried, and there is a strong tendency to stay close to or even hide behind the parent. The toddler may stare fixedly at what is happening, avert the eyes, or hide the face in the parent's body. The child's whole demeanor seems to be saying, "I need some time to process this and to feel safe with what is happening."

Though all toddlers react in this way at one time or another, for some children it is a typical response that may last for twenty minutes or longer. The psychologist Jerome Kagan, who has been studying this set of behaviors for many years, calls it "inhibition to the unfamiliar" or "behavioral inhibition."[1] These children's temperamental features cohere into what is usually called shyness.

The Profile of Slow-to-Warm-Up Temperament

Children who are slow to warm up have three major temperamental traits: they are inordinately wary with strangers, cautious toward novel objects, and prone to withdraw in unfamiliar situations. However, they often do not differ from other children once they are well acquainted and comfortable with their companions and with their surroundings.[2]

In their secure base behavior, slow-to-warm-up toddlers tend more than other children to stay near their parents rather than to explore when they are faced with an unfamiliar setting. Parents learn to prepare themselves for a warm-up period that may involve holding the child or at least letting the child hold on to them or stay very close. Once a slow-to-warm-up toddler adjusts to the new situation, pleasure in exploring may be quite intense. However, toddlers with this temperamental style are more likely than other children to keep an eye out for unexpected changes and go to the parent if any occurs.

There is considerable evidence that slowness to engage with novel situations is a stable temperamental feature with a reliable physiological profile. Kagan compared the toddlers he called "inhibited to novelty" with a group of very outgoing age-mates and found that the timid children had higher levels of arousal of the sympathetic nervous system. For example, they tended to show large increases in heart rate and pupil dilation in response to mildly stressful stimulation, suggesting that they were more reactive to situations likely to elicit wariness or fear.[3]

The possible association of slow-to-warm-up styles with increased wariness and fear is supported by more recent research findings of activation in the neural circuits of brain areas associated with both fear and reward in adolescents who continued to show behavioral inhibition, raising the possibility that slow-to-warm-up children may be more responsive to reward and punishment than other children.[4]

Do children who are slow to warm up continue to be so as adults? Kagan and his colleagues were interested in studying the long-term stability of this pattern of behavior. In one early longitudinal study, 3-year-olds who were extremely slow to warm up were more likely to become introverted adults than were very outgoing peers.[5] A more recent study shows that this trait can be found even earlier in development. Extremely slow-to-warm-up 2-year-olds were more likely to show this behavioral profile and its distinctive physiological pattern when they were 8 years old.[6]

Although there is stability, there is also variability. In another study, less than 30 percent of the toddlers who showed very high social wariness at age 2 continued to show this pattern by age 5. Experiences with caregiving and peers between infancy and adolescence are influential in affecting the stability of these individual characteristics.[7]

The tendency to withdraw from novelty becomes a reliable feature of the child's personality only in the second year of life, but certain responses during infancy may predict that the child will be likely to show the pattern later on. For example, 4-month-old babies who responded to unfamiliar stimuli by crying and increased motor activity continued to be more distressed by novelty at 14 and 21 months than toddlers who had not cried or become physically active when they were babies. Here again, the evidence suggests a physiological basis for the behavioral response.[8]

In spite of this evidence, inhibition to novelty is not completely stable as a personality trait. About half of extremely timid 2-year-olds do not appear to be shy in later childhood. It is possible that this decline in initial slowness to respond to novel situations is a result of social influences, since mainstream American culture values friendliness. As a result, retiring youngsters might be coaxed by parents, teachers, relatives, and peers to overcome their initial reserve in new situations. This possibility is supported by findings that children who used to be shy but no longer behave that way continue to show a higher level of sympathetic arousal. Behavior may be easier to change than physiology.[9]

A Typical Slow-to-Warm-Up Toddler: Erin

Erin fits well the profile of a toddler who in new situations takes her time, watches carefully, and ventures out only after a warm-up period. Erin's mother reports that she developed a standard strategy to mediate between her daughter and strangers eager to make her acquaintance at social gatherings. She told the stranger, "She'll take her time for one hour, and then she'll be your friend." By not using the "shy" label, this mother was preventing a premature categorization of her child's response.

Erin's First Year

Erin was 2 months old when her mother got the first glimpse of her daughter's sensitivity to overstimulation. It happened when she and Erin attended a mothers' group of about eight women and their babies. Erin cried nonstop and could not be consoled. This was in stark contrast with her behavior at home, where she seldom cried and was easily comforted. Ever since the group meeting, Erin's parents could predict how their daughter would behave. In familiar surroundings she was placid and composed; in unfamiliar and busy places she was restless and unhappy.

Even in her earliest weeks, Erin liked to observe her surroundings. The family had a sunny, colorful home with bright walls and interesting ornaments. When Erin was only 3 weeks old, she could spend long periods scanning the room and looking at different objects with eyes wide open and a transfixed expression. Erin's mother, who stayed home for the first six months after her daughter's birth, wondered at such times whether she should try to entertain her daughter more actively. However, Erin herself seemed very content with those private times.

Her interest in looking included people as well. At 6 months, Erin was a very sociable baby who showed only fleeting wariness on meeting strangers. During outings she fixated her big eyes on those around her, and people would fall in love with her as she smiled and cooed in delight while looking straight into their eyes.

Erin's first year was peaceful and uneventful. There were only two areas of sustained difficulty, both of which involved transitions. One was the transition between being awake and falling asleep. Erin cried very hard and seemed to fight off sleep even when she was very tired. The other area of intense distress was being undressed, given a bath, and dressed again. She seemed to hate having her skin exposed to too much stimulation.

Erin's parents found good ways of helping her during those difficult events. The transition to sleep was made easier by movement and sound. The parents put her into a stroller and pushed her all over the house. When that did not work, they rocked her while making wide sweeping movements with their arms. Erin loved sound (her parents were musicians, and music often flowed through the house), and the monotonous sound of the vacuum cleaner had a soothing effect when nothing else seemed to work.

Erin said her first word at 9 months, and language became a major tool for relationships soon afterward. She also began to crawl at 9 months. In fact, she said her first word and began to crawl on the same weekend. Her first steps did not occur until she was 13 months old, and that event formally ushered in the beginning of toddlerhood.

Erin from 13 to 36 Months

13 months. Erin takes her first steps. She seems tentative but delighted with herself. She practices valiantly, falling down and getting up again and again. Her mood as she does this is sober and intent rather than giddy. She seems to be working hard at mastering and controlling this new and unpredictable skill.

Rather suddenly, Erin becomes quite shy. This is when her mother begins to caution people that she will take quite some time to open up to them. Erin's mother remembers her pain when the child changed from outgoing sociability to reserve. She remembers thinking, "People won't even have a chance to find out how wonderful she is."

14 months. Erin becomes clingy and grumpy. Whereas earlier she liked to spend time alone and was in a good mood most of the time, she has now become irritable and difficult to please. She cries when her mother leaves the room and insists on following her everywhere. Her mother finds this change very frustrating and wonders why her child seems so insecure.

Erin has a very good relationship with her babysitter, a warm and responsive young woman who has cared for her since her mother went back to work when Erin was 6 months old. This relationship helps her during her separations, but Erin remains demanding and easily frustrated when her mother is around. There are times when her mother remembers thinking "She has become a pest."

15 months. Erin and her parents go to the birthday party of a little friend, a strictly timed two-hour affair. For the first half hour, Erin stays very close to her mother, intermittently hiding her face in her mother's skirt. The second half hour is spent playing with some toys at her mother's feet. Erin then agrees to go with her father to watch the other six children as they run around in the adjacent family room. The birthday boy hands her a party favor, and that seems to finally break the ice. Erin follows her little friend as he goes to climb on an indoor slide, and she laughs happily as she slides down. She becomes very unhappy when it is time to go home.

Erin remains difficult to please at home. She continues to have happy interactions with her mother and father, but she gets frustrated easily. Contrary to her general good mood during her first year, she now cries easily and needs frequent reassurance. This behavior comes and goes, with two or three weeks of good cheer interspersed with periods of intense dinginess. This pattern lasts until her second birthday.

16 months. Father and Erin go to a small grocery store where the friendly owner exuberantly praises her beautiful eyes and hair, coming close to her and lightly touching her cheek. Erin bursts into tears. Her father explains to the grocer, "She is becoming self-conscious." Erin is using short sentences well and is beginning to talk about feelings. Once, half asleep, she puts her arms around her mother's neck and murmurs, "I like my mommy."

17 months. Erin and her father go to a new playground, and Erin refuses to try the structures for the first half hour or so. Her father walks around the whole perimeter of the playground with her, talking lightly about the scene. He points out a dog peeing against the slide, and they both laugh merrily. They sift sand between their fingers and look for little bugs in the surrounding grass. Then they sit and watch quietly as the other children go up and down the structures. Erin suddenly says, "Me, too." She then plays actively and happily for a long time.

18 months. Erin's mother takes her to a toddlers' gym, where about ten toddlers play on different structures and have a brief "circle time" with songs and a little dance. Erin watches the children intently with a "tight little face," in her mother's word. She does not try anything new. Her mother berates herself for raising such a timid child. "What have I done?" she wonders, worrying that she has been hopelessly overprotective and that she is to blame for making her child feel insecure in new situations. When all the other children are putting their socks on to go home, Erin has a sudden upsurge of activity. She runs wildly from structure to structure, trying everything. She does not want to leave.

(The issue of mothers berating themselves for developmentally or temperamentally normal behavior cannot be underestimated. Mothers are prone to torture themselves with self-blame when their children are having a hard time. Knowing this might help a little when one catches oneself doing it.)

Erin's parents take her to the gym every week because they believe (with good reason) that it makes sense to expose her to a setting where she needs to make some effort to overcome her discomfort with novelty. For a whole year, Erin goes through a similar sequence: a long warm-up period, followed by a surge of activity when no one is looking and then reluctance to leave.

20 months. Erin develops a fear of masks and the full moon. She cries, averts her eyes, and refuses to look at them. She tries to run away from the moon and insists that the masks be hidden somewhere. She cannot articulate what frightens her about those objects, but toddlers do develop seemingly inexplicable fears on the basis of their fantasies about how the world operates. The difference between reality and make-believe is very tenuous at this age, and it is possible that Erin thinks in some half-conscious way that the objects are real but disembodied angry faces that can do her harm. This fear persists for about four months.

There are other examples of Erin's difficulty in distinguishing fantasy from reality. She bursts into tears and cries, "No, no, no, I don't want to go to sleep" when her mother plays a game with her dolls in which the mommy doll tells the baby to go to bed. Another time Erin tries to "scoop" the babies and animals off the pages of her books. These and similar behaviors are very common at this age.

22 months. Erin goes to a party attended by about ten adults and six other children. She behaves very similarly to the way she did in the gym. She stays very close to her parents, watching the other children with wide eyes. She starts playing with them after about an hour of careful scrutiny. When it is time to leave, she complains, "But I did not get to play very much."

Erin's parents develop a strategy to help her leave a social gathering. They give her a ten-minute advance notice when the time to leave is approaching and then keep apprising her of the time: "We'll leave in five minutes; we'll leave in one more minute; now it's time to go." Although Erin still protests departing, the advance notice gives her time to prepare herself for the unwelcome event.

Erin plays happily with individual children whom she knows well when the gathering occurs in her own home or in the home of close family friends. She has early and intense friendships and plays with her friends for long periods of time. She also loves playing quietly with her mother. With her father, she dares to do things she does not try with anybody else: he swings her so high in the swing that her mother can hardly watch, but Erin loves it and asks for more. These examples suggest that Erin needs a secure interpersonal base before she can risk exploring new horizons. Close, one-to-one relationships are her most comfortable and enjoyable forms of social exchange.

24 months. Erin seems to undergo a transformation. She seems more relaxed, confident, and independent. She is less demanding at home and easier to please. Her fear of masks and of the full moon disappears. She begins to ask "Why?" Her curiosity about how the world works seems insatiable. She wants to know why it rains, why the cat licks herself, why pancakes get burned, why Mommy needs to go to work, why So-and-so got angry. She listens with rapt attention to her parents' explanations.

Erin seems to feel freer to be exuberant than in earlier months. A friend's mother comments that "Erin really let go of herself" as she brings her back home from an outing with her little friend. Still, there is a quality of self-restraint to Erin's moods. She can laugh merrily but does not get excited; she does not have intense tantrums; she does not say no very often. The extremes of emotion seem alien to her.

On the other hand, Erin loves to entice her little friends to do exciting things: "jump higher"; "run faster." It seems as though she gets vicarious pleasure from the excitement of others and wants to expand her own experience by watching how others feel.

26 months. Erin's pleasure in strong one-to-one relationships becomes more apparent. When she meets her friend Stephanie after not seeing her for a week, the two children run toward each other with open arms and hug each other tightly.

Erin internalizes her parents' formula of counting down time to help her with transitions. Waiting for her friend Ansel to stop going down the slide so he can play dolls with her, she says, "Two more times, Ansel. Now one more time. Now you come play babies with me."

28 months. Erin begins to spontaneously initiate social contact with other children in unfamiliar situations. At a restaurant, her booster seat is back-to-back with a booster seat at the next table. She leans back, smiles at her little neighbor, and says in a very friendly voice, "Hello."

Being thrust into a large situation is another story; Erin still takes her time before she joins in. These warm-up periods are a stable part of her response to new situations. She does not require coaxing or being won over. As her mother puts it, "She comes around on her own if you don't bug her."

30 months. Erin finds a creative way of saying good-bye to her mother, something she still does not like to do. She invents a separation ritual: she runs all over the house to find a special small object (a leaf, a shell, a marble, a small toy) that she ceremoniously deposits in her mother's hand. This object may represent a precious part of Erin's own self, which she wants to put in her mother's safekeeping while they are apart.

32 months. Erin becomes more assertive in her efforts to be alone with someone special. If her father comes home while she is playing with her mom, she greets him briefly, and if he lingers around them, she says, "Mom and I are playing." After her father returns from a trip, she hugs him tightly, then says to her mother, "Would you go away, Mommy?"

33 months. Erin begins preschool for four hours, five mornings a week. She spends the entire first morning with her mother. Nevertheless, the experience is difficult for her. After returning home, she has one of the few tantrums of her life, and emerges from it sweaty, short of breath, and exhausted.

Erin establishes a very close relationship with a friend at school, Jonathan. They announce plans to get married, and they spend many hours playing dress up and other forms of pretend play. When Erin arrives at school before Jonathan, she sometimes plays by herself while waiting for Jonathan. The friendship with Jonathan continues to be a central feature of Erin's life 12 months later, a testimony to children's ability to form very close, enduring relationships even at this early age.

Erin seems incapable of defending her toys and watches passively when another child takes them away. Her mother blames herself for this trait, thinking that she has encouraged Erin to be "too nice." She begins to encourage her child to be more assertive, and Erin learns to say a forceful and effective "No!" by the time she is 36 months old. This is a good example of how shy children can learn more self-assertive behaviors when they perceive that they are socially approved.

The sleeping problems that Erin evidenced as a baby still persist but in a different form. She has no difficulty going to sleep, but she experiences night terrors two to three hours after falling asleep. At those times, she seems to go through the temper tantrums that she does not indulge in during the day.

After a fight with a friend during which she was very self-controlled, Erin relives the scene at night. She sits up on her bed while still asleep, yelling "I don't want that! Give it back to me! Don't do that!" She gesticulates with great intensity as she talks. Her mother gently tells her that things are fine and talks her back into a calm sleep. Erin is clearly dreaming, and the intensity of the dream spills over into motor discharge. Even at this early age, the dream is fulfilling one of the functions it has through the life span: to enable the dreamer to grapple with unresolved tasks left over from waking life.

36 months. Erin becomes freer in expressing difficult emotions. She now initiates talking about her mother's departures. She asks her mother, "When are you coming home?" If she dislikes the answer, she replies, "That is too long." After her mother returns, Erin tells her, "I didn't want you to go."

Erin seems very aware of feelings and relishes talking about them with her mother. They develop a game: "Tell me a time when you were happy; a time when you were sad; a time when you were afraid; a time

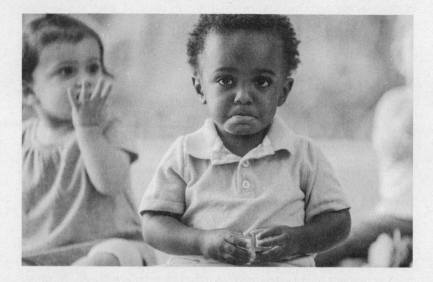

when you were mad." Erin has no problem remembering times when she was happy, sad, or afraid. When it comes to anger, however, she says thoughtfully, "I can't remember a time when I was mad." Anger is not a familiar part of her sense of herself. It tends to go underground and emerges when she is not fully conscious, particularly during sleep. Not all shy toddlers are uncomfortable with anger. However, many shy toddlers try to avoid intense excitement of any kind because it does not fit well with their innate reserve. The feeling is there, but the child may be too self-conscious to express it freely.

Erin's parents (themselves quite comfortable with a full range of emotions—including anger—but not overwhelmed by them) make concerted efforts to encourage their child to become more aware of her anger as a first step toward helping her to feel safe with it. They begin to oppose her more actively when appropriate, and they become less worried about making her angry. They assert their own preferences rather than yielding to her as they did before out of a wish to keep her happy. This turns out to be a very good move. It enables Erin to get more practice with the experience of being angry, with the result that anger becomes less frightening for her.

Erin becomes very interested in pregnancy and babies. After her babysitter gets pregnant, she announces, "I am having a baby in my tummy." She then asks, "When will my baby be born?" When her mother tells her that her baby is not in her tummy yet and that it will be born when she grows up, she asks with much distress, "But where is it now?" She becomes interested in collecting things that she finds during her walks. She treasures pebbles, leaves, shells, and pieces of colored paper, and she gives them away as a special gesture to people she particularly likes. She continues asking "Why?" but now goes to great lengths to come up with her own explanations. When she can't explain something, she says thoughtfully, "It must be magic."

A Well-Developing Slow-to-Warm-Up Toddler

How can we understand Erin's initial holding back in new situations, given her zest in exploring and her pleasure in people once she is comfortable with them? What function does her slowness to warm up serve for her?

We can speculate that this behavior has a physiological origin for Erin, as it did for the children studied by Kagan and his colleagues. Nevertheless, temperamental traits acquire a psychological meaning both for the individual and for her companions. What psychological meaning did Erin's reserve have for her?

We cannot know for sure, but there might be a parallel between Erin's difficulty with the transition from being awake to falling asleep and her difficulty with the transition of going from familiar to unfamiliar situations. Both types of transition involve moving from a comfortable and safe state of being to a different, more demanding state. Falling asleep calls for letting go of one's human connections and venturing alone into a mysterious realm. Going to the gym, to a party, or to preschool involves leaving one's familiar activities in order to engage with other people and other tasks.

From the time she was a baby, it was clear that Erin liked individual people and objects very much and was capable of intense involvements on a one-to-one basis. Individual relationships were her preferred way of relating to the world. Perhaps, in this context, Erin's slowness to warm up was a way of coping when the social situation was so large and complex that she could not be alone with someone special. Holding back and surveying the scene bought her time until she could identify a particular person or object with whom she could be most comfortable (such as Jonathan in the preschool setting).

Conversely, it is possible that she preferred very focused one-to-one involvements because those individual relationships provided a way of coping with the bombardment of stimulation by large situations. In any event, it is quite apparent from her developmental course that Erin's reserve has not impeded her cognitive, social, or emotional progress in any way. On the contrary, it is quite possible that her initial holding back served for her as a helpful mechanism to fend off overstimulation.

Erin illustrates the typical behavior of a well-developing shy toddler. Her preference for close individual friendships rather than group situations, familiarity rather than novelty, and mild rather than intense stimulation is characteristic of healthy, well-adjusted shy children of this age.

There are, of course, individual differences even in these common elements. Some shy children find some new situations so compelling that they forget their reserve and rush forward. One 18-month-old became so thrilled by his first visit to the zoo that he moved from cage to cage as in a daze, calling out to the animals and trying to climb over the fences separating him from them.

Other shy children like specific kinds of intense stimulation. Cindy loved being thrown up in the air by her uncle but not by anybody else. Albert devoured every spicy food, including chili peppers, and seemed to have a sixth sense for detecting it and going for it. Estela adored reggae music and danced like a whirling dervish when it was played, crying "More, more!" when it came to a stop. Maria took quickly to any new situation if there were crayons available that she could draw with.

These examples show that slow-to-warm-up children should not be stereotyped. They are not only shy: they are also curious, energetic, loving, and growing and changing. Their pleasure in exploring can help them surmount their reserve in a new setting. For parents, the important thing is to become familiar with their child's specific range of responses and to continue introducing novelty in gradual, manageable ways in order to cultivate the child's flexibility of response. The final section of this chapter offers suggestions on how to go about doing that.

A Fearful Toddler: Tobias

Sometimes a toddler's natural shyness can become transformed into a pervasive fear of new situations and unfamiliar people. When this occurs, the child refuses to go to new places or cries when meeting new people. Sometimes the child develops multiple apparently senseless fears that can become quite crippling of his ability to explore and learn about the world.

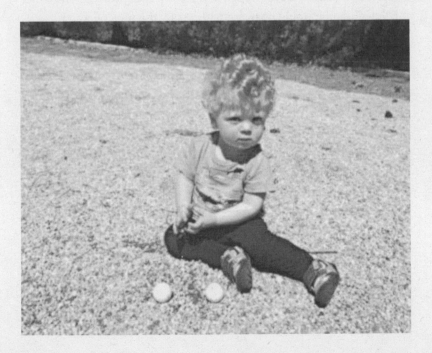

Tobias was a little boy in this situation. His parents asked for a consultation when he was 32 months old because they felt that life in their household was becoming increasingly tense and unhappy due to their child's excessive fears. In the course of a few home visits and playroom sessions, the following picture emerged.

Tobias was a lightly built, pale child with a thoughtful expression. He moved carefully, spoke softly, and liked to spend long periods of time playing by himself. He used wooden blocks to build elaborate structures that he adorned with whatever he had at hand: books, nesting cups, feathers, cans of food from the kitchen. When he was finished, his buildings looked like elaborate masterpieces from many architectural periods. He also liked to look at books, talking to himself as he pointed to the pictures. He was unusually adept at puzzles, and family friends knew that the puzzles they gave him as gifts had to be at least two years above his age level. His manual dexterity was extraordinary, and he loved toys that he could take apart and put together again. His favorite toy was a red plastic car that he could assemble and disassemble with a plastic wrench and a plastic screwdriver. His father predicted that he would be fixing real cars by the time he was 12.

Tobias developed uneventfully until he was 26 months. He was slow to warm to unfamiliar situations, he did not seem particularly interested in people, and he was very cautious in trying new physical feats. On the other hand, he was affectionate with his parents, had a couple of good friends he played happily with, and seemed to be always busy and content tinkering with something or other around the house. His mother commented: "He has a personality all of his own."

The biggest challenge in Tobias's life was his brother, Andrew, 15 months younger than him. Andrew was hell on wheels. Whereas Tobias was light and slender, Andrew was strong and sturdy. Whereas Tobias was slow and gentle, Andrew filled the room with loud chatter and fast-paced movement. Whereas Tobias liked to spend time alone, Andrew craved company. A redheaded, freckled-faced boy with an impish grin and twinkly eyes, Andrew attracted delighted attention and praise wherever he went, while Tobias watched quietly from the sidelines.

Andrew would not leave Tobias alone. This is understandable from an adult's perspective, but for Tobias his brother's intrusions were an endless irritation. Andrew was particularly entranced by the constructions Tobias put his heart and soul into, and he wasted no time in bringing them down. Tobias said no and tried to defend his masterpieces, but his mild manner and soft voice were no match for Andrew's self-assured rambunctiousness. To make matters worse, Andrew could get away with it. Their mother thought of Tobias as a mature little boy who could control himself, and she told him not to get angry at Andrew and to simply rebuild his structure once again. Tobias obeyed dutifully with a resigned, hopeless expression on his face. At those times, he looked much too old for his age.

By the time he was 30 months old, Tobias started displaying multiple fears. He refused to go to his play group, which he had attended for 6 months and had always enjoyed, and he cried for a long time after his mother left. He developed an intense fear of going to sleep and was convinced that there was a monster lurking in his closet. He became literally afraid of shadows and clung to his mother whenever he saw his own shadow or that of another person or object. He refused to try new foods. Each of these fears, by itself, is a frequent enough occurrence in the toddler years. It was their number and intensity that signaled something more serious in this little boy's life.

Every day seemed to bring a new fear. If he was at the corner grocery store, he became afraid of the noisy, old-fashioned cash register. In the park, he was terrified that the dog trotting along next to its owner would bite him. One day he panicked when he saw a man with a totally bald head. Another day he clung to his father when he saw a man dressed as a clown in a toy store. His parents said, "You name it, he is scared of it."

Life became unpredictable as a result of Tobias's fears. The parents never knew whether an outing would proceed smoothly, whether it would become an endless exercise in reassurance, or whether it would have to be cut short because Tobias would insist on going home.

Andrew sailed through the family turmoil. He seemed oblivious to his brother's distress and went on gleefully kicking down towers and snatching toys. Andrew had free rein because of his parents' attitude that he was "too little to know any better." This attitude had very negative consequences for both children: it encouraged Tobias to become a victim, and it allowed Andrew to behave more and more like a bully.

Tobias's predicament can be understood as a heroic effort to suppress his anger at his brother in order to live up to his mother's and father's expectations that he should be a "good little boy."

This effort asked for a degree of self-control that was beyond even his considerable ability in this area. The only way he could be the precociously selfless child his parents wanted him to be was to cut off any conscious awareness of his anger at his brother and his parents. In doing so, he had to suppress the normal ebullience and impetus to self-assertion of this age, because he was afraid that in the process of being assertive he would lose control of his impulses and end up clobbering his brother and losing his parents' love.

Toddlers cannot maintain a total suppression of angry feelings without paying a price. The feelings want out and will find a way of expressing themselves. Tobias could not think of himself as angry without immediately becoming terrified of his own badness. He dealt with the situation by attributing his anger to unfamiliar people and objects. In his eyes, he managed to be good, but anybody he did not know and love was bad and out to get him. He developed a litany when he was out with his parents: "Is that man bad? Is that dog bad? Is that truck bad?" He was simultaneously checking his environment for safety and asking "Am I bad when I cannot be the way my mommy and daddy want me to be?"

At first Tobias's parents did not like my raising the possibility that their older son was angry at his brother but could not express his anger for fear of displeasing them. Anger was an emotion that made them feel uncomfortable. Indeed, those young parents were unusually formal and correct with each other and with their children, as if good manners counted above all else even in family relations. To think of Tobias as struggling to contain angry feelings came too close to their own experience of trying hard to be "good" at the expense of their emotional spontaneity.

With much support, these well-meaning, thoughtful parents began to accept the idea that no 2-year-old could be as self-controlled as they hoped Tobias would be. Watching from behind a one-way mirror, they saw Tobias's initial tentativeness and eventual glee as he threw blocks around the playroom and made two dolls hit each other until they fell to the floor in exhaustion. The parents were moved by Tobias's blissful expression of agreement when I told him that "sometimes it feels good to be angry."

In joint sessions with Tobias and Andrew, the parents had an opportunity to practice new ways of responding to their children. They started to respect Tobias's right to play by himself and to stop Andrew from messing with him. It was a sight to behold the surprised expressions of both Andrew and Tobias when their parents restrained Andrew and took the side of Tobias. The parents themselves were surprised and greatly encouraged that they had the power to tell Andrew what to do. Andrew, in fact, obeyed them when they meant what they said. That relieved the parents because they had been feeling as helpless as Tobias in the face of Andrew's seemingly unstoppable power. It probably came as a big relief for Andrew, too, that he no longer was the most powerful figure in the household at the tender age of 20 months.

A few months after the end of a four-month intervention, the mother called to report on how things were going. Tobias was 39 months old at the time; Andrew had just turned 2 years old. Mrs. Novak had taken Tobias to the playground the previous day, and they had spent a delightful two hours together, in keeping with the parents' effort to build in more time alone with each of the children. After swinging on the swing for a long time, Tobias said, "Mommy, once there was a little boy who was scared of everything. That little boy died, but another little boy was born who is not afraid." He was talking about himself.

Shyness, Suppressed Anger, and Fear

Tobias illustrates a very common occurrence with mild-mannered, slow-to-warm-up toddlers who want to be good but worry that their natural feelings of anger and frustration mean that they are bad. They become afraid of their anger, but in their effort to suppress it they become preoccupied with badness and danger and end up being afraid of the world at large.

Fears have many origins. Some fears have nothing to do with anger but are the result of age-appropriate fantasies and misunderstandings about how the world works. Other fears stem from being exposed to frightening experiences. Still other fears do stem from suppressed anger, and those fears are often the most difficult for parents to understand.

Tobias happened to focus his anger on his brother, although he was also indirectly angry at his parents both for having another child ("Why am I not enough for them? Do they love him more than they love me? Will he replace me? If not, why did they have him?"), for not defending him, and for allowing Andrew to run wild. The parents' permissiveness with Andrew confirmed Tobias's worries that Andrew was the favored one.

Other children become directly angry at their parents and worry about those feelings because they fear losing their parents' love, as the following examples illustrate.

Lenny adores being alone with his mother and resents his father when he comes home. At 22 months, he hits his father when his mother and father kiss. At 30 months, he becomes more articulate. He says to his mother, "Love me, not Daddy." By 36 months, he is even more explicit: "I'll marry you when I'm big, but Daddy can live with us." Lenny loves his father but is also afraid of him. He startles when his father comes into the room, and when he does something wrong, he pleads with his mother, "Don't tell Daddy." The father is a gentle, loving man, and there are no objective reasons for Lenny's fear. It is likely that Lenny is afraid that his father will be angry at him for wanting to be the only one to have his mother's love.

Sonya, 26 months, became very frightened of animals after a one-week separation from her parents during which she stayed with her beloved grandparents. When the parents returned, Sonya turned away from them and buried her face in her grandmother's lap. After about ten minutes, she allowed her parents to hold her and kiss her but seemed constricted and reserved. Over the next few days, she was unusually well behaved and compliant with her parents' requests, but the fear of animals emerged, and at about the same time she refused to go to sleep at night. Sonya's anger at her parents for leaving had to be suppressed for fear that they would leave her again. She became an excessively good little girl, but the cost of that effort was expressed in her fear that she would be attacked by animals when she went to bed and was away from her parents. The fears dissipated when the parents helped Sonya to express her anger at them through words and play and reassured her that they would always come back no matter how angry she got at them.

These examples show that the fear of their own anger is a common response in young children, particularly when that anger is felt toward the most important love figures in their lives. Shy children may not express their anger easily, but they can feel it just as keenly as other children and may suffer silently from their difficulty in showing it. Because of this, it is particularly important for parents of shy children to be aware that their children may be showing anger under the guise of excessive fears.

When Shyness Turns to Aggression: Nadia

Timidity is not ordinarily associated with aggression in people's minds. One thinks of shy children as slow to anger as well as slow to warm up. However, timidity can take an aggressive turn under some circumstances, such as enduring physical or emotional abuse, witnessing violent exchanges between parents, or being overwhelmed by stimulation, including parental demands that the child cannot meet.

Slow-to-warm-up children can also become aggressive when they have not learned to tolerate moderate levels of frustration because they have been overprotected. When parents take their child's vulnerabilities too seriously, they allow themselves to be cowed by them. This can create an expectation in the child that she is entitled to instant gratification because she is too fragile to withstand anything else. When frustration finally occurs (as it inevitably must), aggression becomes the only coping mechanism available to the child to fend off the feared damage to herself.

Shy children become aggressive for the same reasons that other children do. For example, they may be trying to control and master a frightening situation by taking action that makes them feel less helpless. They might also imitate aggressive adults they are exposed to. What is most characteristic of shy aggressive children is the use of aggression to ward off overstimulation. Because children who are slow to warm up are often highly sensitive to stimuli, they may feel forced to strike out to protect themselves when withdrawal does not work.

At age 2, Nadia often scratched and bit her friends. She flew into a rage in response to seemingly minimal frustration. At those times she hit, bit, or scratched the offender and then looked greatly relieved. Unfortunately, the relief lasted only briefly because other adults would rush in to admonish Nadia and protect the victim. When scolded, Nadia cried in anger and shame for a long time.

Nadia did not attack the adults she knew, but she did spit at adult strangers when they tried to make friends with her faster than she could tolerate. She was also quite aggressive with babysitters, and her parents found that potential babysitters were always "busy" when asked to spend an evening with Nadia. This pattern of behaviors developed gradually and was the culmination of a slow process that had begun when Nadia was a baby. The process took different forms at different times.

Nadia was a very alert baby who formed an unusually early and close relationship with her parents. They reported that she refused to be held by anybody other than them from the time she was 6 weeks old. Nadia cried intensely in new situations, turned beet red, and often ended up vomiting from gastric distress. Her parents seldom went out during the first six months of Nadia's life because they felt unable either to take her along or to leave her with somebody else.

As the first year progressed, Nadia began to cry less, but she still took a long time to adapt to unfamiliar situations. She clung to her mother with an anxious expression, scrutinized strangers with an intense and unwavering gaze, and burst into tears if someone she did not know tried to make friends with her too quickly. Her mother commented, "All the books say that stranger anxiety develops at eight months, but Nadia was born with it."

Nadia's parents were very attuned to their child's moods and did their best to keep her happy. They believed that Nadia was a psychologically fragile child and tried hard not to hurt her in any way. Conversation around Nadia was mostly child centered. If the parents were immersed in a conversation and Nadia made some social signal, they immediately interrupted what they were doing to attend to her. Reflecting back on the first year, the father said, "We thought she needed always to come first in order to feel secure."

Though Nadia did feel secure in many ways, she had few opportunities to learn to experience ordinary frustration as an unpleasant experience that was well within her capacity to endure. As a result, she often panicked and turned to her mother to make everything right when she encountered something she did not like. In a paradoxical way, her mother's sensitivity and responsiveness tended to reinforce Nadia's feeling that she was unable to cope with unpleasant feelings on her own.

This situation came to a head when Nadia entered her second year and began to be interested in peer play. Two-year-old peers are fun as playmates but cannot be counted on as sensitive caregivers. They do not set aside their own plans out of deference to a friend's needs and wishes. Playing with friends became Nadia's first consistent encounter with people who refused to do what she wanted. She did not like it, but she could not withdraw (which she preferred to do in unfamiliar situations) because she was too emotionally invested in what was going on. The only response to frustration that was available to her was to hit back because she had not learned to tolerate discomfort or negotiate a way out of it.

A similar mechanism was at work with overly forward strangers and unwary babysitters. Neither situation allowed Nadia to retreat graciously from frustration. A stranger who persisted in his attentions had to be faced; the unwanted babysitter had to be endured. Angry at those impositions and unable to escape, Nadia resorted to physical attack as a form of psychological self-defense.

Nadia learned to modulate her anger when her parents realized that they had been overly protective of her as a result of their intense empathy with her distress in unfamiliar situations. They started training themselves not to become emotionally undone by Nadia's protests, and they began to encourage her to solve small problems on her own instead of rushing to help her at the first sign of frustration. They made themselves wait a little longer before responding to a request or a demand, and they helped Nadia to wait by saying "Just a minute, Nadia. I need to finish this first." This approach helped Nadia to understand that other people's plans and wishes, not only her own, needed to be taken into account.

Nadia's aggression declined as she learned to wait, to tolerate frustration, and to pay attention to the needs of others. She also learned to recognize when she was about to lose control of herself and strike out. At such times her favorite phrase became "You are bothering me." People recognized this statement as an early warning signal and for the most part respected it. Everybody was happier as a result.

Helping Slow-to-Warm-Up Toddlers Enjoy Who They Are

As a temperamental trait, slowness to warm is characterized by high sensitivity to stimulation, gradual adaptation to change, and a tendency to withdraw under stress. Within this general framework, a variety of individual differences is possible, as the personalities of Erin, Tobias, and Nadia illustrate. Depending on the pressures and supports they encounter and on their own talents and vulnerabilities, different slow-to-warm-up children will resort to different coping mechanisms to adjust to the inevitable challenges of meeting new people and facing novel situations.

Cultural influences play an important role in this process. For example, traditional Chinese and Canadian parents showed different predominant responses to their shy young children. Traditional Chinese mothers showed warm and accepting attitudes, while Canadian mothers were more likely to attempt to "correct" or change their children's behavior. In school, shy Chinese children do better academically and are rated more positively by their teachers and peers than are their outgoing peers. Shy Canadian children, on the other hand, do less well than their outgoing peers. The meaning a culture and a family attribute to the child's temperament influences how the child responds.[10]

Erin's ability to form very close, deep relationships with her parents, babysitter, teacher, and a small number of peers shows that shyness need not entail emotional distance from others. Shy children may be more selective but are not less loving than their outgoing peers. Similarly, Erin's glee in trying daring new feats with her father shows that timidity does not preclude boldness if the child feels secure. Erin's ability to take physical risks in her father's protective but encouraging presence highlights the particular importance for slow-to-warm-up toddlers of relying on an adult as a secure base from which to explore.

The sensitivity to stimulation of slow-to-warm-up toddlers means that their parents and caregivers need to strike a careful balance between two extremes of caregiving in serving as a secure base. They have to find a way of protecting the child from overwhelming stimulation without becoming overprotective.

It is only too easy to overlook a child's special need to be buffered from overstimulation. This is particularly the case if, like Tobias, the child is trying hard to be "good" and does not protest in the face of stress. In such circumstances the child may suffer quietly and become increasingly fearful and withdrawn in the effort to put up with a situation that is overtaxing his coping skills. When a child shows excessive withdrawal or too many fears, the parents will do well to look for specific sources of stress in the child's life that they have not been aware of.

On the other hand, it is easy to become overly protective in trying to minimize a child's distress. When parents become anxious, they cannot encourage their child to tackle a taxing situation that is age appropriate and within the child's ability. This can be a setback because slow-to-warm-up children become discouraged with themselves when they see their peers enjoying a situation that is daunting to them, such as playing in a swimming pool or getting onto a swing. If they routinely become hopeless under stress, slow-to-warm-up children can lose their resilience and become overly reliant on adults as a source of comfort. They may also become demanding and angry when their distress is not immediately relieved by a sympathetic adult. Adults can help by reminding children that they usually enjoy themselves after they get used to a new situation.

Perhaps the most useful formula in helping a slow-to-warm-up toddler tackle new situations is "step-by-step, one step at a time." This approach involves gradual but steady encouragement to explore. The following sequence of steps can enable a slow-to-warm-up toddler to surmount the initial hesitation to enter a novel setting.

- Do not send the child over to the new situation. Go with him and draw him in. Take time together to simply observe what is going on. Make little comments about what is happening, focusing preferably on aspects that are already familiar and safe. For example, if a group of new children is playing with some toys, you might want to point to a toy your child already knows and likes: "Look at their beach ball. It is just like yours but orange. Remember how we played with it yesterday? We had to run all over the place just like they are doing, because it bounced so much!"
- Stay near until the child's mood has changed reliably from caution to enjoyment. Then step back.
- Remain "on call" for a while but do not hover in anticipation that the child will need you.
- If the child calls you, modulate your response to match the intensity of his need as you see it. If he seems truly anxious, do not hesitate to approach. More often, a wave from a distance

or some reassuring words may be sufficient to let him know you are available if needed. Try a minimalist approach: start out with the least active response, and see if it works.

- Children are often the best helpers in enticing a slow-to-warm-up child into a novel situation. You might facilitate this by starting a conversation with a child who seems like a compatible partner for yours. The rest may follow on its own.

J. Ronald Lally, a founding member of Zero to Three, and his colleagues suggest that this sequence may be summarized in the following series of moves by the parent or caregiver: "being with, talking to, stepping back, remaining available, moving on."[11] The rhythm of these steps needs to be coordinated with the child's own rhythm, but the adult's confidence will enable the child to "move on" when the time is right.

7

Early Anxieties

Human beings have a deeply ingrained capacity to anticipate and respond to danger. We respond to present and immediate danger with fear. We respond to dangers that we anticipate or imagine with anxiety. Anxiety anticipates, fear responds. Both emotions are related because an imagined danger can materialize very quickly. Both fear and anxiety have a subjective component because we must interpret an event as being safe or dangerous (a process that takes milliseconds). During the early years, while children are learning about what is safe and what is dangerous, anxiety and fear are often indistinguishable because they occur not only in relation to objective danger but also in relation to unfamiliar or unexpected events. The role of parents—not always fulfilled—is to provide a "protective shield" that enables the child to feel safe when anticipating and responding to real or perceived danger. The gifted cartoonist Gary Larson provided a poignant illustration of this psychological process on the first page of his book *The Far Side Gallery 4*, in which he wrote, "When I was a boy, our house was filled with monsters. They lived in the closets, under the beds, in the attic, in the basement, and—when it was dark—just about everywhere. This book is dedicated to my father, who kept me safe from all of them."[1]

Larson evokes in this description Selma Fraiberg's seminal concept of "the magic years," which she described as follows:

> The magic years are the years of early childhood. By "magic" I do not mean that the child lives in an enchanted world where all the deepest longings are satisfied. [The child's] earliest conception of

the world is a magical one; he believes that his actions and his thoughts can bring about events as the child gropes his way toward reason and an objective world he must wrestle with the dangerous creatures of his imagination and the real and imagined dangers of the outer world.[2]

Though it is unpleasant to experience, anxiety has an important role in survival because it serves as a signal of impending danger that gives us time to protect ourselves. The events that trigger anxiety are not always dangerous in themselves, but they get their emotional force from the fact that they often precede danger or are associated with it.[3] For example, waking up to find ourselves alone in our darkened house is not dangerous in itself but can make us anxious if, like Gary Larson, we imagine unseen dangers lurking in the dark. If we turned on the light and saw actual danger, we would move quickly from feeling anxiety to feeling downright fear. Our anxiety is relieved when we find that nothing unusual is happening.

Anxiety is increased by helplessness and lack of knowledge, which makes babies and toddlers particularly prone to it. Very young children face an unfamiliar world that operates in unknown ways. They are small and vulnerable and rely on others to feel safe. Young children also do things that can have unpredictable and even frightening consequences, including making their parents angry at them. For all these reasons, the opportunities to experience anxiety are ever present in infancy and the toddler years.

This chapter describes the origins of anxiety in the first year of life and how the early anxieties change in the course of toddlerhood. The great adventures of the second and third years described in chapter 2—discovering the world, the body, and the mind—have a dark side. With new knowledge comes the fear of harm by being abandoned, unloved, or physically damaged. This chapter describes how toddlers experience expectable and excessive anxiety and the range of coping mechanisms available to them. The next chapter provides specific guidelines to help parents help their toddlers with the more common anxiety-arousing situations of this age.

The Early Origins of Anxiety

Anxiety in toddlerhood can be understood in the context of early development because the child's basic feelings of security or fearfulness are established in the first year of life. This section describes the origins and manifestations of anxiety in infancy as a backdrop for understanding the toddler's anxieties.

It is likely that emotions are felt by the fetus even before birth. Early investigators reported facial expressions of disgust, sadness, happiness, and fear,[4] and those pioneering observations were confirmed with the invention of the ultrasonogram, which allows for close monitoring of the facial expressions of a fetus on a video screen.[5]

Embryos also seem capable of acting on their sensations. For example, they withdraw from noxious stimulation such as a light touch as early as 7.5 weeks gestational age, using a global response that begins with the bending back of the head and then spreads progressively to the hands, trunk, and shoulders.[6] This response suggests that the fetus may be capable of feeling a rudimentary form of anxiety because the same form of physical avoidance is a common expression of anxiety after birth.[7,8] During gestation, the capacity to withdraw from unpleasant stimulation occurs at an earlier age than the capacity to approach using, for example, the prenatal rooting reflex.[9] This may indicate that the motivation for self-protection develops earlier and may be more basic to survival than the motivation to explore.

The fetus, of course, does not need to seek proximity to a source of nurturance and protection. It is already embedded in a secure base: the mother's womb. The healthy newborn's response to departing from this safe haven is a lusty cry that represents both protest and a call for human contact and assistance. This cry may signal the first experience of fear/anxiety after birth.

Once born, the baby cannot take care of herself. She needs the care of a loving adult, who during the first years of life in most cultures and circumstances is primarily the mother. This is no accident. In the course of pregnancy, mother and fetus gradually form an intimate connection with each other.[10] By the time babies are born, they are well equipped to recognize and form a primary relationship with their mothers. For example, newborns recognize and prefer the mother's voice. This was demonstrated in an ingenious experiment in which babies learned to suck for longer or shorter periods of time, as needed, when the reward for sucking was hearing their mother rather than a stranger read from a Dr. Seuss book.[11] Newborns also discriminate and prefer the mother's face within hours after birth.[12] Similarly, they recognize and prefer their mother's smell: they consistently turn their heads toward their mother's nursing pad rather than the pad of a different mother.[13]

Newborns start to make use of these social skills right away because being born involves a major developmental challenge. They need to regulate their cycles of hunger and sleep in a way that complements their mother's expectations and fits in more or less smoothly with the family values and daily routine.[14, 15] Recognizing and preferring the mother's face, voice, and smell help the baby engage with the mother as a partner in the joint venture of regulating the rhythms of the body.

This early preference does not mean that babies respond only to their mothers. It is in the best interest of their early survival and health at a time of high physical vulnerability that they are able to respond to whoever is ministering to them—a flexibility that might have evolved in the course of evolution as an adaptive response to the risk of maternal mortality during childbirth. Preference and flexibility of response are human characteristics throughout the lifetime that are already present at birth.

The dance of reciprocity is accomplished in fits and starts, through trial and error. The baby's earliest anxieties are based on distressing bodily sensations: hunger, the urge to suck, gastric upset, elimination strains, fatigue, and the need for physical contact in the form of touch, holding, and cuddling. Most of the parents' care during the first two or three months of life is geared to helping the baby find relief from these sources of distress. As shown in the chapter on temperament, babies differ in their levels of irritability as well as in their readiness to be soothed. However, each baby can learn to manage anxiety if the caregiver can determine the specific interventions that are most helpful for her child.

Because babies cannot take care of their own needs but have to rely on somebody else, the pleasures and anxieties of the body very quickly acquire a social character. Parent and baby can look at, coo to, smile at, talk with, and cuddle each other while feeding, diapering, bathing, getting dressed, and falling asleep. Conversely, caretaking can be short, abrupt, impatient, or simply matter-of-fact and businesslike.

The sensations created by these early experiences teach the baby a great deal about what to expect from relationships. A young baby who cries when hungry and is fed promptly and lovingly learns that there is a connection between his cry for help and a successful outcome in the form of an appropriate parental response. When this experience is repeated again and again, the baby learns that pangs of hunger or pain will not last forever. He gives a signal, and help is on the way. Such a baby learns to wait with hope in the face of internal stress. The parents' sensitive response helps keep his anxiety within manageable limits. The parents, in fact, protect the baby from experiencing unmanageable anxiety before he can protect himself.

When a baby cries loudly for a long time and nothing happens, a very different internal experience begins to unfold. She finds that her signals of need are not effective in securing help, and she cannot learn a causal connection between needing and receiving. As bodily discomfort mounts, so does anxiety that this state of affairs will go on forever. Despair replaces hope, and the baby has only two avenues of response open to her: disintegrating into frantic, angry wailing or withdrawing into lethargic sleep. Rather than protecting against anxiety, the parent actually becomes the cause of it.

Lack of synchrony between the baby's signals and the parent's response can occur in many areas of interaction. The baby may smile beseechingly and be ignored by the parent; cling to the parent and be summarily put to bed; come close and be pushed away; call for help and not be heard. When these emotional rebuffs become the norm rather than the exception, they shape the baby's sense of herself and her emotional relationships. Babies who receive little help when they are distressed tend to become dispirited or angry and to cry often. They lag behind in experimenting with verbal communication and other social signals because they lose faith in their competence to bring about good experiences for themselves.[16]

Babies with a consistent experience of not having their signals of need attended to can become chronically anxious about the physical and emotional availability of the caregiver who habitually fails to respond or responds abruptly or harshly. They cannot have a confident expectation that the parent will respond to them when they are in need. Gradually, this anxiety gets internalized to become an integral part of their sense of themselves and how they see the world. Conversely, babies whose signals receive consistent and appropriate responses internalize a feeling that they are worthy and deserving of good care. In trusting others, they learn to trust themselves.[17]

The intricate patterns of reciprocity between mother and baby prompted the English pediatrician and psychologist Donald Winnicott to quip that "there is no such thing as a baby."[18] He meant that a baby's individuality unfolds in a particular mothering context, so that his very essence is profoundly affected by the kind of care he receives. At the same time, mothers and fathers may well feel that "there is no such thing as a parent," because all parents respond to the unique characteristics and specific demands of their children in the context of their own specific circumstances. The same parents may respond differently to their different children depending on how safe and confident they feel at different times of their lives, including their comfort with themselves, with being a parent, and with the individual characteristics of each particular child. Parents may also respond differently to their babies and young children depending on how much family and social support they have. The same parents can provide quite different caregiving to their different babies and young children depending on their specific circumstances. Parents who are worried by economic problems, family conflicts, or other reasons while raising one young child might feel quite differently in their personal and parenting roles if those problems are resolved by the time the next baby is born.

How Unique Is the Mother?

Research suggests that on average mothers spend more time with their young children than fathers do[19] and engage in more caregiving and comforting.[20,21] A mother is special to her baby because of the intimate bodily and emotional experiences that they share from pregnancy onward. But this does not mean that only the mother and nobody but the mother can help babies become secure in their human relations. Children can thrive in various child-rearing settings provided that they have satisfying relationships with a small number of consistent caregivers who are responsive to their needs. Fathers, adoptive parents, same-sex parents, single parents, grandparents, and other adults can raise a child equally well.

Fathers have become increasingly more involved in child care in the last two decades, both in heterosexual and same-sex families and by becoming single parents. The psychiatrist Kyle Pruett studied a group of families in which the father was the primary caregiver while the mother worked. He found that the nurturing capacities of the men were more than up to the task of raising their children. The children thrived in their fathers' care.[22]

This does not mean that parents are interchangeable at any time in the child's life. Children who establish strong bonds of love with both their mothers and their fathers may turn differentially to one parent or the other for specific aspects of their lives—for example, to one parent for comfort and reassurance and to the other parent for exploration and play. Mothers sometimes complain that their children see them as caregivers but not as playmates. Fathers sometimes feel hurt when their young children continue crying and insist on wanting their mother when they are hurt. Preferences for the same-sex or the opposite-sex parent may shift at different times in the child's development. Same-sex parents report similar child preferences for one or the other parent at different times and in different situations.

In fact, babies establish distinct relationships with different people from a very early age. At 4 weeks, they already respond in predictably unique ways to both their mother and their father, and these two patterns in turn differ from the much more diffuse responses shown to strangers.[23] By 12 months, an infant may have a secure relationship with one parent but an anxious relationship with the other.[24] These different patterns are strongly influenced by each parent's sensitivity and responsiveness to the child in the preceding months. In this sense, the first twelve months serve as a laboratory in which the baby learns what she can expect from the important people in her life.

How much an anxious relationship with a parent or caregiver affects the child's emotional development depends on the centrality of that person in the child's life. In a group of middle-class children raised primarily by their mothers, toddlers who were anxious with their mothers between 12 and 18 months showed more insecurity at age 6 than those who had a secure relationship with the mother in the first 18 months. In contrast, early anxiety in relation to the father did not predict later insecurity in this group.[25] For these children, the mother was the more central caregiver and their relationship with her clearly influenced their emotional development.

Insecure attachments are particularly forceful indicators of a major normal anxiety of infancy: the fear of losing the mother, or separation anxiety. Between 6 and 10 months, babies begin to protest the mother's departure energetically and are much less willing than they were earlier to accept substitutes with good grace. In the course of multiple interactions occurring in many contexts and moods, the baby has become fiercely, uncompromisingly attached to the primary caregiver, who has become the center of his emotional life.

The quality of this bond has many individual variations. It may be secure or anxious; exuberant or affectively muted; passionate or tranquil; conflictful or harmonious; simple or multifaceted; ambivalent or wholehearted. It may be all of these things or different things at different times. Most of all, it just *is*, and the threat of its not being unleashes intense agonies in the baby's heart and mind.

Once it emerges, anxiety over separation and loss becomes a steady human companion. One cannot have an intimate, intense emotional relationship and be spared anxiety about the stability and permanence of that relationship. Some adults (as well as some babies) are more prone to it and experience it more intensely than others, but fear of losing the loved one is the ever-present, although often hidden, darker side of love. The games of peek-a-boo and hide-and-seek, which occur in some form in many societies, are a beautiful demonstration of the universal cultural wisdom of responding to young children's separation anxiety in the language they understand best: play. By playing appearance-disappearance games, adults help babies and young children learn that people come back after they go away. The assurance that things will happen as they should is an important message for the psychological well-being of very young children.

The Anxieties of Toddlerhood

The 12-month-old baby enters her second year of life with a rich and well-established emotional world. She has a hierarchy of relationships—with mother, father, grandparents, siblings, caregivers, even the family cat or dog—that have special meaning and are not interchangeable. Some of these people are more central to her sense of well-being than others, and she resists and protests separation from them. However, she is also to use other familiar and trusted people as substitutes until the preferred attachment figure returns. The more secure a 12-month-old baby is in her primary attachment relationships, the better equipped she is to negotiate the special challenges of the second year.

As we saw earlier in the book, the developmental course of separation anxiety is such that it becomes most acute at about 18 months. It seems paradoxical that separation anxiety increases just as the toddler experiences the urge to leave the mother's side, but this is as it should be. The momentum away from the mother calls for a psychological counterweight of equal magnitude to keep the toddler within reach at least sometimes. Separation anxiety provides that counterweight.

Like everything else, separation anxiety becomes more complicated in the second year. In the first year of life, the mother's sensitive response was enough to relieve the baby's distress. Now the toddler fights within himself about wanting versus not wanting the mother's help. He wants to be the one to decide, but most often he cannot decide on his own.

The target of that internal struggle is often enough the mother herself, but the issue the toddler is trying to resolve is really an internal one. He is simultaneously saying "I still need you" and protesting, "But I can do it myself!" The inner subtexts indicate the self-doubt underneath the assertiveness: "Can I really do it myself?" and "Will you be there to help, even if I send you away?" Mixed messages are common in the toddler years because the salient emotional issues are usually compound ones.

Fear of Losing the Parent's Love

As the growing toddler acquires a greater awareness of what constitutes right and wrong behavior, another source of anxiety comes to the fore: fear of disapproval and anxiety over losing the parent's love.

> Mario and his mother have a big fight. She yells at him to go to his room. He refuses. She grabs him by the arm, takes him to his room, and shuts the door. He screams. She sits outside the closed door, shaking with anger, helplessness, and guilt. After their tempers calm down, they talk quietly about what happened. The mother tells Mario she is sorry she lost her temper with him. Mario asks, "When you are angry with me, do you still love me?" His mother says yes and asks, "Do you love me when you are angry with me?" Mario is silent for a minute and then says, "Oh, I don't know." After a pause, he adds, "Later I do."

Mario is struggling with the problem of remaining aware of one's love in the midst of one's anger. Toddlers' increasing self-awareness leads them to scrutinize their feelings quite closely and to ask many questions about what feelings occur when and how different feelings fit with one another. They are trying to make sense of ambivalence both in themselves and in others.

Toddlers' anxiety over losing the parent's love is fueled by their experience that they no longer love the parent when they are angry at him or her. Because of their cognitive limitations, young children find it difficult to understand that others may feel differently than they do in a given situation. As a result, a young child cannot believe that the parents still love him even if he is not feeling any love for them at a particular time. This perception may actually be quite accurate, since even the most caring of parents find it hard to feel love in the middle of a fight. The parents' anger is so graphic and real that it can make the child believe that the dreaded loss of love (the ultimate catastrophe) has finally occurred and will last forever. That is why it is so important to make up after a fight: the parent's reassurance is of immense importance to the toddler's emotional well-being.

Body Anxieties

Not all of the anxieties of the second and third years are based on sepa-ration and loss. The body, that old troublemaker, continues to elicit fears. The early anxieties over digestion, hunger, and sucking needs are presumably well enough mastered by now, but as new challenges emerge, so do new uncertainties.

The possibility of damage to the body looms large in the toddler years because young children are simultaneously learning that they can be hurt and that certain parts of the body stay with them but other parts of the body (hair, nails, urine, feces) are cut or flushed away. The feeling of pain during an accident or injury accentuates anxiety over body damage. All cultures seem to have developed a playful ritual to help young children with this anxiety, such as kissing the boo-boo to make it go away.

How real this anxiety can feel for the child is shown in the follow-ing vignette, which illustrates the importance of trying to understand the sources of young children's misunderstandings in order to reassure them.

> Hilary, 3 years old, and her 8-month-old brother are visiting their uncle and aunt, and the baby is happily sucking his toes. As a joke, the uncle puts ketchup on the baby's big toe and starts sucking it noisily. The baby takes this in stride, but Hilary bursts into tears and cries loudly for her uncle to stop. Her father sits next to her and gently asks her what is worrying her so much. Hilary, with great effort, explains between sobs, "Because Uncle will swallow baby's toe when he sucks it!"

Bowel movements and urination can produce much anxiety in toddlers because they cause uncomfortable body sensations that the child cannot control. Particularly when the child is prone to digestive cramps, diarrhea, or constipation, bowel movements can become as-sociated with a feeling of being threatened from the inside.

The pressure of toilet training often generates anxiety in toddlers. When children become toilet trained because they are motivated to grow up, this anxiety is minimized or may not occur. When they are asked by the parents to control their body functions before they are ready, toilet training can create anxiety about who is in charge of the child's body and a feeling of shame for not living up to the parents' standards. Chapter 8 provides specific guidelines for deciding when to start and how to proceed in toilet training the child.

Gender differences are another source of body anxiety. By about 15 months, children become very attentive to differences between boys and girls. They cannot yet ask clear questions or put their worries into words, but it is clear from their behavior that they are aware of body differences, and they can become anxious about having or not having what the other sex has. In a longitudinal study of seventy boys and girls in a nursery school, The psychoanalysts Herman Roiphe and Eleanor Galenson observed that from 15 months onward children watched their own and each other's genitals closely and some of them expressed distress at the differences.[26]

Nursery school teachers are very aware of this phenomenon. One of them described a boy, Timothy, who at 15 months watched with absorbed attention as the teacher changed a little girl's diapers. When his turn came to have his diaper changed, Timothy ran away and hid under a crib, screaming, "No! No!" He had never done that before. It is possible that Timothy, not understanding the source of gender differences, feared that his diaper change would make him look like the little girl he watched. The teacher guessed this fear and said, "Timothy, I won't hurt you when I change your diaper. You are a boy, and you will stay a boy. Lindsay is a girl, and she does not have a penis." The explanation worked. Timothy allowed his diaper to be changed. This exchange illustrates the importance of knowledgeable, unhurried, sensitive child care providers in helping young children with their worries.

Fear of the Unknown

Throughout the life cycle the age-specific sources of anxiety have to do with life tasks we understand only imperfectly and have many fantasies about. For junior toddlers, this may center on movement and toilet training; for senior toddlers and 3- and 4-year-olds, on the differences between boys and girls and how babies are made; for young adults, on the secrets of love; for very old people, on the mysteries of death and the world beyond.

We tend to be afraid of what we do not know, and toddlers are no exception. To compound matters, they often reach faulty conclusions because their reasoning is still based on their wishes and fears rather than on objective information. In addition, toddlers overhear many things they cannot understand. Adults do not routinely edit their conversations so that toddlers can understand them, and often they do not even know that the child is listening. Yet the toddler can be full of anguish over his very personal understanding of what he has overheard.

Philip, 27 months old, started to refuse going to play in the yard or in the playground and developed intense fears of going outside. The source of his fears became clear when his older brother overturned a stone to look at the worms under it and Philip began to scream. After patient questioning by his father, Philip sobbed, "There are bad people in a rock, but I don't know what rock." This was his best interpretation of the anxious family discussions about the war in Iraq.

Anxieties about the parents' love, how the body works, and how the world is made are manageable if the toddler is largely confident that his parents will listen and intervene on his behalf. At any age, fears become magnified if one is alone with them. Philip could trust his father with his information about "bad people in a rock" because his father showed clear and persistent interest in understanding the reason for the child's distress ("Tell me what makes you scared. Did something happen to you outside? Do the worms scare you?"). If his refusal to go out had been dismissed as irrational or ridiculous, he would have suffered silently and unnecessarily for a much longer time.

What Is Manageable Anxiety?

In the most desirable conditions, the child learns to cope with anxiety by being exposed to the right amounts of it, not much more and not much less. This manageable amount of anxiety varies with the child's age and temperament. It may also vary with cultural values. However, even within a particular culture, knowledgeable adults differ in their views of how much anxiety, frustration, or stress is "just right" for an individual child. There is no mathematical formula for calculating the exact amounts of anxiety a child can be expected to tolerate in the course of growing up. This is why child rearing is an art and not a science and why parents need to stay in touch with their personal convictions in deciding how much anxiety their child can tolerate.

Nevertheless, we can entertain some different possibilities to guide our thinking on this topic. Let's go back to the example of a newborn crying with hunger. If the parent responds right away, the baby eats with gusto and falls asleep peacefully. If the delay is long enough so that the crying escalates sharply, the baby will not be immediately soothed when food is offered. He will continue to cry with the nipple in his mouth and may even choke on the flowing milk. If we look at this picture in units of time, we find that when a mother responds to her baby's cry within ninety seconds, the baby calms down in only five seconds. If she waits three minutes, the baby takes about fifty seconds to be soothed.[27] In other words, doubling the response time leads to a tenfold increase in the length of a baby's crying. Once the baby's distress gets out of control, it is much more difficult to help him reorganize emotionally and reengage with the world.

It is not difficult to infer what manageable anxiety means in this context. A hungry newborn does not have the internal resources to wait for food without collapsing in distress. As she grows older, however, she will have more experiences in regulating her inner cues and will have a reassuring inner expectation that her hunger signals will be reliably attended to by the parent. She will be able to tolerate hunger with the parent's verbal reassurances and will distract herself with various activities, including watching the parent prepare his food. She will have learned to wait with trust.

Learning to cope with the anxieties of toddlerhood follows a similar course. Toddlers have tantrums and protest loudly when they don't like what is happening. If they recover from a tantrum and go back to being their regular self, the experience that led to the tantrum was most likely a manageable one. Such an experience is actually valuable because it helps the toddler learn about frustration and anxiety as unpleasant states that can be tolerated as part and parcel of life. If the parents remain available and supportive, toddlers learn to cope with situations of disappointment and distress and become more flexible and sturdy as a result. Tantrums decrease and eventually disappear.

By the time they are preschoolers, children can control their behavior better and begin to speak about what they want and how they feel about not having it. They do not feel as overwhelmed by disappointment and no longer assume that they have an inherent right to have all things their way.

Play and the Mastery of Anxiety

Anxiety can be a very useful emotion if it is managed well enough. The child's impulse to master age-appropriate anxiety is a powerful incentive to learning. Mastery is possible when the child's capacities are tested but not overwhelmed by the challenge. If, on the other hand, the parents are overly lenient and try to spare the child the necessary developmental frustrations, she will grow unsure of her coping skills and may become anxious in the face of even minor trials and tribulations.

How does the toddler learn from anxiety? Anxiety serves as a signal that something dangerous is about to occur but has not yet happened. This gives the child an opportunity to search for ways of coping with the danger. The search, and the eventual solutions found by the child, spur the transformation of anxiety into the pleasure of discovery. This process of transforming anxiety into mastery is a basic component in the development of creativity.

The parents of Cecilie, 15 months old, go out for the evening. She cries even though she likes her babysitter very much. As the evening wears on, she is alternately cheerful and cranky, enjoying games with the babysitter and calling tearfully for her mommy. She then hits upon a game: she crawls under her crib, closes her eyes tightly, waits a moment, and then, unable to control herself, cries out, "Me here!" as she waits for the babysitter to "find" her. She plays this game countless times and laughs gleefully when she is retrieved. This improvised game of hide-and-seek helps her practice and strengthen her fledgling knowledge that Mommy always comes back, just as Cecilie herself can be hidden from view and then be seen again.

Rafi, 20 months old, has just discovered that girls do not have penises. After an unusually long period without hearing from him, his mother finds him sitting in his room, naked from the waist down. He is absorbed in covering and uncovering his penis with a plastic cup. He is checking that it is always there, even when it can't be seen. His anxiety about body integrity has led him to devise a scientific experiment that he repeats systematically in order to be sure that the results generalize from one trial to the next.

Michael's mother has become sick with the flu and is out of commission for a few days. Michael, 24 months, is allowed into her room but cannot go close to her for fear of contagion. He sits watching her quietly for a long time. He then picks up a doll, which he checks from top to bottom, trying to find out "what is wrong with her." He cradles the doll tenderly in his arms. He then turns to his father and announces cheerfully, "All better now."

Play is a major avenue for learning to manage anxiety. It gives the child a safe space where she can experiment at will, suspending the rules and constraints of physical and social reality. In play, the child becomes master rather than subject. She is the one who decides instead of being the one who must abide by the grown-ups' decisions or the one who must endure whatever life brings, from a mother's illness to a troubling discovery. Play allows the child to transcend passivity and to become the active doer of what happens around her.

Erik Erikson proposed the theory that play is the childhood version of a lifelong human propensity: setting up model situations to experiment with different ways of controlling reality.[28] While playing, the child relives past events and in this process alleviates lingering anxiety and fear over what happened by "playing it out," just as adults derive emotional relief by "talking it out."

Jessica, 25 months old, had her tonsils taken out. Although the operation went smoothly from a medical point of view, it involved many stresses for the little girl, including being wheeled away from her parents for the procedure and then being in pain for several days. After returning home, she becomes uncharacteristically clingy to her mother. She also flies into rages at the drop of a hat. During this period she is so anxious that her bouts of play are short lived. Her parents help her by going over

what happened again and again as she listens intently, asks occasional questions, and volunteers her own details. Over the next
four months, as her anxiety over separation and body damage
is assuaged, Jessica does not want to hear about the operation
anymore, but she begins to play it out. She becomes the surgeon
operating on her doll and gets quite angry with her doll as she
"operates" on her, reflecting her perception of the procedure as
an aggressive intrusion on her body. When the parents intervene
in the play and try to give it a reassuring twist, Jessica gets angry
and stops playing. The child's reaction makes Jessica's parents
realize that, although they feel stressed by seeing her play in this
way, she needs to find her own way of expressing and working
through the anger and helplessness she felt during her difficult
ordeal.

Play helps in coming to grips with the past and, just as important,
in giving the right shape to the future: a "happy ending" to a troubling
situation.

> Maria's parents have a loud argument in front of the child. Maria,
> 32 months, watches silently for a while, but then she yells at them,
> "Don't fight! It's not nice!" Later she reenacts the argument using
> her two favorite stuffed animals. She speaks for each of them,
> mimicking her parents' voices and angry tone. Then she brings
> them together in a hug, saying, "We won't fight anymore."

Humor is also a powerful tool in managing anxiety, and toddlers
delight in their growing capacity to make use of it. They even begin to
experiment with practical jokes that play on their own vulnerabilities
as well as on their parents' rules and fears.

> Iden, 28 months, climbs on the kitchen table, an activity his parents
> have forbidden again and again. He stands very close to the edge,
> pretends to fall down, and then yells, "Save me! Save me!" with a
> twinkle in his eye. (His parents were less amused than he by his wit.)

Toddlers can be remarkable at turning immediately to play as a way of coping with a stressful exchange and attempting to repair it, as in the example that follows.

> Kamila, 24 months, had her hair done in a ponytail that her mother was trying to fix. In response, Kamila took off the band that was holding her hair. The mother became impatient, asking sharply, "Why did you do that?" Without saying a word, Kamila sat on the floor with her back to her mother, picked up a toy zebra, and started banging it on the floor while making angry sounds. She then took a toy horse in her other hand and had both animals "yell" at each other, making different sounds for each animal while speaking in a loud, angry voice. She then turned to her dollhouse, took a blanket, and laid an animal down on the bed while wrapping up the other animal in the blanket, saying in a soothing tone of voice, "Shhh . . ."

Children get used to many situations that originally provoked their anxiety when they learn that the event is not associated with a frightening outcome. They find out that their mother's impatience is not final and can be repaired. They learn that having a haircut does not hurt and that their hair grows back. They discover that most unfamiliar situations turn out to be tolerable and can even be fun. Most important, they learn that people and things do not disappear when they are out of sight, that Mom and Dad reliably come back, and that they can have a good time with other people while the parents are away.

What is the parent's role in the child's symbolic play? Parents can help toddlers play out their anxiety about a particular situation by giving them the space to do so, supporting them but not setting the script for them. The essence of play is spontaneity, and toddlers know how to do it better than grown-ups do. Parents can give permission and can follow the child's lead, but they need to be careful not to interfere with the child's own pace by injecting their own agenda prematurely into what the child is attempting to resolve through play. At the same time, parents can provide reassurance by playing with their child and finding ways to introduce protective themes when the child cannot come to them on his own. These playful exchanges can help free the child's imagination by offering new angles and alternatives when the play is becoming rigidly repetitive or out of control because the child cannot use it on his own to find a solution to his fears.

Persistently Intense Anxiety

Anxiety has its uses but also its abuses. It stops being effective as a teaching mechanism when it overpowers the toddler's resources for coping with it. Experimentation, play, and humor are no longer available, and the child cannot learn from the experience.

When toddlers experience fear or anxiety on a routine basis, they must resort to extreme psychological measures in order to keep functioning while minimizing their inner collapse. These measures are defenses against unbearable psychological pain. Although useful in containing anxiety, these responses involve a high psychological cost because they constrict the child's capacities to appraise reality, to feel, and to learn.

What situations give rise to unmanageable anxiety? The answer to this question can vary from child to child. Toddlers with different temperaments experience different situations differently, and some children may become intensely anxious in settings where their peers respond with excited glee because they tend to associate unfamiliar objects or events with the potential for danger. The different responses of toddlers to their first encounter with a swimming pool is a good example of this. Some toddlers are terrified and withdraw in a panic. Others cannot get enough of splashing about. In spite of individual differences, there are situations that elicit intense anxiety in all toddlers.

- Witnessing or experiencing very frightening or traumatic events. The frequency of such occurrences is very high in the first years of life. Contrary to the popular notion that young children live carefree lives, they are more likely than older children to be maltreated,[29] witness domestic violence,[30] and experience accidents.[31]

- Prolonged separations from the parent, particularly in the absence of a trusted substitute whom the child is familiar and comfortable with.

- Threats of abandonment or harsh punishment. Such threats are terrifying because they make children doubt the parent's basic love and commitment to protect them. "I will leave you here if you don't come along"; "I'll call the police to come and get you"; "I don't love you anymore"; "I don't like you anymore" are common but damaging threats used by parents to control their toddlers.

- Global critical comments, which create anxiety because they make the child believe he or she is intrinsically bad. "You are bad"; "Dummy"; "You are so stubborn"; "You never listen" are common examples.

- Blaming the child for how the parent feels. Such blame makes the child believe she is dangerous and can hurt the parent by simply being who she is. "You will kill me"; "You will give me a heart attack"; "You exhaust me."

- Recurrent or harsh physical punishment or threats of physical punishment, which frighten a child and make him watchful in an effort to anticipate when it will happen. Routine physical punishment such as spanking also teaches a toddler that "might makes right" and that it is fine to hit when one is stronger and can get away with it.

- Unpredictable and frequent changes in caregivers, which make toddlers anxious because they cannot rely on a stable substitute relationship when the parents are away.

- Making fun of toddlers' fears. This can make them feel alone with their very real anxieties about how the world works or what will happen to them. Conversely, taking their fears too seriously runs the risk of convincing the child that the danger is so real that the parent is also scared.

- Favoring one sibling over the other. When a parent consistently praises one child over the other or comes to that child's defense, unfavored children may internalize the message that their needs do not rank as high as the favored sibling's needs and may become simultaneously needy, angry, and resentful.

• Parents' overconcern about the child's physical safety, so that they hover around the child and constantly caution the toddler to be careful even when there is no imminent danger: "You'll fall"; "You'll bump your head"; "You'll get hurt." This excessive worry about anticipating danger can be transmitted to the child, who may come to see the world as a dangerous place. Such toddlers become conflicted about the discrepancy between their own impulse to explore and the parental message that exploration is bound to hurt.

• Parents' overconcern about fostering their child's intelligence. When parents become too conscientious about enhancing their child's cognitive skills, they tend to see every aspect of everyday life as an opportunity to teach and to test the child's knowledge. In this frame of mind, it is easy to forget that the most effective early learning occurs in spontaneous, pleasurable exchanges that are responsive to the child's interests. Overly structured efforts at teaching a toddler can create early anxiety about performance because the child starts to associate learning with parental approval and not with the intrinsic pleasure of mastering age-appropriate skills.

• Excessive parental attention to the child's inner life and mental health. Some parents are so concerned about being sensitive and responsive to their child's emotions that they become over-solicitous in trying to understand what the child is thinking and feeling. They may ask many questions and explain at length to the child what he or she is feeling and why, try to minimize frustration in all circumstances, and worry a great deal when their child is sad or angry at them. Young children raised under such close scrutiny can become overly anxious about having negative feelings. The effort to please their parents through a happy, pleasing, cooperative demeanor that cannot possibly be

maintained can become a lifelong source of anxiety that begins
in the toddler years.

This list of anxiety-producing situations is long enough to make
parents wonder whether they can do anything right. The good news
is that it is all a matter of balance. At one point or another all parents
do things that create anxiety in their children. In general, this does not
matter very much. Our children love us enough to forgive our mistakes
and keep on growing. Manageable amounts of anxiety go into building coping resources, and parents and toddlers are the better for it. It
is only when one diverges too much and too often in any one direction
that there is reason for concern, and toddlers tell us eloquently when
the anxiety they are feeling is too much to bear.

Coping with Unmanageable Anxiety

Every child struggling with very intense anxiety develops emotional
strategies for fending it off. Many of these defenses can be understood
in terms of the biologically based "fight, freeze, or fly" response to acute
danger.[32] In other words, children engage in behaviors that result in
withdrawal from the aversive situations become physically, emotionally, or cognitively "frozen" because they don't know how to respond
to the danger or respond with anger and aggression directed against
it. Sometimes the same toddler may show different patterns under different circumstances, for example, withdraw from the parent, become
immobilized when asked to perform, and fight the child care provider
or a peer. Other children may show either withdrawal or anger toward
the same person at different times.

All toddlers show some or all of these behaviors at some time or
another as a response to stress. For example, aggression appears during infancy as a spontaneous way of expressing anger and is considered an expectable developmental occurrence that typically occurs in
response to frustration and the inability to achieve the child's goals.[33]
Noncompliance is also developmentally expectable as a major mile-

stone in practicing autonomy, and it appears in many manifestations that include simple refusal, active defiance, breaking rules, and ignoring the request or directive.[34] A more serious problem exists only when the pattern is so intense and pervasive that it interferes for weeks or months at a time with the child's overall pleasure in emotional relationships and with exploration and play.

Avoidance. Physical withdrawal (or "flight") from the parent is a common defense against intolerable anxiety. It often occurs when a toddler is reunited with a parent after a prolonged separation that has stressed his or her coping resources.[35] The child may fail to greet the parent, avert his gaze, turn away, walk away, or sit with his back to the parent. In more serious situations (for example, after a separation of a week or longer) the child may seem not to recognize the parent, a reaction that can last from a few minutes to a few hours.

In very severe reactions, the toddler may eventually recognize the parent but respond to him or her in an impersonal and distant manner, showing more interest in the toys brought by the parent than in interacting with him or her. This extreme form of avoidance has been labeled *detachment.*[36]

Avoidance can be understood as the child's effort to get control of his anger about the parent's behavior. In the case of prolonged separation and subsequent reunion, the child is caught between his anger at having been left and his excitement and relief at the parent's return. Avoidance may provide a temporary space for the child to sort out these intense contradictory feelings. After a stressful separation, the child is too emotionally vulnerable to risk an overt and immediate expression of anger that, in his fantasy, may drive the parent away yet again.

Many toddlers become excessively clingy and aggressive with the parent after their initial avoidance. It seems that they can allow themselves to express their full range of feelings only after being reassured that the parent is truly back and will not leave them again.

Fighting. Aggression is the most straightforward manifestation of the "fight" response to perceived danger. Although all toddlers engage in occasional aggression, less than 10 percent were reported to hit others "often" in three different studies.[37,38,39] Between 17 and 42 months, there is often a rising pattern of aggression that then declines during the preschool years as children learn to use language and acquire problem-solving skills.[40] Aggression seems to be *unlearned* in the course of healthy development.

Toddlers can also learn to be aggressive as the result of frightening experiences during which they witnessed violence or were the target of it. Toddlers who are often aggressive are given the painful but all too common label of "little monster," "holy terror," or "devil" because adults do not understand that aggressive responses are a defense against fear and chronic anxiety. These children perceive routine exchanges as potential attacks on them and have learned that the best defense is a good offense. They fight when they are being given a bath, dressed, or put to bed; they hit, kick, or bite for no apparent reason; they throw monumental tantrums that go on endlessly and from which they emerge shaky, exhausted, and wet with perspiration.

Self-punishment is another form of aggression. It occurs when the child is angry at the parent but afraid of showing it for fear of punishment. Aggression is then turned against the self in the form of accident proneness, recklessness, and even self-inflicted injury. The child bites or hits himself. An unexplained puzzle in self-punishment is why the pain from the injury does not serve to inhibit this behavior.[41] It is possible that the child does not feel the pain because his emotions are too strongly aroused. Another possible explanation is that the toddler actually seeks out pain because he feels he deserves it.

Disruptive behavior. It is widely known that toddlers often exhibit tantrums, intense protest, and other disruptive behaviors. More than 80 percent of toddlers exhibit tantrums by the age of 2,[42] but although they are common they are not necessarily frequent. Less than 20 percent of 2-year-olds have tantrums every day or almost every day, and by the time they reach age 3 less than 10 percent have frequent tantrums, according to their parents' reports.[43] The quality and context of tantrums, angry protests, refusal to comply, and other disruptive behaviors are important indicators of the child's experience. When these behaviors are the norm rather than the exception, are prolonged, extremely intense, and out of context, and cause damage to the self or others or to objects, there is reason for concern that the child is having serious difficulty with overwhelming emotional experiences.[44]

Transformation of affect. Some toddlers transform their anxiety into behaviors that superficially look like giddy excitement or intense amusement. They run around the room while shrieking wildly, break into silly giggles that cannot be stopped, or escalate a game until they become almost manic. Eventually they cannot withstand the overstimulation and suddenly burst into tears.

What gives these behaviors away as a manifestation of anxiety is that they are inappropriate under the circumstances, as illustrated by the examples below.

- Matias runs around laughing wildly when his father threatens him with a belt.
- Joshua winces and then laughs when his mother angrily throws a ball at him and hits him in the genitals.
- Teresa looks at her mother with a phony smile while throwing toys in her direction in a provocative way.

These three children have all been exposed to high levels of aggression and excessive punitiveness in their home, and they have learned to hide their anxiety behind a mask of false gaiety.

Freezing/inhibition. Some toddlers express anxiety by becoming immobilized in response to an anxiety-arousing situation, as if frozen in space. Their faces become expressionless and impossible to read. Toddlers may also show a generalized inhibition of exploration. They are reluctant to approach, touch, and manipulate objects, and they withdraw from interaction with unfamiliar people.

These children do not show the broad range of emotion from exuberant glee to despair that is so characteristic of this age. Their mood tends to be sober or at best neutral. Some inhibited children cling to their parents and refuse to leave their side even after being familiar with their surroundings. Others tend to keep their distance from one or both parents as well, although they may look at them with a mixture of vigilance and fear. Toddlers can respond with inhibition when they are afraid of what will happen to them if they are spontaneous and carefree.

> **A little girl, Aleta, used this response to an extraordinary degree. She never showed anger, upset, or frustration. She displayed little curiosity or initiative in exploration and remained immobile on her mother's lap for long periods of time.**
>
> **For this little girl, inhibition of movement and emotion was the safest stance. Her mother was very depressed and sat sullenly for long periods of time, unable to stir herself. Her periods of stupor were often interrupted by sharp yelling at Aleta if the child dared to initiate an activity that the mother disapproved of. On one occasion, for example, Aleta moved from her mother's lap to pick up a rubber band from the floor. Her mother yelled, "No!" and slapped the child's hand quite hard. Aleta dropped the rubber band and leaned back against her mother.**

When inhibition becomes extreme, the child seems literally frozen and incapable of feeling or exploring.[45] This "freezing" can come to a sudden end with the toddler collapsing in tears and crying inconsolably while thrashing about. This occurred in the case of Aleta when the therapist gave her a toy. Aleta moved her fingers imperceptibly but did not extend her hand. When the therapist touched her hand with the toy in an effort to encourage her to take it, Aleta burst into tears and fell sobbing onto the floor. This motor collapse is the other side of freezing. The child can no longer contain her inner despair, and her effort at self-control disintegrates in a total emotional collapse.

Inhibition should not be confused with shyness or slowness to warm up. Toddlers who are shy or slow to warm up are fully capable of a full range of emotions, including playfulness and spontaneous joy, when they feel comfortable in their surroundings. They are also just as likely as other children to develop secure emotional relationships with their parents and caregivers. Inhibited children, on the other hand, seem to maintain a vigilant stance, as if they are always ready to flee from danger.

Role reversal in self-care. This defense is manifested through an exchange of roles between parent and child, so that the toddler routinely engages in protective behaviors usually performed by the parents and is unusually solicitous of the parents' (particularly the mother's) welfare. Anxiously precocious toddlers take it upon themselves to keep track of the mother's whereabouts at all costs, even at the expense of playing. They are exquisitely aware of the mother's moods, and they may dry her tears or offer her a cookie when they see that she is sad. They may ask the mother whether she has the keys of the car when they leave the house. In almost uncanny ways, they take on the role of protector in relation to their mother, whom they perceive as vulnerable and needing their help.

Of course, there are many toddlers who are very advanced in their ability to take care of themselves and who are aware of the parents' moods without being overly anxious. In anxiously precocious competence, there is a striking discrepancy between a child's apparent maturity and other behaviors that do not fit this pattern, such as excessive thumb sucking, pulling of her own hair, tics, or compulsive masturbation. The other side of excessive self-reliance can also be seen in night waking and eating disturbances. Many of these children also show a pervasive soberness of affect, perhaps because their need to stay vigilant and act like miniature adults dampens the spontaneity and exuberance typical of this age.

When cultural values stress independence and self-reliance, it is easy to overlook the anxiety that sometimes underlies the precocious coping strategies and to praise children as being advanced or resilient while overlooking the cost of those skills. The most worrisome aspect of anxiously precocious competence is that the child is trying to compensate for a profound insecurity regarding the parents' availability.

The outward show of competence hides painful inner doubts about
her own worth and lovability. For this reason, anxiously precocious
competence can become the foundation of a "false self," in which an
impressive appearance is used to conceal a fundamental fear that one
is not good enough.

Can Toddlers' Intense Anxiety Be Relieved?

The defenses against anxiety previously described can be alleviated if we
understand their meaning for the child. Children can decrease or even
let go of these behaviors when they are no longer needed as a protective
device. As parents become aware of the reasons for their child's excessive anxiety, they can take steps to alleviate it and to decrease the need
for premature defenses that constrict the child's emotional spontaneity.

Some toddlers are prone to persistent and intense anxiety, and professional consultation may be needed to understand the factors at work
and to help the child and the family learn coping strategies to relieve
it. Infant/early-childhood mental health specialists are psychologists,
psychiatrists, social workers, occupational therapists, pediatricians,
and other professionals who are especially trained in the emotional
needs of infants, toddlers, preschoolers, and their families. Their services can be of great help when the child and the family are at a loss to
resolve an emotional impasse through their own resources.[46]

There is, in fact, research evidence that early intervention in problems of anxiety can be effective in resolving them. In a study designed
to investigate the effectiveness of our clinical approach, my colleagues
and I found that toddlers who had been anxious before treatment
functioned just as well after treatment as toddlers who had felt secure
in their relationship with the mother all along.[47] In particular, these
toddlers received high scores in a measure of partnership that assessed
their ability to resolve conflicts with their mothers in a mutually agreeable way. Anxious toddlers in a comparison group not receiving treatment showed no improvement. The positive result of treatment came
about from our working with the parents to understand the causes

of their child's anxiety and to find ways of modifying their approach to child rearing to make it more responsive to the specific needs of their child. There is extensive evidence that early intervention that includes the child and the parents can restore a healthy developmental trajectory for young children in a variety of stressful and traumatic situations.[48]

Encouraging Emotional Security

Perhaps the most succinct formula for encouraging emotional security in toddlers is emotional responsiveness plus clear and firm guidelines. Maternal sensitivity to the baby's signals in the first year of life is strongly associated with emotional security in the infant-mother attachment at 12 months of age.[49] This security becomes a part of the child's sense of self and of the world. As a result, securely attached infants usually grow to cope with the developmental tasks of later years with greater ease and competence than anxiously attached babies. Researchers at the University of Minnesota have been following the same families for more than three decades, starting 3 months before the child's birth and following the mother and child into the children's adulthood, including their becoming parents.[50] The findings show the impressive continuity of beneficial effects stemming from early secure attachments. For example, securely attached 12-month-olds become toddlers who are more cooperative with the mother and more persistent and enthusiastic in trying to master a difficult task.[51] As 3- and 4-year-olds, they have more harmonious relationships with other children and get along better in the nursery school environment as assessed by their teachers.[52] As 5-year-olds, they are more flexible in finding solutions to problems. By age 6, they are less emotionally constricted and have fewer behavioral problems than their more anxious age-mates.[53,54]

Sensitive responsiveness to the child's signals of need remains an important component of the parent-child relationship across the developmental span. In fact, this characteristic is present in all fulfilling intimate relationships. At the same time, some of its manifestations change with age. The infant's signals become more varied and subtle in the course of development, and the parents' responses need to become more discriminating in response to the changes in the child. It would be unimaginable to say no to a crying 6-month-old; sometimes saying no to a crying 2-year-old is the only reasonable response. In forcing us to develop more creative forms of response, children raise their parents as much as we raise them.

As the child grows older and the parent is confronted with an increasing variety of wishes and demands, the natural desire to be sensitive to the child needs to be balanced by the question: sensitive responsiveness to what?

In the second year, it was relatively easier to have a clear-cut answer to this question because 1-year-olds want straightforward things and do not put up too much of a fuss when they are diverted from risky enterprises such as eating dirt, climbing onto the stereo, or putting their fingers into those ever-available electrical outlets.

The third year, ushering in as it does a definite sense of personal will, poses new challenges to the parents. Facing an adamant 2-year-old who is insisting on her rights (either verbally or through that most persuasive of devices, the temper tantrum), any empathic soul is bound to have inner doubts about the wisdom of persisting in denying the child's wishes. One wonders: Is this a contest of wills? A power struggle? Am I being as stubborn and defiant as my child? Am I damaging her psychologically by imposing things on her against her will? Should I negotiate a compromise? Should I be firm no matter what? Will I make her anxious by opposing her wishes?

However one proceeds, it helps to remember that childhood frustrations do not create anxiety if the parents hold a deep conviction that what they do has a personal or cultural meaning that justifies the child's distress. For example, a mother who knows that her working outside the home is important—either for her personal satisfaction or for the family's financial stability—will be able to pass on to her child an understanding that Mommy's work is important and not only a cause for frustration. On the other hand, a mother who feels that what she does outside the home is trivial or selfish will be more likely to be overly apologetic when the child protests her departure. Her toddler in turn will not learn to respect the importance of her mother's outside activities. Toddlers learn meaning from their parents, and they can learn to tolerate distress much better if they have a sense that it is for a worthy cause.

Issues to Negotiate

We saw in the previous chapter that the basic anxieties of toddlerhood revolve around the fear of losing the parents or the parents' love and around the puzzles of how the body is made and how it works. This chapter will focus on some specific manifestations of these basic anxieties.

Every one of the daily events involved in growing and developing can serve as a stage for playing out the toddler's fears. Separation anxiety, sleeping difficulties, refusal to be toilet trained, sibling rivalry, and discipline problems are common manifestations of anxiety about losing the parents or losing control over one's body. The developmental background of these struggles offers an approach that includes the toddler as a junior partner in a shared effort to find satisfactory solutions.

Separation Anxiety

Zoe, at 18 months, attends a child care center for the first time. Her mother has decided to stay with her until Zoe feels comfortable in the new setting. For the first twenty minutes she clings to her mother, but she gradually lets go. She crawls inside a toy cabinet, closes the doors, then opens them boisterously, running to her mother and holding her tight. She repeats this game again and again.

As we saw in previous chapters, young children manage their innermost fears through action. They play hide-and-seek to reassure themselves that things do not disappear when they are out of sight and that Mom will come back when she goes away. They entice their parents to chase them in order to make sure that the parents want them back. They move away to explore but keep tabs on the parent to make sure she does not leave them behind.

Sometimes children's actions are not enough to keep the parent as close at hand as they want. Circumstances may make it necessary for a parent to say good-bye and leave the child with grandparents, in day care, or with a babysitter, sometimes for a few hours and sometimes every day for most of the day.

When the separation is emotionally manageable, the toddler may respond with some distress but be comforted by the substitute caregiver. Even while missing the parents, the child is able to take pleasure in peers, toys, and other caring adults.

In more difficult situations, the child panics and clings desperately to the parent, rejecting efforts to be distracted or consoled while the parent is gone. In even more extreme circumstances, the fear of separation becomes so dominating that the child constantly monitors the parent's whereabouts, refusing to let him or her close the door of the bathroom or be out of sight for even a few minutes. The child loses her zest for playing and social interaction when the parent is gone. Problems of separation anxiety occur when ordinary, expectable distress becomes so acute and all-encompassing that it interferes with the child's overall mood and daily routine.

The Potential Emotional Cost of Major Separations

Everyday separations are an expectable occurrence in the toddler years, and children learn to cope with them even while expressing legitimate protest. Distress does not necessarily mean harm, and parents themselves may be distressed by the child's difficulty separating without feeling guilty about the separation. It is important to distinguish between the actual event (the separation) and the feelings caused by the event (distress).

However, lengthy separations can be a major emotional risk factor in the first three years of life and remain a source of possible stress throughout childhood.

The emotional cost of separation for the toddler depends on many different factors. A separation is most difficult in the following conditions:

- It is prolonged (longer than overnight or a couple of days).
- It occurs abruptly, so that the child is not prepared for it.
- The child is left in unfamiliar surroundings and with unfamiliar caretakers.
- No explanation is given to the toddler about what is happening and what to expect.
- The substitute caregivers do not understand, reassure the child, or pay attention to the child's distress.

Each of these five factors is very stressful in itself, but when all five occur simultaneously, the child is exposed to a potentially traumatic break with everything he holds familiar and dear. Under these conditions, even well-functioning toddlers can deteriorate rapidly in their capacity to trust and may become both angry and distressed. These emotional reactions are often played down by unknowing adults as transitory and reversible, but it is well documented that some toddlers become more prone to long-term depression and anxiety as a result.[1]

Temperamental differences play an important role in a toddler's ability to adjust to separations. An overnight separation may represent a mild stress for one child but be a major source of anxiety for a more sensitive, less adaptable toddler. Similarly, children differ in their ability to be comforted by somebody they do not know well. Individual differences in response to separation are vast, and parents need to learn their toddler's personal style in order to anticipate when a separation will be overly taxing.

Sometimes separation anxiety is the result not of actual separation experiences but of the child's fantasies about not being loved enough.

These fantasies make them afraid of being abandoned. Here again, some children are more prone to these fantasies than others. In general, toddlers tend to interpret their parents' hectic lifestyle, busy work schedule, short temper, or frayed nerves as indications that the parent is angry and does not want to be with the child.

It is sometimes difficult for an adult to keep in mind just how exquisitely attuned the average toddler is to a beloved parent's moods and whereabouts and how quickly the child can become prey to frightening fantasies.

> Marc was the last child to be picked up at day care that day. Later that night, as he was being put to bed, he said to his mother, "I thought you forgot me at school." Only then did his mother realize that it had become dark earlier than usual that evening because of the daylight saving time change. Marc had no way of knowing that she had picked him up only a few minutes later than usual. For him, it was dark and all the other mothers had picked up their children and gone home. Darkness and aloneness triggered the fear of abandonment, which he relived and was able to talk about as the bedtime separation was about to occur.

Alleviating Separation Anxiety

Being mindful of the emotional impact of routine, everyday separations helps to prevent persistently intense separation anxiety. Parents need to prepare themselves and the child for the separation and build a mutual confidence that the experience will be manageable and the reunion joyous. This applies whether the separation involves the child staying with a babysitter for a few hours or going to full-time day care, or the parents' going on a trip for a few days.

Although the specifics vary from one situation to another, the basic parameters for helping a child with a separation remain similar across situations:

- Try to avoid overnight separations until the child is older.
- Think about the separation before it takes place in order to get in touch with your own feelings, so that you can become aware of how you might be expressing those feelings through your behavior.
- Make sure that your child is familiar and comfortable with the substitute caregiver and with the place where she will be staying.
- Help the substitute caregiver become familiar with your child's personal style, likes and dislikes, specific worries and fears, and daily routine.
- Leave the child with tangible reminders of your love: an audiotape on which you speak to her, sing to her, and tell a favorite story; photographs in which you are shown together; a beloved toy that can serve as a transitional object. These measures are particularly useful for younger toddlers because they are concrete reminders of the parents' presence and do not depend on the child's memory and verbal ability.

- For a major separation, such as the beginning of a child care arrangement, tell your toddler what will be happening at least a few days before it actually takes place. Choose language that is simple and straightforward, and use a confident and factual tone of voice. Give your child room to ask questions and express misgivings. Tell him what he will be doing while you are apart. Reassure him that you will be thinking of him, and tell him that he can think about you during the separation. These preparations work particularly well with older, more verbal toddlers, but younger toddlers can understand simpler explanations and a reassuring, loving tone of voice.
- Stress what you will do when you are together again. "And I will come back, and we will hug each other, and I will make your favorite pancakes for dinner, and we will play horsey." Concrete examples carry more emotional force than general statements.
- Encourage the substitute caregiver to speak to the child about you during the separation, to tell him that it is all right to miss you when he is distressed and calls for you, and to reassure him that you'll come back.

Paying attention to what happens after the reunion is as important and helpful to a child as a careful preparation for going away. The separation experience lingers on long after parents and child are together again. Some pointers are as follows.

- After the reunion, be prepared to encounter signs of ambivalence in your child. Some toddlers greet their parents joyfully, but others avoid looking at them, are quite lukewarm and aloof, or show overt anger. These are expectable behaviors and show that the child is making an effort to control his feelings of abandonment by keeping some emotional distance from the returning parent. Do not take offense or withdraw from the child. Often this initial ambivalence upon reunion is followed by anxious clinging and a refusal to let the parent out of sight. Sometimes the expressions of ambivalence are delayed and do not become apparent until days or even a couple of weeks after the reunion.

- Tell the child how happy you are to be back together, and find opportunities to talk about the time you were apart and tell the child that you missed her.
- Be prepared to recognize your child's fear of another separation in behaviors such as night wakings, relapses in toilet training, sudden tantrums, and a low threshold of frustration. Anxiety takes many unexpected forms, and children have different ways of expressing their fears. A little boy whose father was away on a long trip hit his mother quite hard with a toy hammer. After yelling at him, she thought of the father's absence and said, "I think you are angry at me because your daddy went away." He yelled, "You did it!" In his mind, his all-powerful mother was responsible for his father's absence, and his longing was naturally translated into anger at her for her imagined trespass.
- Engage your child in games that help master separation issues, such as peek-a-boo and hide-and-go-seek. Give her room to re-enact the separation experience in playing with dolls or other toys. Children can express in play feelings that are kept carefully under wraps elsewhere. A very well-behaved little girl who seldom got angry scolded her doll, "You bad girl! I will leave you all alone!" She was expressing her fear that the same thing would happen to her if she misbehaved.

Above and beyond paying attention to feelings before and after a separation, never threaten your child with leaving or loss of love in an effort to control her behavior. Children believe their parents' assertions that "I will send you away," "I won't love you anymore," "I'll go away." These statements are terrifying for young children because they make tangible their developmentally appropriate anxiety about losing the parents' love and approval. Instilling fear is a very poor way of disciplining a child because it makes the child mistrust the parents. This mistrust in turn can generalize to other relationships and may cause lifelong anxiety and anger.

Being apart is always experienced by the child, at some level, as the equivalent of being left. This feeling can last into adulthood, as Cole Porter felt viscerally when he wrote:

> Every time we say good-bye, I die a little;
> Every time we say good-bye, I wonder why a little;
> Why the gods above me, who must be in the know,
> Think so little of me they allow you to go.

When we love, we hold an unconscious belief: "If you loved me most of all, if I were the most important thing in your life, you would never leave me." The only way to reconcile a child who has this un-movable conviction is to provide abundant proof, through emotional availability and responsiveness, that he does not need to be the only important thing in your life and you do not need to be always together in order to love and be loved well enough and deeply enough.

The Experience of Toilet Training

In the course of the second year, toddlers learn to recognize more sub-tle sensations in the anal and urethral areas. They also learn to contract and relax the muscles responsible for holding on to and letting go of feces and urine. This increased capacity to notice and control sensa-tions signals that the toddler is getting ready to be toilet trained.

In addition to the child's awareness of anal and urethral sensations, other factors are also influential in the child's readiness to use these sensations to control urination and defecation. The most important of these factors are:

- The child's constitutional regularity or irregularity of the digestion-elimination cycle and overall health of the digestive system
- The parents' tolerance of the child's individual pace
- The quality of partnership that parents and toddler have already established in negotiating earlier developmental issues

Depending on all these variables, toilet training can be a relatively uneventful process or a battleground between parent and child.

For all their earthiness, bowel movements have a profound symbolic meaning. No other body function represents so succinctly the polarities of experience of the human psyche. A BM is a precious treasure because it is part and parcel of one's body and its mysteries, and it is simultaneously something dirty and smelly that the child is taught not to touch or play with. It is both something to cherish and something to discard.

> **Rafi, at age 2, looked skeptically at the potty his mother was offering him for the first time. He sat on it for a few seconds with his clothes on. He then got up, placed a gold-covered chocolate coin inside the potty, smiled lovingly, and said, "There, Mommy." The coin, with its dark sweet inside and its golden allure, was a perfect symbol of what Rafi's BMs meant to him.**

If both these meanings of feces can be respected, toilet training can proceed with integrity. This means that the child's bodily products can be welcomed with pleasure but with no need for exaggerated accolades and can be disposed of matter-of-factly, without marked expressions of disgust.[2]

Above all, feces need to retain their character as something that belongs to the child and that it is in the child's power to produce or to withhold. In this sense, toilet training is the epitome of partnership through give-and-take, withholding, and letting go.

The Child's Readiness

The timing of toilet training has been a topic of much debate among parents and child psychologists alike. There is a wide range among different cultures in social expectations regarding the appropriate age to begin and complete toilet training. A recurrent theme, however, is that of reciprocity: even among cultures that start toilet training in the first

year of life, the actual practices involve noticing children's bodily signals and placing them in the appropriate place and position to encourage elimination. In the United States, there has been a long-standing
consensus that it is best to wait until children are ready to understand
what is expected of them, so that they can become active partners in
the process.[3] This may vary from child to child, but it is unlikely to
occur before 15 to 18 months of age and may not occur until 24 to 30
months or even later.

This focus on child readiness reflects the value that mainstream
American culture places on the child's individuality. As the country
becomes more diverse, other cultural values are increasingly coming
into play and influencing parents' attitudes toward toilet training, such
as how the child fits into the daily rhythms of the family (flexibility of
parents' schedule; the needs of other children) and the financial burden of paying for disposable diapers.

Toward the middle of the second year, children become increasingly aware of the relationship between cause and effect and deeply
concerned with the question of standards. They worry about the consequences of their actions and become disturbed if things are not up to
par, if clothes are dirty or toys are broken. Children may become upset
if their parents leave crumbs on the table or forget shoes in the hall;
they may get upset at themselves when they get dirty or make a mess.
They are quickly internalizing the norms of social behavior that are
being implicitly or explicitly taught to them.

When possible and compatible with family needs, the beginning of
toilet training is best timed to coincide with a child's emerging interest
in standards, which makes them feel invested in living up to them. The
wish to emulate what the parents and older siblings do in the toilet can
then occur naturally and calls for minimal parental encouragement.

Many toddlers initiate the process themselves by calling the parents' attention to the fact that they are making pee or poo-poo or
by becoming upset for being wet or dirty. Even then, some children
are rather lackadaisical in their approach and do not see the point
of making themselves uphold standards all the time. Going in the
potty is something they do when they feel like it; at other times,

going in the diaper works very well for them. These toddlers go back and forth between periods of being clean and dry and periods when they relapse because they are absorbed in other pursuits. Other toddlers are so ready and regular that they become fully trained in a few weeks.

Starting toilet training before the child shows clear readiness can lead to power struggles over who owns the child's body. Precisely because they are interested in standards, children in the second year of life become very upset when they cannot keep up with external demands. Jerome Kagan has shown that 2-year-olds from diverse cultural backgrounds cry or protest when an adult expects them to perform a task that is too difficult for them. Same-age children respond with spontaneous joy when they meet a self-imposed standard, such as building a six-block tower or completing a challenging puzzle.[4]

If we extrapolate these findings to the question of toilet training, we can conclude that beginning this process prematurely can lead to frustration and negativism in the child. When parents feel pressured by circumstances to start relatively early anyway, it is best to involve the child in a partnership by helping her to signal when she is urinating or having a bowel movement. This is easily done: if the parent comments casually on the event ("Mary is making a poo-poo"), the child will soon enough begin to notice it herself because her action brings about that most important of occurrences: the parent's interest and attention. When the child herself tells the parent that the noteworthy event of urinating or making a BM is taking place, she is also signaling an increased readiness to progress to the next step: going to the potty.

Potties are better than grown-up toilets for beginning training and for a long time afterward. A potty is made for the size of a toddler's bottom, sparing the child the fear of falling into the toilet. It enables toddlers to keep their feet firmly on the ground in order to push. Finally, a potty does not come equipped with rushing water, which frightens some children with the unspeakable fantasy that they, like their poo-poos, will be flushed away.

When the child's readiness is not an issue, most conflicts in toilet training can be traced to a combination of the child's irregular cycles (including perhaps a physiologically based tendency toward constipation, loose stools, or a mixture of both) and the parent's misperception that toilet training is a process controlled by the adult. Each of these two factors represents a threat to the formation of a partnership around toilet training.

Physiological Irregularities

Toddlers' physiology can cause bouts of abdominal or rectal pain when they are constipated and feces cannot be eliminated smoothly. The child may withhold to avoid the pain, making the constipation worse. Alternatively, recurrent diarrhea or loose stools make it difficult for toddlers to hold feces back, and they may stop trying and give up. Both with constipation and with diarrhea, the child's confidence in his ability to take charge of his bowels is undermined. Toddlers often personalize their feces, attributing to them malevolent motives when the child experiences pain. As Asher put it, "My poo-poos are very angry with me."

The child's pediatrician is the best person to consult when parents suspect that their child's digestive process is not working well. A special diet and stool softeners may be prescribed if necessary. Suppositories and enemas can be perceived by the child as coercive and intrusive and are best thought of as a last resort. When such a measure is necessary, fear and resistance can be lessened if the parent explains to the child what will happen, why it is needed, and how it will help.[5]

Many healthy children have irregular physiological rhythms and need to eliminate at unpredictable times. This is a constitutional characteristic, and adults need to be thoughtful about not pressuring the child to use the potty at the same time every day simply because it is convenient for them. A portable potty is very useful for children with unpredictable elimination patterns because it is readily available when needed. At the same time, setting a predictable routine to sit on the potty without forcing the child to produce can train the child's body and mind to expect a predictable routine that may in time lead to regular patterns of elimination.

Can Parents Control Toilet Training?

The secret belief that it is up to the adult to control toilet training can creep up in unexpected ways even among parents who consciously believe otherwise. Parents can feel embarrassed if their child is the only one in the play group who shows no interest in even starting the process. Other parents long for a respite from smelly laundry or sizable disposable diaper bills. Still others feel pressure from friends and family to stop "pampering" and help the child grow up. Sometimes adults worry about their own motives in not starting toilet training (wanting him to stay a baby forever? being afraid of not knowing how to do it?).

There is always room for examining one's behavior, but it is likely that if the child has shown no interest in cleanliness, tidiness, standards, toilets, or BMs, he is not ready to start.

On the other hand, if the child seems ready, it behooves the parent to follow, without asking tentatively for the child's permission but with quiet confidence that this is the right time. The child himself can let us know if we have read his cues accurately.

> **Max, age 2, had no interest in toilet training in spite of his parents' entreaties. Eager to start anyway, his mother bought some doll furniture that included a toy toilet and encouraged him to play with it. Max complied—by sticking the mother doll into the toy toilet headfirst.**

Toileting has striking rhythmic similarities with secure base behavior. Both are based on an alternation of holding on and letting go, giving and withholding, opening up and closing down. In both processes, the child's comfort with the parents is reflected and ultimately internalized in her confidence with her body and with herself.

Nighttime Difficulties

Although "sleeping like a baby" is a commonly used expression, it is likely to be more wishful than real for most infants and young children. The average 3-year-old sleeps for an average of about twelve hours per twenty-four-hour day, with one lengthy bout of nighttime sleep and a nap during the day. Most infants and toddlers across the first three years of life do not sleep through the night, but a large proportion of them learn to soothe themselves and fall back to sleep on their own. However, there are significant individual differences in the total amount of nighttime sleep and the distribution of sleep during the day and at night. There are also many cultural variations in what is expected from young children regarding sleep practices, including sleeping space, cosleeping, and parental responses to nighttime wakings.[6] Perhaps because of these complexities, concerns about sleep are among the most common complaints of parents during well-baby visits.[7]

Sleep disturbances include difficulty falling asleep, waking up repeatedly during the night, night terrors, or a combination of all three. In many cases, toddlers with sleep disturbances have a history of early biological vulnerability, for example, they were born prematurely, had other conditions requiring specialized neonatal care, or suffered from colic for longer than three months. These children often have a history of not sleeping well from birth. It is also possible that the child has never acquired a regular sleeping pattern because there has been no predictable nighttime routine.

Many toddlers begin having problems going to sleep in their second year. This may be because daytime anxieties emerge most vividly during the night, when the child is alone and surrounded by darkness. This is the period when the fear of the "monster under the bed" emerges. Taking these fears as an opportunity for problem solving gives the child a dual message of reassurance and control. One parent engaged the toddler in a nightly "monster patrol" that consisted in going systematically through all the places where the child thought there might be a monster in hiding and then closing doors and windows ceremoniously with an admonishment to any lurking monsters that the parent was watching and would chase them away. Here the child was actively enlisted in the solution until his reality testing caught up with his imaginary fears and he outgrew his fear of monsters.

Sleeping Irregularities

Many children get the sleep they need in spite of the awakenings, but their parents do not. The mismatch between the sleep needs of the toddler and those of the parents sets up a tense home situation in which the parents are exhausted, frustrated, and helpless. They become inconsistent and angry with the child, and the toddler becomes scared, angry, and defiant in response.

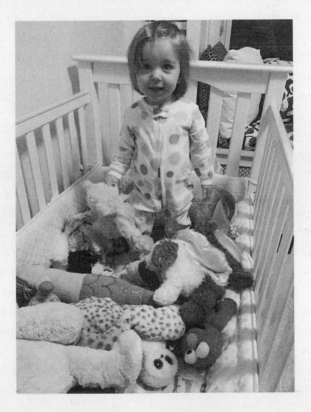

In these circumstances, it might be useful to recognize that toddlers have little control over awakenings. One solution is not to admonish them to "go to sleep"—something they often cannot do at will—but rather to help them understand what they may and may not do while they are awake.

Toddlers should be encouraged to soothe themselves when they wake up at night. Depending on their age, they can hug their pillow or teddy bear, sing softly to themselves, or talk to themselves about the things they will do when it is time to get up. A musical mobile with a soothing lullaby works well for many very young toddlers. These solutions are within the capabilities of even very young toddlers when the parents have the resolve to carry them through.

Mismatches Between Parents and Child

A mismatch between the parents' and the toddler's needs for sleep may occur if the child is a very early riser and the parents are not. Toddlers can learn to take this discrepancy in stride and entertain themselves if the parents convey to them a lighthearted, guiltless sense that this is the way things are going to be.

One mother helped her 11-month-old, Mike, accept her need for early-morning sleep by putting some very enticing toys next to her bed at night. When Mike woke up at 6 a.m., she picked him up, nuzzled and talked to him, took him to her bedroom, set him next to her bed, and told him that Mommy was going to sleep some more and he could play with the toys. Every once in a while he would talk to his mother or pull up to the side of the bed. Each time, his mother gave him a reassuring grunt and a pat on the head, and the child went back to playing. This is an early demonstration of secure base behavior under unusual conditions!

Another mother came up with a different version of this basic solution for her 2-year-old. She set up a child-size table and chair in front of the TV set. Every night she put a piece of banana and some other safe pieces of finger food on the table and set the TV to a channel carrying a good children's program. She taught her child, Logan, to wake up, come to the parental bedroom, and have a prebreakfast snack while watching the children's program. Logan is now 9 years old and has become an unusually self-reliant youngster, in part because of his mother's supportive confidence in his ability to collaborate in taking care of himself.

When Night Wakings Become a Problem

Sleeping irregularities have a constitutional basis. Sleeping problems result when night wakings become charged with strong emotional meaning for the parent and the child. In this situation, the anxiety surrounding the wakings often interferes with finding a solution.

The most common anxiety associated with night wakings in toddlerhood is the fear of separation. This fear exists in both the parent and the child. Nighttime brings about a basic disruption of the secure base patterns so readily available during the day. Instead of easy daytime access, there are now darkness, bedroom walls, and crib sides serving as obstacles between parent and child.

Night, darkness, and physical distance are archetypal triggers of fears and anxiety. This is why many cultures less invested than ours in personal and marital privacy enable mother and child or parents and child to sleep together through infancy and the toddler years. Even in technological cultures, the young child's nighttime cry elicits in the parent an ancient fear that the child's well-being and perhaps his very survival are at stake. The immediate impulse is to go to the child and provide reassurance and protection. This impulse is at odds with the parents' more rational knowledge that the child is healthy, the household is safe, and sleep can be resumed.

Some studies have found that night wakings in toddlers are associated with the mother's own fears of separation and with maternal depression. Many mothers whose toddlers have sleeping difficulties report that they were frightened or were not well cared for as children.[8] They want to spare their own toddlers the anxieties that they felt while growing up, and they respond to night wakings by bringing the child into their bed or going to the child's bed. Of course, every parent does this sometimes. When it becomes the norm, this response may cause problems when it interferes with the adults' relationship and when it gives the child the message that nighttime anxieties cannot be managed without the parents' ongoing presence.

Cultural values and expectations have an important effect on efforts to help toddlers sleep in their own beds and on their own. Although separate sleeping arrangements for parents and children remain the prevalent practice in the United States, cosleeping in a family bed is preferred by many parents. Shared sleeping works best when everybody can sleep soundly in one another's proximity and when both parents are emotionally invested in the arrangement so that it does not generate friction or resentment over loss of adult intimacy. It works less well when it is adopted by default after the toddler's bedtime protests make the parents feel they are harming the child by expecting him to sleep on his own.

The child psychiatrist Klaus Minde and his colleagues reported on the success of a program designed to help toddlers soothe themselves back to sleep when they wake up during the night.[9] This program, characterized by remarkable common sense, helps parents overcome their own anxieties about not protecting and rescuing the child from the anxiety of night wakings. The program involves the following steps:

1. A review with the parents of what the sleeping problems consist of. Is it difficulty settling down to sleep, repeated night waking, or both? The daytime routine is also reviewed.

2. If the toddler does not have a predictable daily routine, the parents are helped to understand that toddlers experience a sense of comforting self-control from being able to anticipate what will happen next. Parents are encouraged to develop a routine in which meals, baths, naps, and other daily events take place at about the same time and in the same place. Daytime naps

should be reserved for soon after lunchtime in order to give the toddler plenty of time to get tired again by bedtime.

3. Once daytime routines are established, the parents are encouraged to focus on soothing bedtime routines that involve quiet activities such as reading, singing bedtime songs, or praying. Creating a predictable "quiet time" as a marker that bedtime is coming helps the toddler to wind down as a transition to bedtime.

4. The sleeping problem is tackled next. Two main techniques are recommended. One is "checking": the parent checks on the crying child at regular intervals that are tolerable for the parent (five or ten minutes), patting the child or using words of encouragement but expecting the child to stay in bed. This "checking" continues until the child falls asleep. If the parent is too overwrought by the child's crying, an alternative "shaping" technique is recommended. This consists of moving gradually from one step to the next. If the child was sleeping in the parent's bed, the next step would be for the parent to go into the child's bed the first night, sit on the bed the second night, on a chair the third night, and so on.

This method was found to improve the sleep of 85 percent of the toddlers with whom it was tried. Interestingly, Minde and his colleagues recommend that fathers carry out this project whenever possible because they tend to be less conflicted about sticking to it. On the other hand, the interventions tend to fail when the father is unwilling to cooperate in restructuring the parents' response to their child's sleeping problem. A major benefit of the program is that solving the sleeping problem tends to give both parents and child the skills to negotiate more effectively other areas of struggle as well.

Enlisting the Child in the Solution

Plans to address sleeping problems can be enriched by helping the child come up with alternatives to crying and calling for the parents. This can work particularly well with older, more verbal toddlers. Such a joint venture between parent and child in finding a solution to the sleeping problem teaches toddlers that their agenda—feeling safe and protected—can be achieved without violating the parents' agenda—to remain asleep.

One possible way of phrasing this approach is saying to the toddler "Danny, you know how you wake up at night and call for Mommy?" (Wait for an answer.)

"Yes, and Mommy is so sleepy that I get grumpy and yell at you to go back to sleep?" (Wait for an answer, which may only be a serious face or a meaningful look.)

"You know, Mommy doesn't like to be grumpy at you. But I'm so sleepy at night, and when I'm sleepy I get grumpy and that's why I yell." (Wait for a response, which does not need to be verbal.)

"It's hard for mommies and daddies to wake up in the middle of the night. I've been thinking, what can you do to feel better when you wake up at night?" (Go over different possibilities with the child.)

"Let's try that tonight. When you wake up, say to yourself: Mommy is sleeping. I am going to hug my teddy bear and talk to him [or whatever alternative you agreed on]. Tonight, before you go to bed, I will remind you. That way Mommy can get her sleep and you can help yourself by talking to bear and we will not be grumpy with each other."

It is worthwhile to have this conversation during the day, when both parent and child are rested, and not in the middle of the conflict they are trying to resolve. In this way, both parent and child can mull over the plan during the rest of the day and be readier to implement it when the time comes.

For some parents and toddlers, talking will be sufficient to establish a meaningful exchange. For others, it might help to have this conversation in the context of play. The adult might set up a bedroom scene in which the baby wakes up and calls for the parents, and the actual nightly scene can then be enacted. As the child becomes involved in the play, the parents may wait for a natural pause and then say, "That is what happens to us at night, isn't it?" This can become a good starting point for a dialogue and for a play enactment of the possible solutions.

Here again, attitude is more important than words. The child needs to realize that the parents are not requesting that she go to sleep; they are helping the child grow into doing something that she is capable of doing. The parents' conviction that they are doing the right thing is the primary ingredient for the recipe to resolve conflicts over sleeping to be successful.

Night Terrors

A child may wake up in the middle of the night screaming in a panic. This deserves prompt parental attention. If she can speak, the child may talk breathlessly and between sobs about "the bad man," "the monster," "the witch," or any of a variety of other scary creatures that are staples of the child's imagination. This is a sign that dreams have made their appearance and have acquired the character of nightmares.

One way to reassure the child is to tell her during the day about the nature of dreams as pictures inside her head that are "make believe" and can do her no harm. Most children go through a temporary phase of having nightmares, particularly at times of unusual stress, such as starting preschool, changing caregivers, making a difficult visit to the doctor, having a scary encounter with a dog or other animal, or being exposed to an overly stimulating story or movie. If the nightmares persist, it is usually a sign that the child is struggling with an unexpressed worry or fear or with more pressure to perform than he can comfortably manage. Exploring what those fears might be usually opens the doors to finding a solution.

There is evidence that some cases of night terror have a biological component and can be hereditary.[10] During an episode, the children's behavior follows a predictable pattern that includes thrashing about, excessively rapid breathing, very fast heart rate, perspiration, and sounds of distress that may escalate to inconsolable crying. The child may respond to the parent's effort to restrain her with intense fear, confusion, disorientation, and efforts to escape. Some children scream for periods ranging from less than a minute to twenty minutes or so. The child seems oblivious to the parent's ministrations and often has no memory of the event the next day. When this pattern is so frequent and intense that it disrupts family life, it is a good idea to discuss the possibility of a sleep disorder evaluation with the child's pediatrician.

Many toddlers start having sleeping problems, including night terrors, following a stressful event or distressing experience. Parents may not link the beginning of the sleeping problem to the event because they may not assign to it the same emotional magnitude that it has for the toddler. The birth of a sibling, starting child care, or changing caregivers may evoke for the child anxieties that emerge during the night. Frightening events—an accident, family discord, being physically hurt—have an even greater potential to trigger sleeping problems. Reviewing recent events can help parents discover links between what happened and the child's response that give new meaning to the child's difficulty with sleep. This new understanding, in turn, can enable the parents to help the child give meaning to and cope with the distressing event.

The Importance of Rituals

Toddlers have many reasons to have trouble with sleep: fear of relinquishing control by letting sleep take over; resistance to giving up the companionship of being awake with the rest of the family; anxiety over being all alone in one's solitary room and solitary bed; or fantasies about what happens in the darkness of the house.

The importance of bedtime rituals in helping with these fears cannot be overemphasized. Rituals provide a container for uncertainty, bind anxiety, and provide reassuring bonds of human connection.

Structuring prebedtime activities can help a child develop a feeling of belonging that will carry off into sleep. Uninterrupted family dinners (without intruding phone calls or other distractions), perhaps a bath or a time for quiet play, and then the ceremonies of getting into nightclothes, brushing teeth, going over the events of the day, anticipating what will happen tomorrow, reading a story, singing a lullaby, saying a prayer—these activities can be woven into a family ritual that becomes associated with feelings of safety and protection that the child can hold on to when the lights go off.

If the bedtime ritual is done with quiet assurance, there will be no need to stay with the child until she falls asleep. A reassuring comment from the living room that "I am here and everything is fine" will be sufficient to convey the message that any anxiety she may feel being alone in her bed is manageable and that the parent is right in expecting her to handle it on her own. Toddlers grow stronger from going successfully through this experience.

Eating Difficulties

Many of the struggles involving eating in the toddler years revolve around the issue of control. Toddlers want to eat what they want when they want it, while parents may worry that the child's nutritional needs will not be met unless they play an active role in feeding the child. Parents may want to introduce some tidiness into the process of eating, but many toddlers want no interference with their control of their hands and spoon and with their freedom to explore the texture of the food by smashing it, squishing it, and putting it into their hair. The very real danger of choking may lead parents to try to manage what children put into their mouths at a slower pace than the toddler would like. The result of these disparate agendas is that toddlers may protest, recoil, and shut their mouths firmly when they don't like what the parent is doing.

The good news is that as a rule parents do not need to worry about their toddlers' nutritional well-being if the child has access to a range of healthful choices. A study of 3,000 infants and toddlers ranging in age from 4 to 24 months found that even children in the lowest 10 percent of the weight curve were meeting their requirements for all nutrients.[11] In spite of these reassuring findings, 50 percent of the parents in the sample described their children as picky eaters, suggesting that parents have a tendency to worry about their children's nutrition even when there is no objective reason for concern.[12] There is also research suggesting that parents may be too quick in labeling their young children as picky eaters. Toddlers who initially refuse a food offered to them eventually try it when it has been offered about ten times, but most parents give up after three or four trials.[13]

Parents who worry about the adequacy of their children's diets often resort to coaxing, forcing, or using food as a reward. These methods not only are unnecessary but also may backfire because they create an association of food with negative feelings and with conflict between parent and child. There is consistent evidence that children develop effective self-regulation in food intake when they are not controlled or coerced to eat.[14] Self-regulation, in turn, is probably the key factor in preventing obesity and eating disorders.

Food has a powerful symbolic meaning as the equivalent of nurturance. The toddler's growing momentum toward autonomy in eating can be perceived by parents as a message that their nurture is no longer needed because the child can now nurture himself. Offering food can become a substitute for offering love, and pangs of sadness can be mistaken for hunger pangs. Adults with eating disorders are helped in treatment to differentiate between physical and emotional

hunger because they equated both kinds of experiences while growing up. Toddlers can be taught that difference from the beginning,
when parents know that the child's refusal of food is not a refusal of
love.

Of course, parents do have an important role in teaching their children to eat. Modeling how and what to eat is an important influence on
children. One study, for example, found that girls ate more fruits and
vegetables when their mothers also ate them, while girls whose mothers pressured them actually ate less of those foods.[15] Modeling works
both ways in the sense that it can also have a negative effect, as shown
by findings that children have less effective self-regulation in eating
when their parents either diet or show out-of-control eating.[16] Eating
is a social activity, and toddlers are more likely to try a new food when
everybody else at the table is eating it. Family meals are an important
social experience that helps toddlers' development at many levels. They
become more competent at feeding themselves when the whole family eats together, and they also benefit in the long term by consuming
less fat, soda, and fried foods and more fruits and vegetables as adolescents.[17] These findings suggest that parents can best support good
eating habits and prevent eating difficulties when they establish the
conditions for *when*, *where*, and *with whom* to eat, when they provide
and consume the foods that they want their children to eat, and when
they use this framework to give the toddler the freedom to decide *what*
and *how much* to eat.

Sibling Rivalry

Having a New Sibling

The birth of a baby brother or sister, even when eagerly anticipated,
can also be quite unsettling for a toddler. This does not mean that it is
psychologically damaging. On the contrary, it can bring about many
important learning experiences and the opportunity for a lifelong
emotional connection with the sibling.

Many toddlers are very loving toward the new baby, displaying capacities for tender protectiveness that are remarkable for such a young child. For example, some toddlers don't want to go out unless the baby also comes along, or they worry about the baby's welfare during a separation, run to tell the parent that the baby is crying and needs help, or gently caress the baby's head, hands, or feet. But having a new sibling can also make toddlers feel displaced and uprooted from their familiar role in the household constellation. If they were the firstborn, they are no longer the one and only child in the parents' lives. If they were the youngest one, they are no longer the baby of the family. Jealousy—the angry fear that one is not good enough and will lose one's place and be replaced by another—is such a deeply rooted human emotion that it has been documented in 5- and 6-month-old infants,[18] and some consider it as important from an evolutionary perspective as love and sex.[19]

Depending on their age, temperamental style, and developmental level, toddlers express their distress in different ways.

Susanna, 15 months, tries to push the baby out of her mother's lap and asks for the mother's breast even though she has been weaned for months. She bites the baby whenever she has a chance. She becomes "hell on wheels," careening through the house even though she has learned to walk only recently. During the day she is aggressive and overactive, but at night she regresses to being a little baby herself, waking up often and asking for the mother's breast or its alternative, a bottle. She clings to her pacifier and is very distressed when it is out of sight.

Benjamin, also 15 months, responds very differently. He becomes withdrawn and subdued, and his face has a sad, worried expression. He bursts into tears at the slightest frustration. He seems to have lost all his smiles, and his movements lack zest and vitality. He becomes very rejecting of his mother but clings to his father.

Nancy, 24 months, hugs her baby brother so hard he turns red. When the mother rescues him, Nancy wails. She wants to hold him constantly but always finds a way of making him cry.

Rebecca, 28 months, is seen walking around with a silk bow and a hammer. Her father asks what she is doing. "A bow for her head," says Rebecca, pointing to her 3-month-old sister's totally bald little head.

Peter, 30 months, looks at his week-old brother and says, "Okay, now he can go back." On other occasions he asks, "Can we put him in the oven? Can we eat him? He'll be tasty!"

The same Peter, now 3½, looks on as his brother tries to blow out his first-birthday candle. He says, "He is very cute, isn't he? We won't kill him, will we?"

Asher, 3 years old, jumps on his mother as she nurses the baby and says, "Put him down, pick me up!"

Janice, 4 years old, has a 5-month-old brother. She confides to a little girlfriend, "Wait till you have one. You will get so mad when your mommy feeds him." She turns her back to the guests who are admiring the new baby and looks at them reproachfully when they try to admire her as well.

These vignettes show the evolution of very young children's expression of anger and ambivalence about having a sibling. Susanna and Benjamin, at 15 months, express their feelings simply and directly using their own temperamental styles: Susanna strikes out, Benjamin withdraws. The older children's responses are more complex. They are struggling to contain and control their aggressive impulses and to integrate them with feelings of love. Rebecca, who loves to wear ribbons on her abundant hair, ostensibly wants to share this pleasure with her bald baby sister and finds no better way of doing it than approaching her with a nail and a hammer "to make the ribbon stay on." Peter struggles at first with opposite wishes to send his brother back and make him a part of himself by eating him; by the time he is 3½, the side of him that loves his brother is gaining over the side that wants to kill him. By age 4, Janice shows that she can reflect on her feelings of anger as an internal state that will not be expressed through destructive action.

The toddler's fear of losing the parents' love receives a powerful impetus with the birth of a new baby. The spectacle of one's very own mother lovingly holding and ministering to another child must be convincing proof to a toddler that this fear has come true. As if this were not enough, the father is also absorbed in the new arrival and every guest pays attention to the baby first. The fear of being replaced by someone better—an anxiety that haunts many adults—has one of its early origins in this experience.

A new baby brings many concrete changes in the toddler's moment-to-moment experience. He now needs to wait more often and longer than ever before for things he wants or needs. He spends more time alone. He is scolded or corrected more frequently as parents try to teach him what he can and cannot do with the baby. Some favorite activities—going swimming, going to the playground, playing a favorite game—often have to be curtailed or postponed because of the baby's needs. Things cannot be done spontaneously anymore because the baby's schedule needs to be taken into account, and the time it takes to prepare the baby's bag can seem interminable.

These are important losses for a toddler. The example below shows how keenly a toddler feels them.

Sammy, 28 months old, began burying his face in his hands and sighing deeply after the birth of the new baby. His father asks, "Why are you doing that?" Sammy replies, "I am sad." His father asks why. Sammy looks at him sadly and says, "I want my mommy back."

These feelings exist even when the parents are patient and sensitive in helping their toddler through the stormy feelings of this period.

Competitiveness toward a new baby may give rise to the toddler's first sustained experiences of jealousy, envy, shame, and guilt.

Even without a new sibling, toddlers feel sometimes younger and sometimes older than they really are. As Linda put it, "I am a baby and a big girl both." Having to tolerate a baby day after day can greatly intensify a toddler's wishes to be a baby all over again. Toddlers may show this by wanting a bottle, losing the gains they made in toilet training, or reverting to baby talk. On the other hand, they also experience pride and a feeling of superiority when they realize that they can do many things that the baby can't.

Parents do well to play along with the toddler's momentary wishes to be a baby. Letting him have a bottle or a pacifier, carrying him to his room, holding him snugly, and talking baby talk—these brief relapses into the modes of an earlier age can reassure the toddler that his baby side is still getting attention when needed. With this knowledge in place, the child can continue to get pleasure from his increased competence.

The toddler's abilities to do things better than the baby can be a good antidote for feelings of jealousy. When parents comment admiringly on a toddler's skill at doing something or point out that the baby cannot yet do that marvelous feat, the toddler gets the comforting sense that she is still special and appreciated.

Perhaps most important of all is the message that a mother's or father's lap is big enough to accommodate both the toddler and the baby. When a toddler is pushed off his mother's lap because the baby needs to feed, this experience can feel to him like a stab in the heart. The father's habit of asking about the baby first when he returns from work can make the toddler feel hopeless about anybody ever again caring for him most of all. At the risk of losing some spontaneity, parents will do their toddler a great service by making themselves think of how he might be feeling when he watches them with the baby. During the difficult initial period of adjustment, including the toddler and even giving him priority whenever possible will help him tolerate the baby and help open the way for love toward the new sibling to develop.

When the Toddler Is the Baby of the Family

Sarah, 4 years old, is playing dress up in her room. A box with a treasured collection of hair ornaments is on the floor next to her. Her sister Robyn, 15 months, comes in, goes straight to the box, and puts one of Sarah's ribbons into her mouth, covering it with saliva. Sarah screams and hits Robyn. Robyn wails.

Mario, 6 years old, is playing ball with a friend. Ronnie, 24 months, wants to join in. "Me, too! Me, too!" he cries.

Ayana, 3½ years old, has been waiting for her mother to read her a story. When she and her mother settle down comfortably and are about to start, Omar, 18 months, whimpers that he is hungry. The reading comes to an end before it even starts.

Rachel, age 4, and Armon, age 2½, struggle furiously over who will sit next to Daddy to watch television.

These very ordinary scenes illustrate the power of toddlers to disrupt the life of an older sibling. They are little, and most of the time they do not know any better. In addition, they often cry in response to frustration, and then they appear so sad and helpless that it is almost impossible not to take their side.

Perhaps the most common mistake parents make in dealing with sibling relations is to favor the younger child too much. This is often done because younger children seem so vulnerable and needy. Another common mistake is to punish either child or both without first learning what happened.

Parents can allow themselves some benign neglect when it comes to sibling relations. Letting children work out their disagreements provides a valuable experience to children of all ages. Negotiations are not always smooth, and the stronger child may win more often than is fair by strict standards of justice. The problem is that parental intervention does not guarantee fairness; it only brings into the conflict an even stronger participant whose word is final regardless of the facts. One can end up with a situation in which the parent is inflicting on the older sibling the same kind of arbitrary power that the older sibling is trying to inflict on the younger one. The parent's action to stop the stronger sibling's power can give the message "Do as I say, not as I do."

Children need to work out their own relationships. Parents can certainly help or hinder this development. One of the parents' roles is to ensure that each child has enough parental attention and care so that there is no need to compete with the sibling for a little place in the sun. The case of Tobias and Andy, described in chapter 6, shows some of the emotional repercussions that may result from excessive or one-sided parental intervention. The more favored child can become a self-righteous bully, ever confident that the parent will come to her defense. The less favored child will either become a secret bully, trying to get away with aggressive acts when the parent is not there, or suppress feelings of anger and resentment in ways that interfere with emotional spontaneity and freedom of expression.

Of course, there are times when parents must intervene. In the first vignette, in which Sarah hit Robyn, their father did the right thing when he told Sarah in a stern voice that she could be angry and scold Robyn but could not hit her. He then told Robyn that she needed to let Sarah play by herself and removed her from Sarah's room. This intervention was concise and to the point, and it addressed both children at their own developmental level. Each of them learned something from it.

Parental intervention is best reserved for times when the squabble threatens to escalate into a major conflagration in which uncontrolled screaming or physical fighting may result. By intervening in a measured, succinct manner, the parent models important values in conflict resolution. The children learn that they can control their more negative emotions and look for a solution that is fair and equitable for all the aggrieved parts. At first, the parent needs to take on the role of moderator. Gradually, the children will internalize this role and learn to exercise it themselves.

Marital Discord

Toddlers become anxious when their parents argue in front of them. Does this mean that couples should have their arguments when they are alone? Should parents try to spare their children the distress of seeing them fight?

Sometimes children are the best judges of what is good for them, and I asked a 5-year-old girl about her opinion. As luck would have it, her parents had just gone through a testy day with each other, so the topic was fresh in Lydia's mind. She took the question very seriously, thought for a minute, and then said with total conviction, "It's better when they fight in front of me. Then I don't get so scared because we can talk about it."

Lydia's answer shows her faith in the power of talking about worries. She equates talking with reassurance. Even when tempers get out of hand, she derives relief from being told afterward a child-appropriate version of what the argument was about and, once it is over, that her parents have made up.

Do toddlers, who are quite a bit younger, respond in the same way as Lydia? Though not able to articulate it, they would probably basically agree with her. Toddlers are very perceptive about cold silences, sarcastic tones, and unspoken tensions. They feel that something is wrong, but they don't know what it is. Sometimes toddlers become cranky and overly demanding when their parents are angry with each other but trying not to show it. Toddlers act out the tension they sense but do not understand.

When marital disagreements do not get out of hand, watching parents argue with each other and then make up is quite instructive for toddlers, because they learn about the cycle of anger and reconciliation as the two most important adults in their lives go through the process. This experience puts into perspective their own episodes of getting angry with their parents and then making up.

However, there are some marital fights that are so bitter and protracted that toddlers are not equipped to witness them without having their trust in their parents seriously shaken up. This kind of fight terrifies toddlers.

Not only are they afraid that the parents don't love each other anymore, they also see the parents at their worst: immersed in their rage, oblivious to the child, and unavailable to the child's needs. The image of the parents screaming out of control or worse evokes the child's deepest fears of abandonment and loss of love. Many adults remember their parents' loud, uncontrolled fights as the most frightening events of their childhood.

The child's very existence calls for a commitment by the parents to work out their differences in constructive rather than destructive ways. Divisive fighting, by its very nature, questions this commitment. Conscientious child rearing includes an awareness of how the parents' actions vis-à-vis each other affect the child and an effort to modulate violent emotions for the sake of the child.

When this effort fails, as it sometimes does, parents need to turn their attention to the aftermath of the fight. Acknowledging the fear, offering reassurance, perhaps even saying "We are sorry" and having a family hug, and trying to do better the next time—all these steps can help contain the damage from an episode one wishes to undo but cannot.

When Traumatic Events Happen

Though it is hard to acknowledge, young children are at greater risk than older children of being exposed to traumatic events that threaten their life and physical and emotional integrity. Frightening events that hurt toddlers' bodies and emotions include accidents (falls, burns, car accidents, dog bites, near drownings, ingestion of harmful products); witnessing violence among adults in the family or in the community or violence against other children; verbal, physical, and sexual abuse by family members or others; and losing someone they love through violent death. The prevalence of these situations in the lives of toddlers and their families is so high and their potential to harm children's physical and emotional health is so well established that the American

Academy of Pediatrics advises pediatricians to screen for their occurrence as routinely as they screen for medical conditions (www.canar ratives.org; www.aap.org).

According to the National Child Traumatic Stress Network, traumatic events involve (1) experiencing a serious injury or witnessing someone's serious injury or death; (2) facing imminent threat of serious injury or death to oneself or someone else; or (3) experiencing a violation of personal physical integrity. All these kinds of experiences can create overwhelming feelings of terror, horror, or helplessness. Traumatic events are considered *acute* when they occur once and are short lived, such as natural disasters, assaults, shootings, or someone's sudden and violent death. Traumatic events can also become *chronic*, occurring repeatedly over a long period of time.[20]

In the moment a traumatic event occurs, the person feels overwhelmed by intense sensations: frightening sights, sounds, smells, and movements that cannot be fended off. Traumatic events can happen in a moment but may have consequences that can last for a very long time, affecting every aspect of the traumatized person's functioning, including the sense of personal safety, trust in others, and the capacity to pay attention, concentrate, and learn. These reactions can occur regardless of the person's age, starting at the beginning of life.

Child traumatic stress occurs when children are exposed to a traumatic event that overwhelms their capacity to cope with what they have experienced. Depending on their age, temperament, and the emotional support available to them, children respond to traumatic stress in different ways, but one consistent feature is their effort to protect themselves by showing distress, withdrawal, or other intense emotional reactions to situations or objects that remind them of the traumatic events. These reminders are called "traumatic triggers."[21]

In toddlers, child traumatic stress has specific manifestations that are related to their developmental stage and can be classified into the following clusters of behaviors: reexperiencing; avoidance; dampening of positive emotions; and increased arousal. Different toddlers may show different configurations of these reactions depending on their temperament and other factors that are not yet clearly understood.

- Reexperiencing includes play or behavior that reenacts some aspect of the trauma; repeated nightmares; significant distress or physiological reactions (change in color; rapid breathing) at reminders of the event; being preoccupied with the event to the extent that the child repeatedly asks questions or talks about it; and becoming still or "spacing out" in response to reminders of the traumatic event.
- Avoidance consists of efforts to avoid people, places, activities, or conversations that are reminders of the traumatic event.
- Dampening of positive emotions includes social withdrawal, reduced expression of joy, interest, and exuberance, and increased fearfulness and sadness.
- Increased arousal includes difficulty going to sleep (bedtime protests, not falling asleep, repeated wakings); difficulty paying attention and concentrating; intense alertness to the environment, as if scanning for signs of danger (hypervigilance); exaggerated startles; and increased tantrums, anger, fussiness, and irritability.

One of the most common mistaken pieces of advice that parents receive when their young children experience a traumatic event is some version of "If you don't talk about it, they will forget that it happened." Scientific evidence from many excellent studies shows that this is far from the truth.[22] A traumatic event can turn a child's world upside down. His expectation that his parents and caregivers will keep him safe can no longer be taken for granted, and traumatized children must reorganize their approach to the world accordingly. Babies, toddlers, and preschoolers remember overwhelmingly frightening events because it is in the evolutionary interest of their survival that they remember and respond to danger. They might not remember the details accurately (for example, they might not understand who made what happen), but they do remember the fear and the pain and try to take steps to protect themselves from the event happening again.

Some of the responses described above represent an effort on the part of the child to fend off another traumatic experience by scanning the environment for signals of danger even in their sleep. These responses represent the activation of the parts of the brain that operate outside awareness and respond automatically to signals of danger. These areas of the brain can become chronically activated following a traumatic event, leading to increased arousal and emotional over-reaction to even mild sources of stress. Other responses represent the child's effort to make meaning of the event by playing it out or asking about it repeatedly to understand how and why it happened, to punish the people the child perceives as the culprits, or to give the event a reassuring "happy ending."

Many toddlers recover uneventfully from exposure to a traumatic event, particularly when the adults acknowledge that what happened was frightening, reassure the child, and take steps to provide safety. This happens more readily when the traumatic event was short lived, did not involve harmful actions by the parents or caregivers, and safety was promptly restored. When traumatic events happen repeatedly, when parents or other close caregivers are involved in inflicting the trauma, and when danger persists, children are more likely to experience serious and long-term consequences, manifested by an intensification of the aforementioned symptoms.

Children need their parents and other caring adults to acknowledge and name the traumatic events they experience in order to feel reassured that their fear is legitimate and their safety is important to the adults. Sometimes adults engage in wishful thinking, hoping that the child is too small to notice or remember a traumatic event. Other times, the parents themselves were traumatized by the events that occurred and do not have the emotional ability to be available to the child in processing the trauma. Fortunately, effective treatments are available that have proven results in helping young children and their parents recover and thrive following traumatic events. Child-parent psychotherapy (CPP), for example, makes use of children's play and child-parent spontaneous interactions to give traumatized young children the emotional space to show and tell their experience of the trauma, correct misinterpretations of what happened, help parents respond protectively to the child, and guide children and parents in rebuilding a sense of safety and trust together.[23,24] Children need to learn that remembering the traumatic event does not mean that it will happen again. When the child encounters a trauma reminder and becomes emotionally overwrought, a calm explanation that the child is remembering what happened but is now safe can be very reassuring. Children and parents alike find relief in learning that "speaking the unspeakable" transforms an initially overwhelming event into a manageable if difficult part of the human experience.

Discipline: Is It Really Needed?

This is the question asked most often by parents of toddlers. Often it is prompted by a secret wish to hear that if children are loved, understood, and sensitively cared for, they will not need to be disciplined because they will be naturally loving and responsive to their parents' wishes.

Unfortunately, being human is not that simple. Toddlers are not clones of the parents, and they have their own wishes, needs, and plans. Sometimes these do not clash with the larger interests of the family; many times they do. The toddler needs to learn from the parents' reactions when a particular behavior is not acceptable and cannot be permitted.

At its best, discipline is a form of teaching inner control. The techniques for doing this vary with the toddler's developmental skills. The preverbal or barely verbal toddler can understand language but is helped best if the parent simultaneously takes action to stop or redirect behavior. The older, verbal toddler has more developed inner controls and can be told what to do and what not to do. However, even senior toddlers (as well as much older children) can test limits to the point that direct and decisive action is needed, to teach them when they have gone too far.

The vignettes that follow illustrate the evolution of different forms of discipline to match the child's developmental needs between 14 and 40 months.

Greg, 14 months, is an active toddler intent on exploring everything that exists at his eye level. He eats the dirt from the living room plants; he sticks his fingers into the electric outlets; he opens the cabinet door below the kitchen sink and rummages in the trash bin; he picks up every little piece of lint or other debris from the floor, looks at it in wonder, and puts it into his mouth.

There is nothing morally wrong in what Greg is doing, but his actions are messy, dangerous, and disruptive. His parents have toddler-proofed the house every way they could think of, but Greg always finds something they did not. This period is very tiresome for most parents. Again and again they need to say no and redirect the child to acceptable pursuits.

Sometimes it looks as if a child is learning nothing, but every bit helps. Soon Greg begins to hesitate before approaching the forbidden goal. He then starts to check the parents' faces before proceeding. These behaviors indicate that the memory of the parents' prohibitions and redirection is beginning to compete with his irrepressible impulse to do what he wants.

Although the process will continue for a long time, Greg is beginning to acquire the rudiments of what will eventually become a conscience. He is starting this process by learning to obey external directives of right and wrong to guide his behavior.

Joel, 2 years old, bites his parents and friends when he is angry with them. This has caused friction between his parents and the other parents, who do not relish seeing the marks of his teeth on their children's faces and arms. Some children are now reluctant to play with Joel even when he is not angry. His own parents are sometimes uneasy about coming close to him for fear of his bites.

Joel is a little boy who always enjoyed sucking and gave up his mother's breast and the bottle with great reluctance. His anger at having to relinquish those pleasures is expressed in an urge to bite when his feelings become too difficult to control. The mouth, that old receptacle of pleasure, has become a handy instrument for revenge.

Understanding Joel does not mean condoning what he is doing. His parents tell him firmly that he cannot bite and remove him from the situation when he does. In response, Joel begins to bite himself. His behavior is telling us that he understands his parents' disapproval and is trying to comply, but his impulses are too powerful for his fledgling mechanisms of inner control.

We can help a barely verbal toddler flooded with emotion by providing him with an alternative way to channel his urge to bite or to strike out. His parents provided Joel with a teether and told him he could bite that. It took Joel a while to make the transition, but after a week or so he was biting his teether with gusto. It worked: he stopped biting himself as well as others.

The ongoing evolution of his inner controls became clear a year later, when at 36 months the now-verbal Joel looked at his newborn brother and said, "Mom, it's true I can *want* to bite, but I cannot bite, right?" His wishes to bite are still ready to resurface, but he can now stop himself from doing something he knows to be wrong. He is beginning to have an internalized sense of right and wrong—namely, a conscience.

Sonya, 2½ years old, is at dinner with her parents and four dinner guests. She begins to sing loudly, making it hard for the adult conversation to continue. Her mother humors her, diverts her attention from the guests, and sings along for a couple of minutes. When the mother goes back to talking with the adults, Sonya shrieks, "Sing with me!" Taken aback, the mother returns to singing. The father says, "Don't sing so loudly," but he listens on. Everybody's attention is on Sonya. This continues for the next thirty minutes. Sonya protests loudly whenever the parents try to go back to the adult conversation, and each time the child protests, the mother resumes singing with her. The guests smile tightly, torn between wanting to pursue their adult conversation and unsure whether or not Sonya should be humored, given her young age.

How should we think about this scene? Should adults yield to little children who want attention? Are the dinner guests unreasonable to want to carry on an adult conversation in the presence of a toddler?

Different people may respond differently, but 30-month-olds are capable of learning that everybody gets a turn. If the parents had told Sonya at the first loud interruption that she should lower her voice because she was hurting people's ears, and if they had sung along with her for a couple of minutes but then gone back to their guests, it would have taught her that she was a participant in a social situation but not the only one.

Of course, most parents know that they have to split their attention in many social situations—one ear and eye for responding to the toddler, the other for the social scene. This is one of the most trying aspects of having a toddler. Tiring as it is, this split parental attention is needed to teach toddlers to become emerging participants in social gatherings.

> **Cynthia, 40 months, is having a bad afternoon. She has just learned that her parents are going out that night. Although she will be staying with a teenager she knows and likes, she takes her parents' outing as a personal offense. Instead of using the advance notice to prepare herself for the good-bye, she engages in a full-scale guerrilla attack to convince her mother not to go. Every twenty minutes or so, she sobs, "I don't want you to go." Being gifted with an unusual ability to put feelings into words, she elaborates handsomely on her inner experience: "I will miss you too much"; "Why are you going without me?"; "I will be too sad."**

Cynthia's mother herself feels saddened by her daughter's experience but also manipulated by the child's precocious ability to make her feel guilty by describing in such detail how bad she feels. Caught between these two sets of feelings, the mother alternates among cheerful reassurance that Cynthia will be fine, admonishments that the child should get herself together and stop whining, and threats (not pursued) that she will be sent to her room if she continues with her complaints. Cynthia's behavior continues unabated, and it escalates when the babysitter arrives and the parents get ready to leave. The child clings to her mother, screaming, "Don't leave!"

Cynthia's mother is unwittingly playing into her daughter's difficulty containing her anxiety. The indecisiveness of her efforts to respond to her daughter's complaints is interpreted by the child as an agreement that it is indeed a problem that the parents are going out for the evening.

Cynthia would be helped by a less accepting response. She needs a self-confident assertion on her mother's part that she can manage the separation and that it is okay for the parents to go out. This is a situation when a socializing approach may help the child learn to control herself.

One may ask, won't Cynthia feel guilty if she is told that the mother does not approve of her behavior? If she does, her ability to feel guilty at 40 months will actually speak well for her emotional development. As they grow, children (like adults) need to experience remorse when they do something that is not acceptable to others. Guilt is a useful emotion when it is felt in response to specific damaging behavior. It is unhealthy only when it is pervasive, as in the case of children who constantly worry about doing something wrong and become inhibited in their ability to assert themselves.

Peers and older siblings are sometimes better teachers than parents in this regard. They show in no uncertain terms that they do not like what the child is doing, and the child learns from that response. Parents are often too worried about inducing guilt feelings or making a child feel unloved if they express disapproval or withdraw affection. Parents cannot act as if they feel equally loving regardless of the child's behavior. This cannot be true, and neither the parent nor the child really believes it. The pretense of ongoing benevolence and affection in the face of objectionable behavior is actually quite damaging, because it is not genuine and toddlers can see through it. Real emotion is an important element in helping children understand how their actions affect others and build inner controls.

In summary, toddlers cannot become socially competent and emotionally healthy human beings without their parents' help in modulating, containing, and finding alternative ways to channel their negative emotions. Preverbal toddlers need to direct their impulses to hit and bite into activities that will not hurt others: hammering on a toy bench instead of on a baby, biting a teether instead of a peer. As a child becomes more verbal, the parents' expectations for appropriate behavior can increase. The child can be expected to put feelings into words instead of acting on them, and the parents can express disapproval when the child fails to do so. Even with verbal children, however, energetic action will be needed at times to curtail objectionable behavior. As the case of Cynthia illustrates, a very articulate child can talk about feeling as a form of badgering. When the parent feels verbally battered by the child, it is just as appropriate to stop verbally inappropriate behavior as it is to stop hurtful physical acts.

Far from threatening the parent-child partnership, clear guidelines actually strengthen it. A partnership is based on the ability to encompass a full range of feelings and the knowledge that harmony is not destroyed by a good fight.

Managing Social Change: The Example of Screen Time

Every generation of parents and children finds ways of adjusting to the impact of new social trends and new products in their lives. Screen time and social media are recent arrivals that are generating intense debate about the risks and benefits of access to very young children. Worry about deleterious effects on young children's health, relationships, and cognition is a dominant theme in the recommendations by a large number of sources, in spite of the lack of methodologically sound longitudinal studies to uphold these concerns. These recommendations are also often at odds with how parents use screen time in their own lives. Screens have become so ubiquitous that they are now an integral environmental presence in the home and other settings where young children spend large portions of the day. Toddlers and parents frequently engage in pleasurable exchanges by making things happen on the screen. Screen time has become one more way of spending time together for toddlers and parents, on a par with reading books, playing with building blocks, or assembling puzzles.

There seems to be something hypnotic about screens that mesmerizes even babies. On a recent cross-country flight, an 8-month-old baby spent time first on his mother's lap and then on his grandmother's lap, playing with a range of toys, turning the pages of a book, and paying attention to the pictures as the mom and grandma took turns reading to him. As the hours of flying went monotonously by, and after eating and taking a nap, the baby had had enough of being constrained and started fussing and squirming, pushing away every effort to entertain him. And then . . . his mom reached into her purse, brought out her cell phone, and showed him the screen. The effect was instantaneous:

the baby started patting the screen as he and his mom looked at it together. After a while, he was ready to go back to having a book read to him. Similar scenes, with variations, are playing out in restaurants and public places all over the world with infants, toddlers, and preschoolers.

Sometimes a distinction is made between what children do and learn during "screen time" and what they do and learn in "real time." That might be a distinction without a difference. All time is real time, and what children learn in different venues might or might not generalize to other venues but invariably teaches them something about the world. A screen is as "real" as a toy or a book but has different properties that the child explores and learns to manipulate. Parents who give their toddlers access to screens often explain that they want their children to be prepared for the digital world that surrounds them and that they will need to be competent in as they grow up. This is an important point of view. Parents are routinely advised to introduce books during the first few months of their baby's life as a tool for social interaction, relationship building, and early learning. For many parents, there is a clear parallel between this advice and the early introduction of digital tools.

How screens are used is also a topic for discussion. Is it for entertainment? Learning? To give parents a breather? The answer most parents would give is probably "All of the above, at different times." Screens need not hold a unique place among all the activities available to children. In fact, parental values and common sense are probably the most reasonable guidelines for deciding when, how, and with whom the toddler is given access to screens.

Parents engage actively in learning from each other about how to use digital tools with their children through blogs and other forms of communication. The London School of Economics has issued a report, "Families and Screen Time: Current Advice and Emerging Research," that includes a review of what different organizations currently recommend and findings from interviews with parents about their own ideas and practices. Some key points are itemized here.[25]

- Screen time advice for parents focuses primarily on risk and harm, with only a small proportion of advice addressing the potential of digital media as a medium for learning, creativity, and connection.

- There is a wide variation in how parents use media. Some parents restrict their use, while others use media together with their children and talk with them about them.
- Instead of focusing on amounts of screen *time*, it is more useful to think about screen *context* (where, when, how, and with whom digital media are accessed), *content* (what is being watched or used), and *connections* (whether relationships are facilitated or undermined by the use of media).
- Advice to parents is usually generic and does not take into account the decisions parents must make based on the child's age, interests, and resources available in terms of time, finances, and other considerations.
- There is a role for public policy and industry to help parents in making decisions. This role involves providing training to professionals working with children (e.g., teachers, health professionals) to equip them to offer useful advice to parents; working to ensure that inappropriate content is made less accessible to children; and independent evaluation of products marketed as "educational" to ensure the appropriateness of the label.

The report provides the following five key recommendations for parents:

1. Parents can use their experiences, values, and expertise—both digital and nondigital—as a resource to learn and not be intimidated by new technologies and as a basis for modeling constructive and balanced digital practices and habits for their children.
2. Parents should adjust their strategies to the age, interests, and needs of their children, supporting them through the age range from infancy to adolescence.
3. Parents should understand that restriction of screen time may avoid risks but may also limit opportunities to learn. This awareness will enable them to tailor their decisions accordingly.

4. Parents should feel free to develop their own approaches rather than "keep up" with what other parents do because every family is unique in how it uses digital media.

5. There is no reason to assume that children's digital media use is automatically problematic. Instead of using an arbitrary time limit, parents can consider the context, content and connections involved in screen time using the following guidelines: (1) Is the child physically healthy and sleeping enough? (2) Is the child socially connected with family and friends? (3) Is the child engaged with school/child care? (4) Does the child have a range of interests and activities? (5) Is the child enjoying and learning while using digital media?

The website Zero to Three provides recommendations that are geared specifically to infants and toddlers and consist of balancing access with parental involvement. The recommendations involve parents' participation with their young children in an active "whole-body," "three-dimensional" use of media that includes watching together; talking about what they are viewing; asking the child questions; acting out the scenes being viewed; singing, dancing, and moving along with favorite characters; playing screen games together; and using games and apps to model patience and persistence and learn from mistakes.[26]

Media content addressed to children needs to be reviewed and approved by parents before being shown to the child. Parents are often tempted to download free apps, only to find out that they contain advertisements, in-app purchases that the child can click on, or material that parents find inappropriate for their child. Guides such as Common Sense Media, which review and rate content for all ages, can be helpful in navigating the many choices available. Digital media can be used to foster learning and development when they address issues that are relevant to the child and the family, such as songs or apps that feature going to child care or saying good-bye.

How parents themselves use media is an important factor in the decisions they make about their young children's use of media. Many new parents rely on cell phones, tablets, and apps for advice and support from other parents, for work, and for their social life. The centrality of digital media in their own lives has repercussions for their child rearing because nothing is as compellingly attractive to young children as doing what their parents do. Imitation is the highest form of admiration, and if they see their parents immersed in their screens, they will feel the urgent need to do the same because they want to be just like their parents. As parents reflect on how they want to socialize their toddler's screen use, they need to take into account how their own screen use is influencing the context of their decisions.

It is worth noting the parallels in the historical evolution of research about children's use of digital media when compared to three other social processes that introduced major changes in family life: the increase in the number of working mothers, full-time child care for young children, and parental divorce. It seems that social change is assumed to be risky as a first research response: in each of these three examples, the first wave of research used a deficit model. The hypotheses tested during the first years of research in these topics posited that, as a group, children of working mothers would fare less well than children of stay-at-home mothers; that young children in day care would show more problem behaviors than home-reared children; and that children of divorced parents would do less well as a group than children of parents who stayed married. The research findings failed to confirm those expectations. Instead of deficits, the findings showed enormous variability of child responses. When the anticipated negative effects failed to materialize, researchers adopted a more sophisticated research methodology that takes into account the many factors that influence how children respond, such as individual differences in children, parents, and family circumstances, to predict different aspects of the child's development. The current consensus is that there is no simple cause-effect link between single factors such as working mothers, day care attendance, and divorce and child functioning. Across these conditions, it is factors such as the quality of the parent-child relationship, parental social and psychological well-being, and family emotional climate that tend to be most associated with child functioning. Families adapt differently to new circumstances, and the child's well-being is best predicted by the quality of this adaptation and the extent to which the child's developmental needs and individual characteristics are taken into account in the decisions that parents make for themselves and their family. Screen time is no exception but rather the latest example of parents leading the way in teaching researchers and child professionals that they can make savvy decisions that balance their own needs and practices with what is good for their children.

9

When Parents Divorce

Toddlers are deeply affected by family strife and by their parents' divorce. I remember a little 18-month-old who stood between his parents as they fought, yelling at them to stop. After the parents separated, he called out tearfully for whichever parent was not with him at the time. When his father took him back to his mother's house, the child clung to him and refused to let him go. After the father managed to leave, the little boy hit his mother, threw himself onto the floor, crying loudly, and angrily fought off her attempts to console him. This went on for many weeks. His anguish subsided only after much reassurance by both of his parents that they continued to love him and would always come back to him.

Not all toddlers are equally overt in showing their distress. Individual temperament, as well as the parents' comfort in allowing expression of negative emotions, has a strong influence on each child's particular way of showing pain, anger, and fear. Sometimes adults needs to glean the toddler's innermost feelings from the subtlest of cues.

Regardless of how readily they express their distress, it is safe to assume that to some degree all toddlers worry about what will happen to them when their parents separate. The family constellation that represented the world as they knew it is now broken, and they miss the absent parent and the predictability of the daily routines. They are afraid that they, too, are on the verge of being left. They are angry, for different reasons, at both the parent who stays and the one who leaves.

The child's distress need not be a source of crippling guilt for divorcing parents, although some degree of remorse and regret is probably inevitable. In the long run, children may well be better off when they're spared the daily experience of witnessing anger, tension, or aloofness between the parents. Follow-up studies suggest that most children of divorced parents develop in healthy ways when the parents are attuned to the child's responses and remain emotionally available in spite of their own distress. Mavis Hetherington, a leading researcher on divorce who conducted three longitudinal studies involving 2,500 children in 1,400 families—some of them studied for as long as thirty-two years—summarized her decades of experience by emphasizing the enormous variability in children's responses to their parents' divorce. She wrote:

> When I began studying divorce, like most investigators I had a pathogenic model of divorce. I was focused on the deleterious consequences of divorce for families and especially for children. Now, after 35 years of studying divorced families, what impresses me is not the inevitability of adverse outcomes, but the diversity of adjustment in parents and children in response to marital dissolution. Divorce presents family members with stressful life changes and challenges. It may also present them with an escape from an unhappy, conflictual, or abusive family situation, a chance to build new, more fulfilling relationships, and an opportunity for personal growth and individuation.[1]

This chapter focuses on the sources of this variability of children's responses in order to offer tools to help toddlers and parents cope with the difficulties of parental divorce. Some of the toddlers' reactions to divorce occur because young children tend to put themselves squarely at the center of whatever happens around them. A happy, well-adjusted little girl, watching a lion roar in the zoo, reflected, "He's roaring because he wants to eat me for breakfast." She could not imagine that the lion had its own private reasons to roar. In her mind, such an impressive display had to involve her in some way. The Swiss clinical psychologist Jean Piaget referred to this feature of early thinking as "egocentrism,"[2] not because young children are selfish but because they understand an event subjectively, through their own reactions to it. Their understanding of the relationship between cause and effect is centered on their own capacity to make things happen. As a result, they react to an event in terms of how it affects them. In other words, they reason by applying to themselves the real or imagined consequences of an event. On the basis of this rudimentary form of logic, a toddler's unspoken (and unspeakable) train of associations in a case of divorce goes approximately like this:

- "If Daddy left, then people can go away, and if so, maybe Mommy will leave me, too."
- "If Mommy stopped loving Daddy, maybe she will stop loving me, too."
- "If Mommy and Daddy got angry and don't want to live together anymore, maybe they won't want to live with me either when they get angry at me."

These inferences are, of course, inaccurate, but they are emotionally compelling nevertheless. A toddler whose parents are divorcing is discovering, much too prematurely, the bitter truth that human relations can be brittle and that bonds of affection and commitment do not always hold.

Once the toddler's basic trust that Mom and Dad or both same-sex parents will always be there is shaken, other anxieties follow. The toddler's emerging ability to fantasize enables her to imagine scenarios that may frighten her even more than the reality she is experiencing. A child who was frightened by her parents' fighting fantasized that wild animals would attack her; another child, caught in the middle of a custody battle, developed fears of being kidnapped by a stranger. Divorcing parents face two key challenges in the midst of their personal upheaval. The first is placing what is good for the child above their individual preferences without confusing one with the other. The second is collaborating in showing the child, through actions and words, that they will continue to love and take care of her because parents may leave each other but in their hearts they never leave their child. At all ages, children of divorcing parents must feel free to continue loving both parents. Toddlers, whose trusting attachments are easily derailed by fear of loss and disapproval, need explicit, sincere assurances of each parent's acceptance of their love for the other parent.

The best place to start is an explanation, given calmly but with feeling, that the parents will no longer live together, followed by a simple description of where and with whom the child will live. Some toddlers ask many questions when given this basic information. Others are too little or too frightened to ask. The parents' receptiveness to spoken and unspoken questions (both immediately and as the questions change in the course of development) will convey to the child that this is not a taboo topic and that he has permission to try to understand it as well as he can.

Divorce as Secure Base Disruption

Divorce can be viewed as the toddler's loss of the secure base represented by the family constellation. This is because toddlers do not only use their individual parents as a source of security; they are also acquiring a sense of the family as a unit of care and establishing equally intense but qualitatively different relationships with each family member.

This means that in the normal course of events toddlers are learning to relate to more than one person simultaneously, to share attention, and to relinquish exclusiveness in family interactions. They are not only active participants in the family dynamics but also watch intently from the sidelines as family members interact with one another. In doing so they learn much about their parents and siblings and begin to make generalizations about human relations. When the complex relationships and interactions among family members are sharply modified and often curtailed following marital separation, both the toddler and the parents face the task of re-creating a secure base adapted to the changed family conditions.

Like all change, this loss and rebuilding of a secure base seldom proceeds uneventfully. Grief and anger are inseparable components of family dissolution, just as they are inseparable components of any other form of loss. The toddler cannot be spared the experience of witnessing strong emotions in her parents or feeling them herself. She can, however, be helped to go through this difficult situation with relatively little emotional damage if her parents remain emotionally available in spite of their own pain.

Bodily movements often carry strong psychological meanings. With young children in particular, motion conveys emotion more powerfully than words. In the second year of life, motion is centered on the achievement of balance, and the risk of losing this balance becomes a central concern. Physical balance stands as a symbol for emotional balance both in child play and in adult imagery. Just as they spend endless hours trying to master the fear of falling, toddlers often set up situations in which balance is precarious as a way of expressing uncertainty and mastering the anxiety that goes with it. Two children referred for help during their parents' divorce used this avenue of expression quite graphically.

Barbara is with her mother in the therapist's office, playing with some toys. The conversation turns to the parents' conflicting wishes about Barbara's custody. Barbara stops playing and asks her mother to lift her up and place her on the fireplace mantelpiece. Her mother complies and then stands nearby. The child spends the rest of the session on the mantelpiece, clearly afraid of falling but refusing to get down.

Terry's father wants to build a better relationship with his son and hopes that the therapist will help him achieve this goal. However, he is so angry at his wife for leaving him that he cannot stop himself from cursing her even in his son's presence. After listening for a few minutes, Terry walks silently toward the play staircase, climbs up, and perches himself precariously at the top. He seems both afraid of falling and determined to stay where he is. When he finally gets down, he systematically turns all the contents of the dollhouse (dollhouse included) upside down and throws the mother doll, father doll, and baby doll across the room.

These two children are showing that they feel off-balance, barely able to hold on. They are wordlessly asking the parent to stay very close and to help them feel secure.

Sometimes children feel overburdened by the need to keep themselves in balance and long for happier, simpler times. At the end of an intensely emotional therapy session with his father, Terry buries his head in his lap and says, "I am just a baby."

What Do Toddlers Understand?

Divorcing parents often hope that their little ones are unaware of what is happening around them, that they do not notice the strife and dissension and unexplained absences from the dinner table or the parental bedroom. But toddlers do notice, and they form their notions of what is happening long before they are able to speak. The following excerpt from a home-based therapeutic session provides a clear illustration of a mother's wishes to protect her daughter from knowing about her father's departure and the child's very clear feelings on the matter.

[T]his led into a discussion of Moira's nightmares and [the therapist] asked if Moira had been sleeping better. The mother answered that Moira was still waking up and often cried in her sleep. She then started talking about her husband. The therapist asked what Moira had been told about the separation. The mother answered that she had never spoken to Moira about it because the child had been only 18 months at the time and too young to understand it. Moira, now 26 months, was sitting next to her mother during this conversation. The therapist turned to her and said, "Mommy and I are talking about your daddy, Moira." At that Moira looked directly at the therapist, then at her mother, jumped out of her chair, and began to race wildly from the living room to the adjoining kitchen, hall, and back again. The therapist asked the mother how she understood Moira's behavior; the mother replied that she had never seen Moira so agitated. The therapist asked whether perhaps Moira was scared and needed to feel safe. At that point Moira was running into the bathroom and fell down. The mother picked her up and cuddled her, and after a while she asked, "Were you scared because we were talking about your daddy?" Moira looked straight at her mother and said, "Yes." The mother continued, "Does it hurt you because Daddy is gone?" Moira looked down but again said, "Yes." The mother asked yet again, "Does it make you mad because Daddy went away?" Moira again looked directly at her mother and said, "Yes." She then got up and ran into the bathroom. The mother turned to the therapist and commented, "I didn't think she could ever feel that way. Is it possible for someone 18 months old to understand that? He was hardly around, and he paid so little attention to her." She was continuing to talk about her husband when Moira returned and started crawling all over her mother. The mother asked, "Do you want me to stop talking about your daddy?" Moira nodded her head in a silent yes. Her mother said, "Moira, listen to me. I want you to know that I love you and I will never leave you. Do you understand?" Moira shook her head and buried it deep into her mother's shoulder. They rocked each other silently for a while.

This sequence shows clearly that even very young toddlers notice that a parent has left the home, and may grieve without ever saying a word about their loss. Many children harbor secret worries from a very early age, just as Moira did. When not recognized and alleviated by an understanding adult, these worries reappear in disguised form as nightmares, fears of separation, inexplicable terrors, frequent and intense tantrums, negativism, renewed bed-wetting, or a myriad of other symptoms that can be best understood as the child's cry for help. The symptoms are in effect saying "Pay attention, Mom and Dad. All is not well with me."

Symptoms may change their appearance. A fearful child may become overly aggressive, and nightmares may disappear but be replaced by biting. Symptoms may shift, but they do not go away until the underlying problem is relieved. As Reginald Lourie, a pediatrician and child psychoanalyst, once put it, "Babies are very patient. They keep on showing us the problem over and over until we understand. The more we understand what children need, the better we will do in helping them."

It is worth noting that Moira's nightmares did recede when her mother started talking with her about her father, empathizing with her anger and sadness about losing him and reassuring her that Mommy would not go away. At first she felt awkward speaking about these difficult topics, but she became progressively more self-confident as her child's positive response helped her realize that the issues needed to be addressed. This mother also found, paradoxically, that talking about how hard it was that the father wasn't there actually made his absence more bearable, both for her child and for herself.

Longing for the Way Things Were

Infants and toddlers have well-developed memories. They remember people, events, and experiences even when they cannot describe them in words. In fact, the earliest memories are based on perceptual rather than linguistic events. Newborns are able to recognize the smell of their mother's milk and the sound of her voice.[3,4] By 5 to 7 months, infants can store visual memories and retrieve them on cue. For example, babies who watched the photograph of a stranger's face for less than one minute were able to recognize that same face more than a week later.[5] Moreover, at this age babies are already able to recall the specific emotional experience associated with an event. In one study, babies smiled at the mere sight of a silent puppet that had actively "played" with them and made them laugh a week earlier.[6]

If infants can do all this in the first six months of life, what can we expect of toddlers? There is much observational evidence that they remember emotionally tinged events many months after their occurrence. At 18 months, Rafi pantomimed the exact sequence of his last

medical checkup six months earlier as soon as his mother told him
that they were going to the doctor. He did not speak fluently, but he
lay down on his mother's lap, pulled at his ear, opened his mouth with
gasping sounds, motioned with his hands as if someone were looking
into his throat, and said, "No, no." It was clear that he remembered
what had happened and did not wish to repeat it.

"Out of sight" does not mean "out of mind" for toddlers; they remember clearly and keenly. This continuity of experience exists also
when their parents separate. Children hold in their memories the family routines that took place when the family still lived together, and
they may feel an acute sense of longing for the way things were.

Sammy refuses to get out of the car when he and his mother arrive at a favorite restaurant. He puts up a fight when she tries to
coax him out. It dawns on her that this was a cherished family
outing when the parents lived together. She asks, "Does it make
you miss Daddy when we come here?" Sammy sobs, "Yes."

Tanya clings to a stuffed animal her father gave her and hugs it
tightly when she goes to bed.

Sylvia refuses to listen to her mother's lullaby. She says, "That's
Daddy's song!" Her absent father sung her the lullaby when he
put her to bed.

Cameron puts up a fuss when a dinner guest sits at the table in
"Daddy's place." He also wants to keep everybody from sitting in
"Daddy's chair" in the living room.

Gabriel puts the mommy doll and daddy doll in bed together. He
says, "All right now."

Marina and her mother go to a summer resort where she had
watched her father hunting ducks the year before. Marina says,
"Daddy, duck, bang, bang."

These quick glimpses into children's inner lives, their memories, and their longings are often missed or, more sadly, *dis*missed by people who believe that toddlers cannot remember or feel as intensely and genuinely as adults. Yet it is these glimpses that capture most eloquently the child's experience. Toddlers do not make speeches about their inner lives (or about anything else). They rely on symbols, games, facial expressions, sudden silences, body language, and half sentences to convey what they remember and how they feel about it. They also rely on adults to decode those messages and respond to them.

This need to be "felt with" means that it is helpful to talk reassuringly to the child about past experiences. This applies to cherished routines that are no longer viable in the new family composition as well as to the less palatable scenes that tend to precede a divorce, such as arguments, tears, even physical fights.

Toddlers feel emotionally torn by the parents' separation. On the one hand, they may experience relief that the household is calmer and the difficult confrontations have come to an end. On the other, they miss the moments of togetherness that did exist, and most of all they miss the parent who left but feel guilty that this longing betrays in some obscure way the parent who has stayed. They worry that loving one parent will make the other parent angry at them.

It is confusing to have all these contradictory feelings at the same time, yet this is the very stuff of emotional life. Talking with the child, *while the child is having these feelings*, about missing the absent parent, being angry, or being scared enables her to cope with them without feeling overwhelmed by them. Reminiscing about the good times ("Remember when Daddy played horsey with you in the park? We laughed and laughed!") and explaining the bad times ("Daddy and I yelled at each other. Sometimes I can't stop yelling when I'm angry, but I don't like it. I still love you, and I will not go away even when I am mad") helps integrate the past with the present instead of banishing it to the underground caves of the child's imagination, where the unspeakable memories fester while becoming increasingly out of reach but continuing to exert a malignant influence on the child's inner life.

Though helpful to the child, broaching these topics can be taxing for the parents. They have to make themselves put aside feelings of anger and resentment toward their spouse in order to protect their child's relationship with the other parent. This is difficult—even excruciating. It calls for a conscious effort to distinguish between one's ex-spouse and the child's other parent, although both roles are played by the same person. It also calls for an effort to keep in mind the positive attributes of the other parent and to remember that those attributes can help the child even if the marriage is doomed.

In the following sections we will examine some of the factors that interfere with parents' ability to protect their child from the anger and bitterness they may feel toward each other. The language used addresses the experiences observed for children of divorcing heterosexual couples, who have been studied more extensively and for longer periods of time. Emerging evidence indicates that children of divorcing or separating same-sex couples have comparable emotional experiences in adjusting to the family dislocation that follows parental separation.

The Divorced Mother's Situation

Although every woman's situation is different and uniquely personal, most women's experiences are influenced in some way by the demographics of divorce. The figures are sobering:

- Divorce has a negative effect on women's finances. More women than men live in poverty and receive public assistance within a year after the divorce, according to the US Census Bureau.[7] Data from Australia and Great Britain also show that women's income declines in comparison to men's income after divorce.
- About 75 percent of children whose parents divorced in 2009 live with their mothers.[8]
- Divorced fathers often lose contact with their children, a situation that places sole responsibility for raising the children on the mother. In a survey of 1,423 children from divorced families

funded by the National Institute of Mental Health, 52 percent
had not heard from their fathers in the past year and 35 percent
of them had had no contact with their fathers for five years.[9]

These interlocking sets of facts can have a profound influence on the
everyday life and emotional experience of divorced mothers regardless
of their children's age. Financial worries, major changes in lifestyle as
the result of reduced economic resources, and primary responsibility
for the children put serious stresses on the lives of divorced mothers.

Women with babies and toddlers may have an even more difficult time because child-rearing habits and routines are not yet fully
established, because child care is scarce and expensive, and because
very young children place high demands on their mothers' energy
and emotional resources. In spite of these difficulties, the majority of
women successfully meet the challenges of being single mothers to
their young children.

The Divorced Father's Situation

Fathers' feelings about their divorce tend to center around two major
issues: the financial burden of support payments and the psychological
burden of limited access to their child or children. These issues are often
intertwined in conflict situations. Many fathers believe that the mother
withholds visitation to enforce support payments and that the children
are used as ransom to achieve financial aims. A common complaint is
that fathers have to work longer hours or even take an additional job
to meet their court-ordered obligations for child and spousal support.
Some men argue that the increased financial burden leaves them with
less time and energy to remain active in their children's lives.

The census data do not support these perceptions of the impact
of divorce on men as a group. However, a subset of divorced fathers
is certainly faced with these predicaments. They may find themselves
having to support two households on a single income. Their access to
the children may be restricted or closely regulated by the mother, either

as a form of pressure or because of disagreements about child-rearing styles. The father may be rebuked or criticized by the mother in front of the child for failing to fulfill financial or parental responsibilities.

Regardless of the legitimacy of the mutual complaints, the bitterness between the parents can set up volatile situations in which conflict escalates, often without warning. This is not difficult to understand. Divorce touches parents at their very core, making them feel alone, vulnerable, and unprotected. These are the very conditions that trigger tantrums in toddlers, and the same conditions lead to angry battles between adults.

Divorce can bring out the worst in us, and it usually does. Feelings of resentment, victimization, and rage often gain the upper hand, leading to a desire for revenge and efforts at settling old scores. These impulses can easily override the parents' best efforts at retaining self-control. Sometimes the only hope for containing punitive action is remembering that the children are the first to suffer from parental strife, both within the marriage and after the divorce.

"Divide the Living Child"

> And the king said, Divide the living child in two,
> and give half to one and half to the other.
> —Kings, 3:24

Could King Solomon foresee that his predicament in deciding the fate of a contested child would one day become a commonplace event as parents sue each other for the right to their child? We will never know, but it is sobering to consider how often we face this biblical dilemma in modern garb.

In fact, we may think that the great king's quandary was trivial when compared to present-day legal conflicts. Solomon could count on the rapacious self-interest of the false mother, who was blinded by her own desire to the point that she acquiesced to a verdict that would destroy the child. Today's custody battles are often less clear cut because both parties sincerely believe that they are trying to protect the best interests of the child.

Perhaps the most useful way of applying the wisdom of Solomon to current circumstances is to think of the biblical drama in psychological terms. Every parent fighting for his or her child's custody personifies the three characters of the story at one and the same time. Every parent carries within the potential to become the false mother, who cannot distinguish between the child's welfare and her own needs, and who would rather see the child destroyed than renounce her claim. Similarly, every parent can embody the loving true mother, whose wish to protect her child overrides her own self-interest.

Every parent also has available within him- or herself the wisdom of Solomon, who represents the point of balance between two extremes: the readiness, on the one hand, to sacrifice the child to one's own needs and the willingness, on the other, to renounce a legitimate personal claim for the child's sake. By transforming a clash of personal wills into a test of the mothers' deepest motivations, Solomon found a solution that was based not on the right to possess but on the willingness to protect and love.

Children do best when they have access to two parents who can put aside their personal grievances to work together on behalf of their child. This need not mean becoming friends or remaining lovers. It does not mean brushing aside legitimate demands. It does entail recognizing that each parent has a unique part to play in the child's life, that neither parent can fill the role of the other in the child's development, and that neither parent can replace the other in the child's affection.

The child's relationship with each parent needs to be kept separate from the relationship of the former spouses to each other. A toddler should not become one parent's ally against the other and should not have witness the parents' mutual complaints and recriminations.

In spite of this, putting each other down in front of the child is the most common mistake made by divorcing parents. They often find fault with every detail of the former spouse's parenting and berate each other for feeding the child junk food, not keeping her clean, overstimulating her, not having a predictable schedule, being overly permissive or harshly restrictive. They also complain that the other parent does not provide a thorough account of what transpired while the child was in his or her care: what they did, whom they saw, where they went.

Those problems often lead to active efforts to curtail or restrict visitation. In most cases, this is a serious mistake. In the long run, eating one or even four cookies too many or missing a nap is far less important for a toddler's welfare than being allowed to establish comfortable relationships with both parents.

Parents who criticize each other are seldom arguing specifically about the child's diet or daily routine; they are actually struggling for sole control over the child's life. Each is unconsciously setting him- or herself up as the ideal parent, the one the child should love the best.

In accepting the importance of their child's separate relationship with their former spouse, parents must come to grips with the sad realization that they will have no access to a major part of the toddler's life. They will not be able to watch as the child forms a relationship with the other parent and with a new and different circle of that parent's friends. They will not share the child's developmental milestones and daily joys and tribulations with a partner who is just as passionately committed to the child. There will be large areas of the child's experience that they will neither understand nor oversee.

These are some of the enduringly painful consequences of divorce. In an effort to avoid them, many parents try to make themselves the one and only center of their child's life and to push the other parent into a peripheral role. When they do so, they unwittingly impoverish their child's emotional development and deprive themselves of a valuable source of support: the other parent's emotional investment in the child.

Toddlers are immeasurably relieved when they can watch their parents join forces on their behalf. A mother who greets her returning child by saying "My goodness, your boots are all muddy! You and your daddy must have had quite an adventure!" is contributing to her child's peace of mind much more profoundly than a mother who greets him with an angry comment about his father's thoughtlessness in leaving her with the job of cleaning up the boots (right as she is to be annoyed).

A father who can say sympathetically to his daughter, "Mommy takes a long time saying good-bye because she loves you so much" is protecting his child's mental health much more thoroughly than another who responds to the identical situation by snarling at the mother, "Stop clinging to her."

Even when one parent infuriates the other, it is possible to frame the situation in a way that supports the child's self-esteem. One mother, seriously inconvenienced by the father's tardiness in picking up the child for the weekend, responded to the toddler's clear worry and discomfort by saying, "Don't worry, honey. Sometimes your daddy has to work late. I am sure he is trying to get here soon because he wants to see you." (Later she discussed the situation with the father when the child could not hear.) Another mother responded to a similar situation in a less constructive way. She blurted out, "He only cares about himself. He doesn't care that you and I are waiting!"

The first mother kept herself focused on her child's need to be reassured about the father's continuing (if imperfect) love. The second mother could not contain her anger at feeling abandoned and exploited by her child's father. She was unable to allow her daughter to develop a different and more positive relationship, and coached her to feel as exploited and unloved by him as she did.

Toddlers need their parents' assistance to restore some confidence that in spite of the divorce, each parent can continue serving as a secure base in the absence of the other. If the parents support each other, the child will be able to integrate their separate contributions into a cohesive sense of himself as cherished and protected by the two people most important to him.

If, on the contrary, the parents undermine each other, the child will internalize each parent's mistrust of the other and will become anxious about her own well-being while in their care. She will also worry about betraying one parent when she is having a good time with the other.

These anxieties are much too burdensome for a young child. Each parent needs to reassure him—and mean it—that it is okay to love and enjoy being with the other and that both his mother and his father love him and will help each other to take care of him.

Mismatches in Children's and Parents' Perceptions and Wishes

Partnership in the parent-child relationship in the toddler years is predicated on the effort to understand each other's perspective. The experience of divorce represents a disruption of those efforts because the intense emotions of the different family members can interfere with the clarity of mind they need to entertain the perspective of the others.

A study of preschoolers whose parents had divorced when they were toddlers provides insights into the different experiences of preschoolers and their custodial mothers two years following the parents' divorce.[10] Mothers were asked to describe their personal experiences and their social network, including their relationship with the child's father as coparent and ex-spouse. Children were asked to tell stories involving mother, father, and child dolls. The researchers presented the mother and father dolls as living in different houses but made no explicit mention of the divorce when they asked the children to tell the stories.

The findings show the extent to which children and their mothers tended to have different perceptions and attitudes of the child's father. Mothers tended to speak about the father much more often as a source of stress than as a member of their social support network. More than three-quarters of the mothers perceived the father as insufficiently available or insufficiently attentive to the child. They often described the father using terms such as "unreliable," "selfish," and "insensitive." They also worried about the children's safety and exposure to inappropriate experiences in the father's house, including witnessing alcohol or drug use or sexual behavior and failure to attend to the child's health needs. Approximately half the mothers disapproved of the father's parenting practices and were upset when the children relayed derogatory remarks he had made about the mother. Many mothers also spoke about how difficult it was for them to speak positively to their child about the father.

The children's stories as they played with the dolls represented a different perspective on their fathers when compared with their mothers' descriptions. Both girls and boys tended to play out themes of support- ive parent-child relationships, and positive themes were much more prevalent than themes of hostility, aggression, or violence. Children tended to incorporate the father doll into their stories as a caregiver, authority figure, or companion. The children often enacted scenes of family reunification. They placed the mother, father, and child dolls very close together; showed positive interactions among the three characters; pushed the two houses together or on top of each other or said that there was no need for two houses and asked for one of the houses to be removed; showed affection between the two parent dolls; and had the two parent dolls sleeping, dancing, going on a trip, or doing other activities together. Although themes of conflict, loss, and conflicting loyalties were present, the themes showing both parents as effective caregivers were much more predominant.

Unfortunately, fathers were not included in this study, and as a re- sult there is no information about how they saw themselves and how they perceived their child's mother as ex-spouse and coparent. In spite of this limitation, the study offers a window into young children's long- ing for family harmony and their tendency to have positive percep- tions of both parents in spite of the divorce. The following sections expand on these themes by looking more closely at different aspects of the child's experience.

Missing the Father

Most children of divorced families live with their mother and have varying degrees of contact with their father.[11] Because of this, missing the father and waiting for him to call or visit are often major compo- nents of their divorce experience.

Though ideally children of all ages would profit from regular and frequent access to their fathers, toddlers are in special need of a reli- able visitation pattern because of their unique cognitive and emotional needs.

The toddler's attachment relationships are still being formed, and the emotional quality of these relationships is highly influenced by external circumstances such as changes in the parents' physical and emotional availability. An attachment that had been secure may become tinged with anxiety if the parent withdraws from the child. Conversely, an anxious attachment can improve significantly if the parent becomes more emotionally attuned.[12,13]

A few days of no contact with the parent can be far more unsettling for a toddler than for an older child, who has a better internalized image of the parent, more sophisticated coping mechanisms (including language, symbolic play, and capacity to delay gratification), and a broader network of relationships and activities to help in withstanding the separation. Toddlers respond strongly to broken promises and failed visitations. The day before Terry and his father went to a scheduled therapist's session, the father had failed to show up for a visit with the boy. At the session, Terry expressed his feelings about his disappointment. This is what the therapist reported:

> Terry and his father arrived a few minutes late. It was immediately clear that there was a great deal of tension between them. Terry was not looking at his father, and Mr. F. in turn seemed angry with his son. Mr. F. started the session by complaining that Terry had put up a fuss when he picked him up to come to the session. [The therapist] asked what might make Terry put up such a fuss. After much digression, it emerged that Mr. F. had missed his regular visit with Terry the previous day. While Mr. F. talked to [the therapist], but not to his son, about the reasons for this, Terry went about overturning every chair in the room and then began to lightly kick every one of them. As his father continued to talk without paying attention to him, Terry muttered very quietly, as if to himself, "Motherfucker!"

Most toddlers do not have Terry's opportunity to express how they feel in the safety of a therapeutic session, where their behavior can be observed and understood and where they can be helped to experience and cope with their feelings. Even in these favorable circumstances, it was ultimately Terry's father who could best help his son, by becoming more aware of his importance to the child and by arranging his schedule so that visits were given the priority they deserved.

Toddlers who miss their father and have no consistent access to him may develop a longing for him that manifests itself in sleep disturbances and other symptoms. The child psychiatrist James Herzog reported that in a six-month period he saw twelve little boys, ranging in age from 18 to 28 months, who were brought to the clinic because of night terrors. The children would wake up at night screaming and calling for their fathers. In each of the cases, the parents had separated or divorced in the previous four months. Herzog found that the mother alone was unable to help the child, but the assistance of the father or another male figure did bring about a decrease in the child's fears. He concluded that the toddlers were responding to a developmental need for a father figure with whom they could identify and who could serve as a model as they moved from the mother-oriented world of infancy to finding a gender-specific identity as boys.[14]

Girls, too, are in need of a father as they learn about their femininity and practice how to relate to the opposite sex. Their longing for their father may be expressed in less dramatic ways than the boys studied by Herzog. It may also be more easily overlooked, because girls as a group are more likely than boys to internalize negative feelings and to make often superhuman efforts to be "good" (which they identify with being undemanding). They may manage their longing for their father by developing an idealized fantasy of an imaginary father who is perfect and unfailingly loving. They may also insist that another male figure in their life is their real father.

Antonia, a bright 30-month-old, had not seen her father or heard from him for two months. She knew that he lived far away and often kissed his picture, which she had placed carefully by her bed. At the same time, she developed an ongoing dialogue with an imaginary father who lived in the garden just outside her room and who knew all her secrets. She also insisted that either her loving maternal grandfather or her uncle was her real father. She was able to maintain all these contradictory beliefs at the same time. It seemed as if her efforts to find another daddy helped her to compensate for the loss of her father, because when her mother spoke to her about "your daddy," the child knew exactly who was being talked about. When the father finally called Antonia, she refused to speak to him on the phone but later asked to send him a Valentine's Day card. She needed to gain some control over his comings and goings. Taking the initiative in refusing or accepting contact enabled her to do so.

Antonia's grief over her father's elusive role in her life was apparent in other areas as well. She cried inconsolably over minor incidents at nursery school and became overly anxious when she could not immediately find an object that she was looking for. The anger inherent in her grief was expressed in stubborn defiance of her mother and in her gleefulness when she killed the ants that abounded in her garden. Like the little boys described by Herzog, Antonia woke up crying at night, complaining of monsters that threatened to attack her.

Blaming the Mother

Antonia's defiance of her mother illustrates a common phenomenon among toddlers: they automatically blame their mothers for whatever goes wrong in their experience.

This unpalatable tendency is a logical by-product of the mother's centrality in the young child's emotional life. She is all-powerful in the baby's and toddler's eyes simply by virtue of her ability to evoke good and bad feelings. She can make a hurt go away with a kiss, and she can make her child's world crumble with a glare. Her absence brings sadness and worry, and her presence restores buoyancy and joy. This is understandable. For as long as the toddler can remember, Mommy has been the one who most often feeds and diapers, holds and cuddles, praises and admonishes, ministers and punishes. She is inextricably bounded with the child's sense of who he is. Who else could possibly be responsible for all that happens in his world? Some telling examples:

Mark's aunt, an old-fashioned type, is shocked when she finds him naked on the beach, covering his penis with sand and triumphantly retrieving it again. Like a classical witch from the annals of psychoanalysis, the aunt hisses, "Your penis will fall off if you keep playing with it." Mark's mother shrieks, "That is not true, Mark. Aunt Helen is just being silly." But it is too late. For the next few hours Mark repeatedly pulls at his penis, as if testing his aunt's prophecy. His mother tells him, "Mark, I think you are still worried about what Aunt Helen told you." "What did she tell me?" asks Mark. "That your penis will fall off," stammers the mother. With utter conviction, Mark replies, "It wasn't Aunt Helen. You told me that." His chagrined mother cannot make him change his mind. For Mark, only his mother could be the origin of such dramatic news, and he changed the facts to fit that perception.

Lisa is severely injured by her father when he suffers a psychotic episode. When she recovers consciousness and sees her mother next to her, she screams, "Why did you hurt me like that?"

Mina is clumsy in her efforts to climb a wooden structure and falls on the ground. When her mother rushes to rescue her, Mina hits her, yelling "Bad Mommy!"

Mothers are also often seen as the culprits when it comes to divorce. Not only are they all-powerful, they are also most often the ones who stay and are therefore ready targets for the child's anger and grief. When that happens, they need to be careful. Their own distress over the divorce can trick them into accepting the child's blame. They need to find within themselves the calm conviction to say, "I know you are angry at me, but it is not my fault."

Protecting the Mother

Sometimes the reverse happens: the toddler is keenly aware of the mother's pain and depression and feels compelled to protect her. A child may dry her mother's tears or may try to cajole her out of her sadness by being artificially jolly or extraordinarily good. When a child responds like this, a role reversal takes place. It is the child who attempts to protect and nurture the parent, and the parent may take on the role of a needy, vulnerable child. When this role reversal colors the whole relationship, toddlers become precociously competent and overly mature at the expense of their own age-appropriate emotional spontaneity in asking for help or expressing their needs. The most common expression of precocious competence is a toddler's worry about the mother's welfare or excessive solicitousness. A toddler may tell the mother not to worry or ask her if she is all right.

When these behaviors occur repeatedly, it is worthwhile to reflect on their meaning and to assure a child that the mother can and will take care of herself and that the child is too little to take care of her. This can be done in simple ways: telling a child what one did while he was gone ("When you were with your daddy, I went for a nice walk and saw a very cute puppy."), commenting on pleasant plans or even telling a child not to worry ("I am big and strong, and it's my job to be the mommy. It is not your job to take care of me.").

When a Parent Is Unfit to Care for the Child

There are, of course, situations in which the child is at substantial risk of physical or psychological harm while in a parent's care. These situations are invariably complex and call for thoughtful evaluation of all the factors involved before devising a long-term plan that is protective of the child. No two situations are alike, and it would be inappropriate to search for a single formula that would magically do away with the anguish, hard work, and painful compromises that are usually called for.

The services of an infant mental health professional (a child psychologist, child psychiatrist, developmental pediatrician, child social worker, or other professional specializing in the emotional issues of the first three years of life) can be most useful and are often crucial in such situations. Talking with an experienced and sympathetic professional can help a frightened parent sort out his or her worries about the former spouse's liabilities as a parent from the strong emotions associated with the divorce process itself.

Even when the fitness to parent is not at stake, many parents engage in thoughtless, uncaring, or even objectionable actions. Personality problems, impulsive actions, and angry outbursts are exacerbated in the course of a failing marriage and its aftermath. Some parents suffer from chronic character flaws that were manifest even in the happier times of the family. For aggrieved spouses, it is often difficult to watch their toddler adore and admire a mommy or a daddy they know to be undeserving of such uncritical love. They may experience a wish to set the child straight, to tell the child what Mommy or Daddy is "really like." Often this impulse is experienced as a wish to protect the child from disappointment later on. However, this is hardly ever a task that parents should take upon themselves. Children learn to discern the weaknesses of their parents as they grow older and become readier to see them with more objective eyes. A toddler needs to idealize her parents because through their perceived strength and goodness she learns to find those qualities in herself.

There are times when toddlers witness or experience parental actions that are frightening and destructive, such as physical aggression against the other parent or against the child. Condoning these actions or ignoring their damaging effects would distort the child's unfolding understanding of right and wrong and undermine the child's moral development. In these situations, it is necessary to acknowledge what the child knows: that the parent did something hurtful and wrong. The emotional tone of this acknowledgment is an important component of the message. It can be said in anger or in sadness. It can be said as if the wrong actions described the parent in his or her entirety, or it can be embedded in an acknowledgment of the positive aspects of the parent that are loved and missed by the child. The examples below are statements made by parents in describing to their young child the reason for the divorce.

- "Your daddy forgets to use his words when he gets mad, and then he hits and throws things. It is too scary. I can't let him hurt you or hurt me. That is why we can't live with him anymore."
- "Your mom drinks too much wine, and then she doesn't think right and can't take care of you. She needs to get better before she can spend time alone with you."
- "Your dad loves you, but he doesn't know how to be a dad; that's why he went away. It is very sad because you are a wonderful boy and he would be very happy if he knew how to be a dad."

These explanations are honest, correct, and straightforward. They are also protective, describing a regrettable situation factually but leaving room for other aspects of the child's experience. Giving permission to remember, feel, and speak about the negative aspects of the parent while also allowing room to recall positive aspects and happy moments is a great gift to children struggling with a parent's shortcomings. It helps children learn that good and bad coexist, humans are fallible, and one can have a range of loving, sad, and angry feelings about the people one loves while taking action to protect oneself when necessary. It also gives them permission to grieve for not having the parent they wish their parent to be.

Lack of fitness as a parent is not always permanent. People can change for the better, and many parents who have difficulties with substance abuse, violence, and emotional problems are motivated by their love of their children to work on themselves and overcome or manage those problems. Interventions geared to repairing the parent-child relationship following stressful and traumatic experiences show promising results when parents are able to understand the impact of their behavior on their child.[15,16] This understanding can be linked to their ability to retrieve memories of how they were raised and their own fear, anger, and loneliness while growing up. Reconnecting emotionally with those memories can help parents realize that they are now doing to their children what was once done to them. This insight can serve as the impetus to change the trajectory between generations from one of fear and alienation to one of intimacy and hope.

Introducing a New Partner

Sometimes the divorce is intertwined with the presence of new partners in the parents' lives. These partners may have children of their own who are of the same or different sex and age as the toddler. Circumstances vary greatly, and each situation has its own specific challenges and rewards for the child.

In spite of the diversity, general rules are worth keeping in mind. It is best not to rush toddlers into making a close emotional connection with a new partner and his or her children. Particularly if the adults' relationship is new and still tentative, the pressure of bringing children into it too fast can strain it in unhealthy ways. Sometimes divorcing parents long to reconstitute a family and move swiftly into a new commitment, bringing the toddler into it. A gradual deepening of the connection is preferable because it protects the toddler from yet another loss if the new relationship does not work out.

Sometimes a new partner wants to become the child's emotional parent. If the toddler's own mother or father is not involved, this willingness to fill a parental role is of course a wonderful opportunity for the toddler. If, on the other hand, both parents are active in the child's life, it is not a good idea to try to replace them. The stepparent does not need to compete with the "other" parent and vice versa. Each has a valuable part to play in the child's life.

Toddlers in divorced families fare best when the adults respect each other's importance to the child. Toddlers are usually not confused by their relation to more than two parenting figures if the adults themselves are confident of their roles. Stepparents and their children can enrich toddlers' lives, both directly and by being a source of emotional support and stability to the parents.

Is There an Ideal Custody Arrangement?

The search for a perfect custody arrangement is like the search for the perfect mate or the perfect diet: elusive, ultimately futile, but also tantalizing.

Custody arrangements go through fashions. It used to be taken for granted that the mother's care was the best and that the children should stay with the mother and have periodic visitations with the father. Then joint custody became the arrangement of choice, until it became clear that the parents' various schedules often called for more cooperation and flexible negotiation than they could muster even while married.

There is no "quick fix" for custody arrangements. All of them call for hard work, flexibility, willingness to accommodate, and ability to negotiate. It is even possible that one type of arrangement may work better at one time and a different type may be desirable later, as the child's needs and family circumstances change.

Following are some factors that are useful to consider in arriving at arrangements consistent with a toddler's needs.

- What is the child's temperament? Is she easily upset by changes in routine, or does she adjust to comings and goings relatively easily? Are separations and reunions emotionally draining for her, so that her responses to transitions affect her general functioning?
- Does the child markedly prefer one parent over the other?
- How verbal is the child? Can she understand verbal explanations of who will pick her up and when? Can she ask questions about what will happen and when?
- Is one parent much better able to provide quality time than the other?
- Can the parents cooperate with each other in setting up transitions and helping the child through them?
- How far apart do the parents live? Will transitions involve long trips that will be tiring for the child and difficult for the parents to maintain?

- Are there siblings who can help provide continuity for the toddler during the transitions?

In general, joint custody arrangements are likely to work best with
relatively flexible children whose distress during transitions can be
contained with the parents' help, who can understand verbal explanations and ask even rudimentary questions, who are emotionally invested in both parents, and whose parents cooperate with each other so
that separations and reunions occur in a supportive emotional climate.

If these conditions do not exist or if well-intentioned trials show
that the child does not fare well in a split-custody arrangement, it
might be best to consider a single-home arrangement with liberal
opportunities for the noncustodial parent to have access.

It is quite likely that the actual custody arrangement is less important than the spirit in which it is carried out. Custody can be a fertile
ground for acting out the unfinished business of the failed marriage. If
this is the case, no custody arrangement will serve the child well. If, on
the other hand, custody is understood as what it should be—namely,
a reasonable arrangement to protect and preserve the child's relationships with both parents—many different arrangements can work basically well.

Helping the Toddler with Transitions

Transitions from one parent to the other and back again epitomize
what is most difficult about divorce: the lost togetherness of the family
unit. As the spouses face each other to exchange their child, both of
them are confronted most clearly with their mutual resentments and
recriminations as well as with their grief over the parting of ways. They
are immersed in their own emotions and hardly at their best to attend
to their toddler's urgent need for support as he is asked to say good-bye
to one parent and get ready to adjust to the other.

Separations and reunions can be difficult for toddlers in the best of
circumstances. When they take place in a tense emotional climate, the

burden on the child increases and she often falls apart. The scenes that ensue can be heartrending, as the toddler clings first to one parent and then to the other, crying and unable to either stay or go.

The child's distress is often paralyzing for the parents. Unable to help, they may resort to blaming each other for the child's difficulties. One parent may suspect that the other is influencing the child against him. The other may see the child's distress as evidence of negligent care or worse.

Transitions from one home to the other may always remain painful events for children. If the parents feel confident that the transitions are necessary because contact with the other parent is valuable, this conviction will be transmitted to the toddler and separation distress will be greatly reduced in time. Some suggestions that may help:

- Find a private time to speak with the child's other parent about the transitions. Explain that you believe the child needs to spend time with each of you and profits from it, and that you would like the transitions to be as free of stress as possible for all concerned. Try to identify the sources of problems, and offer constructive suggestions that apply to both of you. Do not lose your temper or your willingness to continue trying if this approach is not immediately welcomed by your former spouse or partner.
- Before a transition, prepare yourself for it. Try to get in touch with your emotions about the child's departure or return. Do you feel relieved? Anxious? Angry? Overburdened?
- Prepare your child for the transition. Tell her that the other parent will pick her up for their time together. Whenever possible, spend some quiet time with the child before she is due to leave. However, do not start an engrossing pastime that will be interrupted by the other parent's arrival.
- Use a confident and supportive tone of voice when you talk to the child about going with the other parent. Be ready to acknowledge that it is sad to say good-bye, but be equally ready to remind her that she also has a good time with the other parent.

- Make use of transitional objects, for example, a favorite toy or blanket that the child can take along and bring back.
- Agree with the other parent that phone calls will not be restricted. Offer the child the chance to call the other parent when she is with you.
- Speak positively to the child about the other parent and the parents' relationship.

Parents who live apart represent for the child a split in the secure base of an undivided home. The child needs to bring together the split halves to form a cohesive secure base that is internalized and becomes a reliable part of him. In actions and in words, the parents can help in this endeavor by remaining coparents in child rearing.

10

The Toddler in Child Care

Damian is sitting at a table in his day care center, slowly moving his jaws and mouth while staring into space. "What are you chewing, Damian?" asks his caregiver. "I'm chewing Mommy," replies Damian dreamily.[1]

Damien's answer tells us with haikulike conciseness about a major aspect of the toddler's child care experience: missing the parent, yet holding on to her through a combination of memory, hope, and imagination. By chewing on his mother's image, Damian is carrying her in the most reliable place of all—inside himself.

Damian is reminding us that child care is first and foremost about relationships. It is about how to separate from the parents while trusting that they will come back. It is also about forming new relationships with the caregiver and with the other children that will be enriching and sustaining in the course of the day.

These experiences—learning to say bye-bye and enjoying the new hellos—are closely intertwined. When toddlers can separate from their parents with a sadness that is manageable, they are more able to engage with other people than if they are overcome by distress. Conversely, enjoying the child care setting helps relieve their apprehension and distress when the parent leaves.

For the parents, child care is also about relationships. It is about how to let go of their little one with the trust that they are not hurting the child by not being together full-time. It is about going through the day with confidence that the child is safe, well cared for, and having a good enough time, so that this knowledge can compensate for the waves of longing and guilt that may be a regular part of the working parent's routine. It is about developing ways of communicating with the child's caregiver that will lead to a solid partnership on behalf of the child.

A successful child care experience calls for careful attention to three major aspects of nonparental care: (1) the daily transitions of departing and reuniting, (2) the quality of the child's emotional experiences in the course of the day, and (3) the quality of the parents' relationship with the caregivers. These three factors remain important regardless of where the child care arrangement takes place: in the child's home, in the caregiver's home, or in a day care center.

Making the Transition: Saying Good-bye

Let's examine two contrasting scenes that illustrate some of the pressures of parting for the day.

On Monday, Charlie and his mother enjoy a lovely early morning together. The whole family had spent a relaxed weekend. The chores were disposed of without too much tension between the parents, and there was time to go to the park, play games, and watch a family movie together. This particular Monday morning, everybody woke up easily and the father took the older children to school in time and without the need for raising his voice about the need to hurry up. Charlie's mother is feeling that family harmony is possible after all, even when both parents work. She dresses Charlie for the day in a playful manner, tells him she will miss him during the day, and chats with him about what they will have for dinner that evening. They sing silly songs on the way to Charlie's child care. When they get there, Charlie's mother lingers a while, telling the caregiver about Charlie's cute behavior during the weekend. She then tells Charlie, who had drifted off toward the other children, that she needs to leave. She approaches him, hugs and kisses him, tells him she will see him that evening, and leaves. Charlie looks at the door for a few seconds as she disappears. He sighs with a brief expression of sadness and then rejoins the other children in their play.

On Thursday morning, things do not go so smoothly. The whole family is tired from a week of work, school, chores, and nightly homework for the older children, and the weekend seems a long way off. Tempers are short. To compound matters, Charlie puts up a fuss while getting dressed because he wants to wear his green overalls, which are in the laundry. Later he spills his bowl of cereal on the floor. (Fortunately, the dog, a good friend, laps it up.) The mother yells at Charlie, and he, not to be outdone, yells back. On the way to the car he trips and falls and cries inconsolably, as if this small accident gives him the chance to release the accumulated tension of the morning. His mother picks him up and cuddles him, but she is keenly aware of the time. They are already fifteen minutes late. On the way to child care, she drives fast, changes lanes frequently, and goes through every yellow light. She is totally focused on getting to work as soon as possible and cannot pay attention to Charlie, who is whimpering in the backseat. The good-bye at child care is rushed and perfunctory. Charlie's mother spends the day with a feeling of guilt and longing for her little boy. She finds herself having trouble concentrating on her work. Images of Charlie's sad face as they said good-bye keep crossing her mind, and she wishes she had spoken with him about the difficult time they'd had. She wishes she had told him she loved him and was no longer mad at him. At his child care setting, Charlie mirrors those feelings in his own way. An assertive child with a strong will, today he is particularly prone to get into struggles with his peers. He fights taking a nap and cries bitterly when the caregiver lets another child rather than him sit on her lap. Fortunately, his mother calls him on the phone and tells him she loves him. The mood of both of them picks up a great deal as a result.

These two vignettes illustrate how the same parent-child pair can have different kinds of separation experiences at different times depending on their mood and the circumstances involved. The vignettes also show that a separation begins long before the actual event takes place and its effects may linger for a prolonged period of time afterward. Being conscious of this process can improve things considerably for both parent and child.

Separation has at least two developmental meanings for toddlers. First and foremost, it triggers the fear of losing the parent that is so prevalent at this age. Closely connected with this fear is the fantasy that something the child did is prompting the parent to go away; in other words, that he is to blame for this loss because of his bad behavior. A long day away from the parent gives a toddler plenty of time to embroider on those fears and to worry that her parent will not pick her up today because she bit the baby or did not go potty or spat out her cereal or refused to wear the dress that was picked out for her.

Acknowledging separation feelings directly and sympathetically is the best way of coping with them. It is actually helpful to tell a toddler,

"I will miss you," "I will think of you during the day," "It is hard to say good-bye," or "I can't wait to see you at the end of the day." These messages tell the child that he is important to the parent even when they are not together and that "out of sight" need not mean "out of mind." Making up after an early-morning conflict is also an important way of reassuring the child that daily conflicts have no lasting bearing on the enduring emotional connection between parent and child.

When parents try not to experience the feelings aroused by separation, they tend to avoid the experience altogether. They may sneak out while the child is not paying attention or say that they are going to the bathroom and coming right back when, in fact, they are leaving for the day.

Lying to a toddler is usually done to protect the adult's feelings rather than the child's. There is nothing a toddler cannot hear and assimilate if it is age appropriate and explained in a calm, supportive way, leaving plenty of room for the child's reaction and the questions he might have as he assimilates the news over time.

Toddlers who are lied to about separations cannot trust what their parents tell them. Some become hypervigilant and clingy because they never know when they will be left. They need to monitor the environment for signs of abandonment because they cannot trust the adults to be forthright about what will happen and when. Other toddlers become dismissive of the importance of relationships. They avoid close emotional ties and adopt an indifferent "Who cares?" attitude as a way of coping with the uncertainty of the parents' comings and goings.

Parents who have trouble leaving may do the opposite of sneaking out; they may be unable to leave at all and linger around the child, postponing the moment of saying good-bye. They are persuaded again and again by their child's pleas to stay "a little longer," all the while telling the toddler that they really need to leave. This contrast between what they say and what they do can be quite confusing to their child, who keeps asking them to stay because the strategy is clearly successful in getting what he wants.

Staying a little longer can certainly be a sensitive response to the child's need if the parent uses this time to talk about the separation and to help the child make the transition to the caregiver, to a peer, or to a favorite activity. If, on the other hand, parents become trapped in an indecisive sequence of efforts to leave followed by halfhearted decisions to stay longer, the effect is actually counterproductive because children get the message that separations are as emotionally unmanageable as they fear them to be.

Spending the Day in Child Care

The act of saying good-bye is the most noticeable aspect of the parent's departure, but it marks only the beginning of the separation process. The child is now faced with a long day away from the parent. Being apart arouses anxiety and taxes the child's coping resources, but there are ways of keeping the parent's reassuring image alive in the toddler's heart and mind.

Bridging the Parent's Absence

Within the toddler period there are developmental differences in the ease with which the child can adapt to being away from their primary parent figure. Between 12 and 18 months, there is an increase in the child's distress over separation. After 24 months, most toddlers have an easier time being away from the mother, and this ease becomes more pronounced after the middle of the second year. The toddler's sustained progress in the areas of memory, language, and symbolic play means that she can bring more sophisticated cognitive and emotional skills to the task of coping with the parent's absence.

This developmental trajectory can guide parents' considerations about when to start child care for a toddler. The later it begins, the more likely it is that the child will adjust to it more smoothly.

Regardless of when it begins, full-time child care is more taxing to the child than shorter daily separations. There is good observational documentation that part-time child care puts less strain on the child's resources for adaptation than a full eight- or ten-hour day away from home. For most toddlers, their parents are their first and best loves, and they experience a sense of relief (even if they do not show it) when they are reunited at the end of the day.

This situation makes it particularly important to build bridges between the child care setting and the home. When the child care setting is the home—that is, when the caregiver comes to the child's home—the child is surrounded by familiar and reassuring reminders of the parents' presence and of their life together. When child care occurs outside the home, the bridges need to be consciously and conscientiously built and maintained.

Sally Provence and her colleagues at Yale University pioneered the use of many simple yet effective means of helping young children with separations in a day care center called Children's House, which they opened in New Haven in 1967 with a grant from the US Children's Bureau.[2] To this day, their work remains a model of what developmentally oriented, family-focused child care can provide for infants and toddlers and their families. Clinicians, child care workers, and researchers have built upon this model to apply, expand, and adapt the techniques to a variety of child care settings.[3] How many of these measures are feasible will depend on each family's circumstances, but the following is an outline of optimal efforts to ease the transition between home and child care.

1. Make yourself familiar with the child care setting and the daily routine. This will enable you to talk about the routine with your child. It will also help you understand your child better when she talks about what happened during the day.
2. Acquaint your child with the caregivers and the new setting before child care actually begins. How intensive and extensive this period of familiarization needs to be depends in part on the child's temperament, previous experience, and ease of adjustment to new situations. Your child's responses are the best barometer of this.

3. Discuss with the caregiver your child's individual preferences, her areas of strength and vulnerability, and your child-rearing values, including your approach to discipline. This will enable the caregiver to use the knowledge in her own relationship with your child. Tell the caregiver about any special events when they occur so that she can talk about them with your child in the course of the day. (Are Grandma and Grandpa visiting? Did the dog run away? Did you watch a special movie last night?)

4. If at all possible, start out with briefer separations that become progressively longer as the child adjusts to the new setting. How brief the initial separations need to be depends on many factors, including your child's prior experience with separations and ease of adjustment to the new setting.

5. Avoid dropping the child off and leaving right away. Try to stay for a while, until your child has settled in.

6. Try to establish contact with your child during the course of the day if possible. This may mean dropping in at lunchtime or making a phone call. Telephone contact is particularly useful with toddlers over 2, but it can be helpful as early as 18 months to provide a sense of continuity. Even if your child does not speak very much, he can recognize your voice and cherish the connection with you.

7. Encourage the caregiver to let the child call you on the phone at times of unusually intense distress if this is realistic in terms of your availability. Many caregivers feel that this takes away from their own role as a substitute parent or that it disrupts the child care routine. This may call for a talk with the caregiver in which you can acknowledge her importance in the child's life without relinquishing yours.

8. Give your child something from home to take to the child care setting. It may be a toy, a security blanket, or something that belongs to the parent. Such a transitional object serves as a concrete representation of the parent and helps the child remember that his home has not disappeared from his life.

9. Give your child a photograph of yourself. This photograph can be kept in the child's locker, with ready access to it in the course of the day. Toddlers know just how to use this precious resource. They go to it at times of stress and may not look at it for weeks at a time when things are going well.

10. Talk with your child about what it is like to be apart and about the pleasures of being together. This will help to make separation feelings a legitimate area for parent-child communication.

11. Play games that build on the mastery of separation experiences, such as hide-and-seek, the hiding and recovery of objects, and play with dolls around themes of going away and coming back. These games strengthen the child's sense of object permanence—the knowledge that people and things continue to exist when they are out of sight.

Different parents will find some of these suggestions more compatible with their own style than others. Similarly, different caregivers and child care settings may lend themselves more easily than others to some of these efforts to build connections with the child's home. The specific configuration of what is done matters less than the spirit of partnership between parent and caregiver in arriving at workable ways of helping the child feel at home even while away from home.

The Child-Caregiver Relationship

Child care is the toddler's home away from home for a major portion of the day. Many of the major developmental milestones may take place while the toddler is in child care: new motor skills such as jumping and running; toilet training; learning about objects through play and manipulation; and learning about the larger environment through exploring and roaming about.

All these developments occur in the context of human relationships. Just like children raised full-time by a parent, the toddler in child care needs a secure base from which to explore the surroundings. In the home, this secure base is usually the parent; in child care, it should be the caregiver.

The toddler's relationship with the caregiver is the single most important component of the child care experience. Young children internalize the quality of their interactions not only with their parents but with other important people as well. The relationship with the caregiver becomes an important model of what human connections outside the family have to offer.

If the child-caregiver relationship is nurturing, reliable, and often even joyous, the child's confidence in human relationships as a source of comfort and reciprocity will be strengthened and expanded in spite of the parents' absence. The child will learn that the parents are not the only people to be trusted and that other people are trustworthy as well.

If, on the contrary, the child feels emotionally lost in the child care relationship, with no reliable adult to turn to when he needs help or wants to share a discovery, the experience will mar his emotional investment in himself, in others, and in the world at large.

Different children respond to inadequate conditions in different ways. At best, more competent and resilient toddlers fall back on their own budding coping resources and make the most of whatever the environment has to offer. They may become precociously self-reliant or form an intense relationship with a peer to help them find challenge and interest in the course of the day. They may also develop a single-minded pursuit of something they can do on their own, such as fantasy play or building structures. These activities are constructive and growth-promoting in themselves, but they can result in emotional isolation when the child uses them as a defense against anxiety.

Other toddlers cope less creatively with the absence of an invested and available caregiver. They may roam about listlessly, becoming fleetingly interested in one or another feature of the environment but unable to sustain their interest through the supportive presence of a caring adult. Such children spend the day marking time until the parents return. It is as if they put their hearts, souls, and minds into storage until "real" life begins again. Some toddlers can regain a relatively intact sense of themselves at the end of a long and emotionally depleting day in child care. Others carry the losses into other settings as well, in the form of mistrust, aggression, or emotional withdrawal.

This should not do. Jeree Pawl of Zero to Three put it succinctly: "As parents, we can allow our child in day care to miss us, but she should not miss herself."[4] The child needs ongoing access to her sense of being emotionally alive in order to flourish as a human being.

It behooves parents to assess the child care setting for its ability to provide meaningful human relationships. First and foremost, this means finding a caregiver or small set of caregivers who can get along with toddlers for a major portion of the day.

This is probably easier said than done. Provence and her colleagues acknowledged that they found it harder to create a program geared to the developmental needs of toddlers between 15 and 30 months than to devise a program for younger or older children. They elaborated on this difficulty as follows:

> To live exclusively with a group of toddlers is not easy. They tend
> to impinge sharply and more or less continuously upon adults and
> upon each other. Their rapid shifts from helplessness to indepen-

dent behavior, from negativism to angelic compliance, from adamant holding on to explosive casting out, from wishing to be as
one with the adult to insisting on separateness and standing alone,
from tenderness towards others to hostility, from taking initiatives
to acting passively—this radically varying behavior is physically
and psychologically taxing to adults.[5]

All parents will recognize this catalogue of the toddler's inner states
and outer behaviors. If parents, who love their child with all their
hearts, have trouble coping with these swiftly changing and often contradictory moods, what can we expect of a caregiver, who even under
optimal conditions may be very fond of the child but does not hold
him at the very core of her being, as do the parents?

It is difficult to find adults (parents included!) who can derive a
sense of fun from being with toddlers all day and who can negotiate the developmental challenges of the toddler's newfound mobility,
genital curiosity, toilet-training requirements, separation anxiety,
and experimentation with self-assertion. Still, such adults do exist.[6]
In searching for them, it is good to remember that caregivers (like
parents) need not be omnipotent or omniscient. They do need to know
and empathize with the needs of toddlers and be able and willing to
give of themselves in relating to the children in their charge.

Things to Do

Relationships do not unfold in a vacuum. They are most rewarding
when they become a vehicle for learning about oneself, about each
other, and about the world. For toddlers, having things to do is a pre-
requisite for all these kinds of learning.

Child care arrangements vary a great deal in their structure. Some
settings offer a highly structured curriculum with emphasis on academic topics such as learning to recognize and use numbers and letters. Others have no organized program and rely largely on free play
and spontaneous activities.

Similarly, individual caregivers vary greatly in their ability to stimulate and entertain a child when she is cared for in the home. Some caregivers are wonderfully resourceful in coming up with interesting projects; others are so lackadaisical that the child can become quite bored as the hours go by.

The specific structure of the day matters less than the spirit with which it is carried out. An academic focus can challenge a toddler's intellect but carries the risk of becoming overly structured at an age when spontaneity is a key factor in developing a love of learning. Conversely, a totally unstructured atmosphere that emphasizes spontaneity can degenerate into chaos and anarchy if the caregivers lose touch with what is happening around them.

It is likely that different toddlers will do best in different settings. Some toddlers crave the safety of a predictable schedule; others are brimming with the impetus to do what most fascinates them at any given time and find it hard to comply with circle time.

The optimal toddler child care environment combines structured activities with plenty of attention to the child's individual needs.[7] Toddlers are unlikely to spend an inordinately long period of time at any activity, no matter how entranced with it they may be at first. A child care schedule organized around the idea that toddlers may spend about fifteen minutes in any one pursuit is realistically geared to the attention span of this age. Of course, even within this time frame there should be flexibility to enable one toddler to finish "putting the baby to sleep" or give more time to another toddler for putting the last touches to her block structure.

This means that the child care setting should provide opportunities both for free play and for mastery of the environment through the development of new skills. The following materials and activities help toddlers to become engaged in different kinds of discoveries and accomplishments.

- Construction toys and puzzles that help develop fine motor manipulation and visual-motor coordination
- Housekeeping utensils that encourage reenactment of the daily home routines and imaginative variations on domestic chores

- Dolls and play furniture to stimulate play around themes of caregiving and nurturance
- Play-Doh, painting equipment, and other "messy" materials and water-play toys that represent the bodily processes the toddler is struggling to master
- Musical instruments to encourage singing and dancing as a form of aesthetic expression through the body
- Dress-up clothes to allow the child symbolic experimentation with other ways of being
- Playground equipment for outdoor play to enable the child to release energy and to acquire, expand, and refine gross motor skills

A child care setting that provides at least a sizable proportion of these opportunities for play and exploration is likely to have a good understanding of toddlers' developmental needs. When the child care takes place in the home, outings to the park, to community centers, or to play groups can add variety to the daily routine.

The physical safety of the child care setting is an essential ingredient. Without it nothing else can work well. Physical safety is important in itself, but it also serves as an index of the quality of the setting. Carollee Howes, whose research on child care has set a standard in the field, found that physical safety is related to the caregiver's attitude toward the children. Safer settings allow the caregiver to be less restrictive of the toddlers' activities and give them more freedom to explore. When the setting is safe, caregivers are also more physically affectionate with the children in their charge, perhaps because they feel less need to be vigilant and can be more relaxed and spontaneous as a result.[8]

Relationships with Peers

Toddlers in child care form stable, reciprocal, and meaningful relationships with other children. In fact, friendships with other children alleviate the distress caused by the daylong separation from the parents.

Furthermore, toddlers in child care interact more with one another and learn one another's names at an earlier age than toddlers who are raised full-time by their mothers. They also engage in more sophisticated pretend play.[9,10] This greater cognitive and social complexity of peer play in toddlers who attend child care suggests that friendships with other children enable the toddler to cope more effectively with the daily stresses of separation from the parents.

The stability of these friendships is helpful. Toddlers who have long-term relationships with the same group of peers tend to be more popular and more socially interactive in the child care setting.[11] Just like adults, toddlers feel more comfortable with friends they have known for a long time. Similarly, losing a friend in toddlerhood has noticeable effects on the child's sociability. Toddlers whose friends have left the child care setting tend to be less socially involved one year later.[12]

These findings highlight the importance of striving to provide the child with stable child care. Although parents cannot control the departure of their child's friends, they can try to minimize the number of changes that they themselves initiate. Toddlers, like adults, miss their friends and may become more self-protective after losing a cherished relationship.

The child's relationship with the mother and with the caregiver has a significant effect on the ability to form friendships with other children. As a group, toddlers who have secure, nurturing, mutually satisfying relationships with both their mother and their caregiver tend to be more sociable with peers than are children who feel insecure in their relationships with both women.[13] This finding highlights the continuing importance of the parent as well as the centrality of the caregiver in enabling toddlers to expand their social horizons. The secure base provided by emotionally available parents and parent surrogates sustains the child's confidence in exploring relationships with peers.

Saying Hello: The Joys and Stresses of Reunion

Coming together again after a long day apart can be an experience in which joy, relief, anger, and fatigue are all present in different degrees for both the parent and the child. Because of their importance in marking the resumption of direct contact, reunions deserve as much attention and care as separations if they are to enhance the relationship between parent and child.

Reunions can be eagerly anticipated and still be something of a let-down when they finally occur. The parent and the child may be in different moods. One may be exuberantly active, the other tired and low key. Worse yet, they might both be grumpy and needy and have few emotional resources left to share.

Toddlers often do not show pleasure on being picked up at the end of the day. They may be involved in play and figure that the parent can wait for them for a change. They may be angry at the separation and show it through turning a "cold shoulder" or through outright aggression. They may have intense positive and negative emotions raging inside them and try to cope with those feelings by keeping some distance from the parents until they can offer a genuinely warm hello.

For a parent who is looking forward to a loving reunion, these responses can feel like a dismal welcome indeed. Feeling unneeded and unappreciated, the parent may withdraw emotionally in return. This sequence of child reaction and parental counterreaction may set the tone for an evening of emotional distance between parent and child.

A reunion is colored by the emotional baggage of the separation experience, and some ambivalence is inevitably attached to it. Because of this, it is a good idea not to overinvest the reunion with the hope for instant and complete emotional reconnection. It takes some time to process the reality of the separation, to let go of the coping mechanisms used for dealing with it, and to relax into being together again. When the parents are preoccupied by what happened at work during the day, their minds might still be processing adult issues while they are "on autopilot" in reestablishing a connection with their child.

Parents can help themselves and their toddlers by becoming aware of the range of feelings that come up during reunions and accepting them without guilt or blame. Lingering a while in the child care setting, greeting the child warmly but giving her space to wind up an activity while staying near, chatting with the caregiver and the other children—these small but meaningful gestures can go a long way to create an atmosphere in which both parent and child feel permission for taking their time in being together and enjoying each other again.

The Parent-Caregiver Relationship

Child care providers often report that their relationships with children and coworkers are the most satisfying aspect of their work. This response is yet another reminder that child care is primarily about relationships.

Parents are potentially valuable partners of the child care circle, yet their relationship with the caregiver does not receive the attention it deserves. Some studies show that parents spend an average of seven minutes a day in the child care setting, and 10 percent of parents do not even go in. When parents are so minimally involved with their child's caregiver, they are losing an opportunity for a satisfying partnership on behalf of their child.

There are concrete factors that account for this perfunctory contact. In the morning, the parents are in a rush, and by the end of the day, everybody is tired and wanting to go home. However, there are also built-in tensions in the relationship between parent and caregiver that contribute to the lack of communication between them.

Perhaps the most salient source of tension is a certain unease over who "owns" the child. When the toddler is at home, the parents' values and child care routines are clearly the order of the day. In the child care setting, the provider's guidelines take over. There are multiple opportunities for conflicting attitudes and practices about the appropriate age to give up the bottle, when and how to begin toilet training, how to respond to the child's curiosity about bodily matters, how to mediate conflicts between peers—the list could go on and on.

Areas of disagreement can easily become sources of tension and even enmity between parent and caregiver, with feelings of disapproval and defensiveness experienced simultaneously by both sides. If these feelings are not modulated by a certain amount of goodwill, each party might come to feel that the child should be raised in a particular way (the way he or she favors) and that the child does best while in his or her care.

It is easy for caregivers to feel exploited by the parents, who often have better salaries and a more sophisticated lifestyle. The caregiver might feel that she is treated like "hired help"—expected to take care of the child but not given the respect and deference that such a responsibility should command. This experience is heightened if the parent is late making payments or picking up the child at the end of the day. It is also heightened when the child care provider is from an underrepresented minority with a history of discrimination and the parent is from a mainstream cultural group.

It is also easy for parents to feel criticized by the child care provider, particularly if they are already feeling guilty or insecure. Mutual dissatisfaction often leads to mutual avoidance in an effort to prevent a fight that could end the child care arrangement.

Enhancing the parent-provider relationship improves the quality of life for all involved: the parent, the caregiver, and, most of all, the child. The suggestions that follow can be helpful in facilitating this process.

- Set up one or more interviews with the caregiver before you decide on a child care arrangement. Elicit her views on the areas of child development and child rearing that are important to you. Ask her how she handles particular situations that are likely to occur, such as the child's refusal to obey or the child's calling for you. Ask also about her expectations regarding contact with you. For example, will you be able to drop in unannounced while your child is in her care? If you feel satisfied and reassured by her responses and by her affective style during this talk, it is a good sign that the two of you can form an effective working partnership.
- Try to set up regular times to talk with the caregiver and exchange views about your child. The frequency and length of these talks may vary depending on circumstances and how smoothly things are going. It is imperative, however, that you

keep an ongoing sense of being able to talk to each other whenever an issue of importance arises.

- Remember that the caregiver is a stable presence in your family life. Do not restrict your interaction with her to child care topics. Allow yourself to be friendly with her. Chat with her. If she looks tired, make a supportive comment about that. If she was sick, ask her how she is feeling now. Inquire after her children. Feel free to explore the limits of what is feasible and appropriate between the two of you. The warmer your relationship, the greater the continuity your toddler will experience between child care and home. Toddlers are keen observers of the adults they care about. Your child will notice how you and the caregiver relate to each other, and the conclusions she reaches will in turn influence her comfort in her relationships with both of you.

- If your child tells you something about the caregiver's behavior that seems unusual or worrisome, do not dismiss it as a figment of his or her imagination. Toddlers can be amazingly accurate observers and reporters. On the other hand, remember that young children can misinterpret events: a caregiver who is trying to dislodge a piece of food stuck in a child's throat might be perceived by a young observer as hitting the child. Try to get a sense of the context in which the event reported took place. Then bring it up with the care provider in a calm, nonaccusing manner.

- If a conflict emerges, give some thought to strategy before you attempt to deal with it. If you can buy some time, let off steam by talking with the trusted people in your life and taking time to sort out your feelings. When you discuss it with the caregiver, try to frame the problem in a positive context. If at all possible, start out with the things that you value about her caregiving style, and work your way gradually to the area of concern. People (caregivers and parents included) respond much better when they are reassured that their areas of strength are noticed and appreciated.

Signs of Trouble

There are times when a toddler is not doing well in child care. How can we tell? The signs can be as varied as children's personalities, but some recurrent warning signals are listed below.

- Sudden changes for the worse in the child's behavior that persist for longer than a few days and that cannot be attributed to increased stresses at home. For example, the toddler might become unusually aggressive, clingy, fearful, defiant, or negativistic. An increase in symptoms of anxiety described throughout the book should alert the parents to look more closely at what is happening in child care.
- Avoidance or fear of a particular child care provider.
- Persistent and sustained refusal to go to child care, particularly when the onset of this refusal is sudden and occurs after the child has settled into the child care arrangement.
- Loss of zest for learning and exploring, sadness, and emotional withdrawal.
- Repeated statements about not liking a caregiver or another child or reports that somebody did something scary, such as yelling or spanking.

Children might misinterpret adult behavior, but more often they report accurately what they experience. It is always important to pay attention to the child's verbal reports and behavioral changes. The two examples that follow make this point even more strongly.

Kerri, 36 months, says to her mother, "My teacher lies on top of us to make us take a nap." The mother believes that Kerri is exaggerating. Two weeks later, she comes in at nap time and finds the assistant caregiver "containing" a struggling child by placing her body on top of his.

Trim, 2 years old, struggles every morning on being taken to his grandmother's house. "No hit, no hit!" he cries. When his mother finds a bruise on his leg, she realizes the grandmother has been hitting him.

Children's distress in child care is not necessarily the result of abuse. One child refused to go to her day care center for a week after listening to a story that frightened her. Another one developed nightmares as the result of daily confrontations with an older, stronger, and more aggressive child who bullied him. A third child relapsed in toilet training and became clingy and whiny after her favorite caregiver left suddenly without notice.

Signs of distress need to alert parents to look more closely at the child's experience of child care. This is when the efforts at building a relationship with the caregiver really pay off. The more parents and caregivers can cooperate with each other in tracing the reasons for the child's distress and in working toward a solution, the more effective they will be in making the child care situation a secure base that sustains the child's emotional growth.

The Emotional Effects of Child Care

Does child care affect the toddler's attachment to the mother? There has long been a lively debate among child development specialists about the effects of child care on the young child's development. Some experts worry that long daily separations may create anxiety in the infant and toddler over the mother's availability. Other experts counter that young children acquire important social skills in the expanded social context of child care.[14,15]

The debate revolves around disagreements over theoretical and methodological issues, but two decades of research have failed to yield reliable findings that early child care has substantially negative effects on the relationship between mother and child. The majority of infants and toddlers with early day care experience are securely attached.[16]

These findings make sense from many theoretical perspectives, including that of attachment theory. As the psychologist Alan Sroufe remarked, one would expect infants to do well when they can learn over time that separations are predictable and lead equally predictably to reunions, that caregivers are emotionally available, and that parents and caregivers are accepting of the child's ambivalence about separations.[17]

Under normal circumstances, the emotional connection between parent and child is too powerful to be dampened by a family's need for two incomes or by the mother's desire to pursue other interests in addition to motherhood. Even when they cannot be always available, the parents' fierce, unique love for their child makes them different in the child's heart and mind from all other caregivers. In spite of a long working day, a parent's passion for his or her child retains its many nuances of emotional intensity, ranging from rapture and delight to impatience and even rage, that no other relationship in the child's life can match. Even very young infants are smart enough to recognize this passionate commitment and to reciprocate it in kind. Researchers may argue, but young children know best.

The question "Is early child care detrimental to the child's relationship with the parents?" should be turned on its head. The question should be "What are the emotional costs to the child of not providing adequate substitute care when both parents work out of the home?"

A large majority of mothers in the United States return to work within their baby's first year.[18] In this context, it is high time to transform the academic debate on the effects of early child care on child development into public policy actions to eliminate the human costs of not providing good substitute care to a young child when both parents need or choose to work. The scientific evidence is now compelling in showing that early child care does not have detrimental effects and that good quality child care can have beneficial effects on child development. This leads us to the question of what constitutes good substitute care.

Choosing Good-Quality Child Care

It is difficult to determine exactly what constitutes good child care because this care comes in many forms. The child care provider may be a cherished relative (an aunt, a grandmother) or someone hired especially for the purpose. The child might receive individual or group care. The setting may be the child's home, the child care provider's home, or a day care center. There might be one or several child care providers. The setting might be licensed or unlicensed, and it might be for profit or sponsored by nonprofit organizations such as a church or community center.

Within this diversity, quality criteria that apply to one setting may not be relevant to a different type of care. The most obvious example is group size, which is not an issue when the child is the single charge of a single caregiver but becomes an important factor in judging the quality of group care.

Some settings are easier to study than others. Day care centers are more open to systematic research because they are formal settings at least nominally accountable to state standards. Private providers and family day care homes are less likely to be licensed and more likely to argue that they are providing informal, homelike care not amenable to systematic evaluation research. For these reasons, most of the research on quality indicators has been conducted and validated in day care centers. The following factors have emerged as reliable indicators of quality group care.[19, 20]

1. Stability of care. The ongoing availability of the same caregiver or a small number of caregivers is a requisite to establish trusting emotional relationships that are not marred by a continuous process of loss and replacement. In addition, caregivers who are committed to their jobs for the long term relate to children in more stimulating and developmentally appropriate ways than those who see child care as a temporary job.[21]

   For these two major reasons, the stability of the child care provider is a pivotal factor in the quality of care. Optimal group care settings assign a primary caregiver to a small group of toddlers in order to maximize the child's use of a specific caregiver as a secure base. Clearly, caregiver stability is just as important in individual care as it is in group situations.

2. Caregiver training. Child care providers are better able to give quality care when they have specific training in child development. Knowledge of age-specific issues enables the caregiver to keep a broad perspective on the child's behavior. A toddler's negativism or temper tantrums, for example, can be handled with greater sensitivity by a caregiver who is aware of the autonomy strivings and intense emotions of this age.

   Training is particularly important when the caregiver must attend to several toddlers with competing individual needs and demands. If she does not have specific knowledge about child development, the caregiver can only rely on her personal experience, which might not equip her well for the challenges of her task. A well-trained provider is also better qualified to identify early signs of behavioral problems and to share her perceptions constructively with the parents.

3. The child-to-adult ratio. Each caregiver can interact frequently and harmoniously with only a small number of toddlers. When they are asked about their work, caregivers report that being responsible for too many children is a major source of job-related stress. They cope with the situation by putting more emphasis on routine and cutting down on spontaneous, individualized exchanges. A ratio of three to five toddlers per adult allows for playfulness as well as ready attention to child distress before it becomes unmanageable. The higher this ratio becomes, the more difficult it is for the caregiver to maintain individualized care.

4. Group size. Even with an adequate number of children in the care of each adult, a large group of toddlers can eas-

ily become draining and unmanageable. There is too much noise, too many simultaneous demands, too much distraction. A group size of no more than eight or ten toddlers allows the caregivers to focus on playfulness and emotional availability and diminishes the need for rigid group management.

5. The presence of another adult. Individual caregivers are supported both concretely and emotionally by another adult who can pitch in, help out, and provide some companionship. The presence of a second caregiver can also reduce the likelihood of child abuse both because there is a potential witness and because each caregiver is less likely to lose control if she can delegate responsibility before she is pressed to her limits and events get out of hand.

Does the Quality of Child Care Matter?

The shortest and most accurate answer is: *yes*, quality matters very much. Good-quality child care enhances the child's well-being, and poor-quality child care is damaging to it. At least a dozen recent research studies document this conclusion. Infants, toddlers, and preschoolers feel more secure emotionally and have more advanced social and cognitive skills when they attend good-quality child care.[22,23]

While the quality of child care matters, so does the family's input on the selection of child care. Parents who are overburdened may not be able to do extensive research before choosing a setting and may unwittingly place their children in centers of poor quality, regardless of their income and of tuition costs.[24] Since there is a greater abundance of mediocre care than of high-quality care, parents need help in sorting out the various factors they should consider. In addition to the information in this chapter, the leading early-childhood websites, such as the Child Care Resource Center (CCRC), National

Association for the Education of Young Children (NAEYC), and Zero to Three (ZTT) provide useful guidelines for making informed choices.

The Social Realities of Child Care

As a society we know what constitutes good-quality child care, but we have not yet made a collective decision to provide it to all our children. The criteria for good-quality care, painstakingly gleaned from extensive and expensive research, are routinely overridden because there is no national mandate to follow up the money for research with money for service delivery.

As a result, we acquire more and more academic information that remains unused because we are eager to collect it but not to apply it. The knowledge stays in books and journals and is disseminated in professional conferences without fulfilling its potential value in enhancing the lives of millions of children and their families.

The effectiveness of the various states in setting and enforcing standards of quality is a case in point. Licensing is under state control, and it provides a primary means of regulating the quality of care. States that do have guidelines often frame them in terms of such minimum standards that the goal is simply to prevent physical harm to the child rather than to ensure a developmentally appropriate environment. In this sense, the research findings regarding quality of child care have not been systematically incorporated into state regulations.

This situation has a direct effect on quality of care. Child care workers are among the lowest-paid workers in the country, and many earn below the official poverty rate.[25] This dismal situation cannot be excused as the natural consequence of lack of training because substandard wages apply to child care workers regardless of educational level and years of experience. However, caregivers who can earn more money elsewhere tend to leave the field, with the result that there might be a net decline in the availability of highly trained child care providers.

What accounts for this state of affairs? Most likely a combination of factors involving deeply rooted societal attitudes about "women's work." Child care was traditionally provided by mothers at no cost before they joined the workforce as the result of changing economic and social conditions. We have been slow to relinquish our idealized image of caring for children as a nonprofit activity deeply rooted in the maternal instinct and unrelated to economic concerns.

This stereotype is reinforced by the fact that women, particularly minority women, are overrepresented in the field of child care. The most recent available data show that between 95 and 98 percent of all child care providers are women, and a large percentage belong to ethnic minorities.[26] Women and minorities are traditionally underpaid, a factor that compounds the built-in tendency to regard child care as an occupation untouched by the market forces of supply and demand.[27]

These considerations provide the background for understanding child care providers' daily experience. Caregivers who are underpaid and overworked are less able to provide quality care because those stresses detract from their energy and emotional availability. On the contrary, caregivers who are at ease with their working conditions are more likely to provide appropriate care. As the Center for American Progress noted in a 2015 report, "Research shows that the most important indicator of quality in early learning environments is the interaction between children and their caregivers. When caregivers provide a warm, nurturing, and language-rich environment that structures learning and exploration in a developmentally appropriate way, children thrive."[28]

Providing higher wages and better working conditions for child care providers increases their sense of stability and enhances their ability to provide a nurturing environment for the children in their care.

In summary, good-quality child care results from an effective partnership that includes all of us: society as a whole, caregivers, and parents on behalf of their children. A national commitment to financing and upholding the standards of good-quality child care is essential to providing the stability and continuity that all children need to become well-functioning adults. Such a social framework will benefit each parent, each child, and each family because it will support the day-to-day and moment-to-moment efforts of parents and caregivers to be physically available and emotionally responsive to the children's needs. As is often stated, our children are our future, and the future begins in each present moment through the actions we take.

Conclusion:

Staying Close and Letting Go

As babies become toddlers and begin to assert their need to establish an autonomous sphere of action, parents learn to face their own limitations in nurturing and protecting their child. The fantasy that the parents' physical and emotional presence is enough to keep the child safe and content gives way to the realization that there are disappointments, challenges, and even dangers that we are helpless to wish away.

The desire to do well by our children goes hand in hand with the inevitability—even the usefulness—of failing them sometimes.

Many knowledgeable and well-meaning parents have tried to anticipate every sorrow and put into words each nuance of what the child is thinking and feeling in the belief that this would prevent loneliness and fear. In the process, they may rob their child of the experience of struggling with inner uncertainties and coming up triumphantly with very personal insights and solutions. By injecting themselves excessively into their children's inner life, parents may deprive them of the opportunity to develop selves of their own.

Not until adolescence will parents face as many dilemmas in raising their children as they do in the toddler years. In fact, the second and third years of life are excellent practice for the challenges posed by a teenager. Toddlerhood resembles adolescence because of the rapidity of physical growth and because of the impulse to break loose of parental boundaries. At both ages, the struggle for independence exists hand in hand with the often hidden wish to be contained and protected while striving to move forward in the world. How parents and toddlers negotiate their differences sets the stage for their ability to remain partners during childhood and through the rebellions of the teenage years.

Toddlers, like adolescents, need to forge an identity that integrates a solid sense of personal initiative with a reliable feeling of communal belonging. Parents are faced in both periods with the task of deciding when to respect aloneness, when to offer companionship, and when to exercise firm authority. When the parents' choice is responsive to the child's needs, the negativism of toddlers becomes the self-assured assertiveness of the preschool years, just as the emotional storms of adolescence resolve themselves in the self-worth of young adulthood.

Communication is important in growing up, but so is the chance to think and feel on one's own. Letting the child be is at times just as important as being with him or her. The lifelong lesson of the toddler years involves learning that sometimes letting go—within limits—is the surest way of staying close.

References

Chapter 1: The Emotional Importance of Early Relationships

1. Bowlby, J. (1969) *Attachment and Loss, Vol. 1: Attachment.* New York: Basic Books.
2. Ainsworth, M. D. S., M. C. Blehar, E. Waters, and S. N. Wall. (1978) *Patterns of Attachment: A Psychological Study of the Strange Situation.* Hillsdale, NJ: Lawrence Erlbaum Associates.
3. Powell, B., G. Cooper, K. Hoffman, and B. Marvin. (2014) *The Circle of Security Intervention: Enhancing Attachment in Early Parent-Child Relationships.* New York: Guilford.
4. Lamb, M. E., ed. (2010) *The Role of the Father in Child Development,* 5th ed. Hoboken, NJ: John Wiley & Sons.
5. Boldt, L. J., G. Kochanska, J. E. Yoon, and J. Koening Nordling. (June 2014) Children's attachment to both parents from toddler age to middle childhood: links to adaptive and maladaptive outcomes. *Attachment & Human Development* 16(3): 211–29.
6. Kochanska, G., and S. Kim. (January 2013) Early attachment organization with both parents and future behavior problems: from infancy to middle childhood. *Child Development* 84(1): 283–96.
7. McHale, J., and E. Fivaz-Depeursinge. (2010) Principles of effective co-parenting and its assessment in infancy and early childhood. In *Parenthood and Mental Health: A Bridge Between Infant and Adult Psychiatry,* eds. S. Tyano, M. Keren, H. Herrman, and J. Cox. Chichester, UK: Wiley-Blackwell, 383–97.
8. *Lesbian & Gay Parenting* (2005) Washington, DC: American Psychological Association.
9. Farr, R. H., S. L. Forssell, and C. J. Patterson. (2010) Parenting and child development in adoptive families: does parental sexual orientation matter? *Applied Developmental Science* 14(3): 164–78.
10. Burt, T., A. Gelnaw, and L. K. Lesser. (January 2010) Do no harm: cre-

ating welcoming and inclusive environments for lesbian, gay, bisexual, and transgender (LGBT) families in early childhood settings. National Association for the Education of Young Children. https://www.naeyc .org/files/yc/file/201001/LesserWeb0110.pdf.

11. Harris, R. H. (2012) *Who's in My Family?: All About Our Families.* Somerville, MA: Candlewick Press.

Chapter 2: Who Is the Toddler?

1. Kierkegaard, S. (1938) *Purity of Heart Is to Will One Thing: Spiritual Preparation for the Feast of Confession.* New York: Harper Brothers.
2. Center on the Developing Child at Harvard University. (2017) Brain Architecture. http://developingchild.harvard.edu/science-key-concepts/ brain-architecture.
3. Grall, T. S. (December 2011) *Custodial Mothers and Fathers and Their Child Support: 2009.* US Census Bureau, Current Population Reports. https://www.census.gov/content/dam/Census/library/publications/2011 /demo/p60-240.pdf.
4. Center on the Developing Child at Harvard University. (2007) *In Brief: The Impact of Early Adversity on Children's Development.* http://developingchild .harvard.edu/resources/inbrief-the-impact-of-early-adversity-on-child-rens-development.
5. Zero to Three. (2016) Policy & Advocacy (2016) *The Impact of Early Adversity on Child Development.* zerotothree.org/policy-and-advocacy.
6. Ainsworth, M. D. S., M. C. Blehar, E. Waters, and S. N. Wall. (1978) *Patterns of Attachment: A Psychological Study of the Strange Situation.* Hillsdale, NJ: Lawrence Erlbaum Associates..
7. Bowlby, J. (1982) *Attachment and Loss, Vol. 1: Attachment,* 2nd ed. New York: Basic Books.
8. Bowlby, J. (1973) *Attachment and Loss, Vol. 2: Separation: Anxiety and Anger.* New York: Basic Books.
9. Uematsu, A., M. Matsui, C. Tanaka, T. Takahashi, K. Noguchi, M. Suzuki, and H. Nishijo. (October 2012) Developmental trajectories of amygdala and hippocampus from infancy to early adulthood in healthy individuals. *PLoS ONE* 7(10): e46970.
10. Gunnar, M., and K. Quevedo. (2007) The neurobiology of stress and development. *Annual Review of Psychology* 58: 145–73.
11. Buss, K. A., R. J. Davidson, N. H. Kalin, and H. H. Goldsmith. (July 2004) Context-specific freezing and associated physiological reactivity as a dysregulated fear response. *Developmental Psychology* 40(4): 583–94.
12. Anderson, J. W. (1972) Attachment behaviour out of doors. In *Ethological*

Studies of Child Behaviour, ed. N. Blurton Jones. Cambridge, UK: Cambridge University Press, 199–216.

13. Slade, A. (June 2014) Imagining fear: attachment, threat, and psychic experience. *Psychoanalytic Dialogues* 24(3): 253–66.
14. Erikson, E. (1950) *Childhood and Society.* New York: W. W. Norton.
15. Mahler, M. S., F. Pine, and A. Bergman. (1975) *The Psychological Birth of the Human Infant: Symbiosis and Individuation.* New York: Basic Books.
16. Grall. *Custodial Mothers and Fathers.*
17. Mahler et al. *The Psychological Birth of the Human Infant.*
18. Marvin, R. S. (1977) An ethological-cognitive model for the attenuation of mother-child attachment behavior. In *Attachment Behavior: Advances in the Study of Communication and Affect, Vol. 3*, eds. T. Alloway, P. Pliner, and L. Kramer. New York: Plenum, 25–60.
19. Brazelton, T. B. (1989) *Toddlers and Parents: A Declaration of Independence*, rev. ed. New York: Delacorte/Seymour Lawrence.
20. Lewis, M., and J. Brooks-Gunn. (1979) *Social Cognition and the Acquisition of Self.* New York: Plenum.
21. Tronick, E. Z., and J. F. Cohn. (February 1989) Infant-mother face-to-face interaction: age and gender differences in coordination and the occurrence of miscoordination. *Child Development* 60(1): 85–92.
22. Lewis, M. (2000) Self-conscious emotions: embarrassment, pride, shame, and guilt. In *Handbook of Emotions*, 2nd ed., eds. M. Lewis and J. M. Haviland-Jones. New York: Guilford, 623–36.
23. Barrett, K. C., C. Zahn-Waxler, and P. M. Cole. (1993) Avoiders vs. amenders: implications for the investigation of guilt and shame during toddlerhood? *Cognition and Emotion* 7(6): 481–505.
24. Furman, E. (1992) *Toddlers and Their Mothers: A Study in Early Personality Development.* Madison, CT: International Universities Press.
25. Chukovsky, K. (1963) *From Two to Five*, trans. M. Morton. Berkeley: University of California Press.

Chapter 3: The Challenges of Being (and Raising) a Toddler

1. Patterson, G. R., and E. E. MacCoby. (1980) Mothers: the unacknowledged victims. *Monographs of the Society for Research in Child Development* 45(5): 1–64.
2. Fawl, C. L. (1963) Disturbances experienced by children in their natural habitat. In *The Stream of Behavior: Explorations of Its Structure and Content*, eds. R. G. Barker and L. S. Barker. New York: Appleton-Century-Crofts.

3. Minton, C., J. Kagan, and J. A. Levine. (December 1971) Maternal control and obedience in the two-year-old. *Child Development* 42(6): 1873–94.

4. Forehand, R., H. E. King, S. Peed, and P. Yoder. (June 1975) Mother-child interactions: comparison of a noncompliant clinic group and a non-clinic group. *Behaviour Research and Therapy* 13(2–3): 79–84.

5. Fawl. Disturbances experienced.

6. Patterson and MacCoby. Mothers.

7. Dix, T., A. D. Stewart, and E. T. Gershoff. (July/August 2007) Autonomy and children's reactions to being controlled: evidence that both compliance and defiance may be positive markers in early development. *Child Development* 78(4): 1204–21.

8. Craig, L., and M. Bittman. (January 2004) The effect of children on adults' time-use: analysis of the incremental time costs of children in Australia. Paper presented at the Conference on Cross National Comparisons of Expenditures on Children, Princeton University, Princeton, NJ.

9. Craig, L. (January 2005) How do they do it? A time-diary analysis of how working mothers find time for the kids. *Social Policy Research Centre Discussion Papers, no. 136*, 21.

10. Siegel, D. J., and M. Hartzell. (2003) *Parenting from the Inside Out: How a Deeper Self-Understanding Can Help You Raise Children Who Thrive.* New York: Jeremy P. Tarcher/Putnam.

11. Fraiberg, S. (1959) *The Magic Years: Understanding and Handling the Problems of Early Childhood.* New York: Scribner.

12. Woodhouse, S. S., J. R. S. Beeney, A. E. Doub, and J. Cassidy. Secure base provision: a new approach to links between maternal caregiving and attachment. Manuscript under review.

13. Bowlby, J. (1982) *Attachment and Loss. Vol. 1: Attachment*, 2nd ed. New York: Basic Books.

14. Lecuyer, E., and G. M. Houck. (July/August 2006) Maternal limit-setting in toddlerhood: socialization strategies for the development of self-regulation. *Infant Mental Health Journal* 27(4): 344–70.

15. Greenspan, S. (1989) *The Essential Partnership: How Parents and Children Can Meet the Emotional Challenges of Infancy and Childhood.* New York: Viking.

16. Stern, D. N. (1985) *The Interpersonal World of the Infant: A View from Psychoanalysis and Developmental Psychology.* New York: Basic Books.

17. Letter from Kevin Frank, quoted in Murphy, L. B. (December 1988) When a child is inconsolable: stay near. *Zero to Three, Bulletin of the National Center for Clinical Infant Programs* 9(2): 15.

18. Bowlby, J. (1988) *A Secure Base: Parent-Child Attachment and Healthy Human Development.* New York: Basic Books.

19. Lieberman, A. F., P. Van Horn, and C. G. Ippen. (December 2005) Toward evidence-based treatment: child-parent psychotherapy with preschoolers

exposed to marital violence. *Journal of the American Academy of Child & Adolescent Psychiatry* 44(12): 1241–48.

Chapter 4: The Question of Temperament

1. Brazelton, T. B. (1969) *Infants and Mothers: Differences in Development.* New York: Delacorte/Seymour Lawrence.
2. Brazelton, T. B. (1973) The neonatal behavioral assessment scale. *Clinics in Developmental Medicine* no. 50. https://www.abebooks.com/Neonatal-Behavioral-Assessment-Scale.
3. Thomas, A., S. Chess, and H. Birch. (1968) *Temperament and Behavior Disorders in Children.* New York: New York University Press.
4. Stern, D. N. (1985) *The Interpersonal World of the Infant: A View from Psychoanalysis and Developmental Psychology.* New York: Basic Books.
5. Goldsmith, H. H., A. H. Buss, R. Plomin, M. K. Rothbart, A. Thomas, S. Chess, R. A. Hinde, and R. B. McCall. (April 1987) Roundtable: what is temperament? *Child Development* 58: 505–29.
6. Thomas et al. *Temperament and Behavior Disorders in Children.*
7. Ibid.
8. Thomas, A., and S. Chess. (1977) *Temperament and Development.* New York: Brunner/Mazel.
9. Thomas, A., and S. Chess. (1980) *The Dynamics of Psychological Development.* New York: Brunner/Mazel.
10. Chess, S., and A. Thomas. (1984) *Origins and Evolution of Behavior Disorders: From Infancy to Early Adult Life.* New York: Brunner/Mazel.
11. Brazelton, T. B. (1973) Neonatal behavioral assessment.
12. Escalona, S. (1968) *The Roots of Individuality: Normal Patterns of Development in Infancy.* Chicago: Aldine.
13. Greenspan, S. (1989) *The Essential Partnership: How Parents and Children Can Meet the Challenges of Infancy and Childhood.* New York: Viking.
14. Fox, N. A., H. A. Henderson, K. H. Rubin, S. D. Calkins, and L. A. Schmidt. (January–February 2001) Continuity and discontinuity of behavioral inhibition and exuberance: psychophysiological and behavioral influence across the first four years of life. *Child Development* 72(1): 1–21.
15. Kagan, J., N. Snidman, M. McManis, and S. Woodward. (December 2001) Temperamental contributions to the affect family of anxiety. *Psychiatric Clinics of North America* 24(4): 677–88.
16. Erikson, E. (1950) *Childhood and Society.* New York: W. W. Norton.
17. Thomas et al. *Temperament and Behavior Disorders in Children.*
18. Thomas and Chess. *Temperament and Development.*
19. Thomas and Chess. *The Dynamics of Psychological Development.*

20. Chess and Thomas. *Origins and Evolution of Behavior Disorders.*
21. Crockenberg, S. B. (September 1981) Infant irritability, mother responsiveness, and social support influences on the security of infant-mother attachment. *Child Development* 52(3): 857–65.
22. Gandour, M. J. (October 1989) Activity level as a dimension of temperament in toddlers: its relevance for the organismic specificity hypothesis. *Child Development* 60(5): 1092–98.
23. Parmar, P., S. Harkness, and C. M. Super. (2004) Asian and Euro-American parents' ethnotheories of play and learning: effects on preschool children's home routines and school behaviour. *International Journal of Behavioral Development* 28(2): 97–104.
24. Ghosh Ippen, C. M. (2012) The sociocultural context of infant mental health: toward contextually congruent interventions. In *Handbook of Infant Mental Health*, 3rd ed., ed. C. H. Zeanah. New York: Guilford, 104–19.
25. Bush, N. R., and W. T. Boyce. (2016) Differential sensitivity to context: implications for developmental psychopathology. In *Developmental Psychopathology, Vol. 2: Development Neuroscience*, 3rd ed., ed. D. Cicchetti. Hoboken, NJ: John Wiley & Sons, 107–37.

Chapter 5: High-Activity Toddlers: Racing Ahead

1. Provence, S., and R. C. Lipton. (1962) *Infants in Institutions: A Comparison of Their Development and Family-Reared Infants During the First Year of Life.* Madison, CT: International Universities Press.
2. Lieberman, A. F., and J. H. Pawl. (1988) Clinical applications of attachment theory. In *Clinical Implications of Attachment*, eds. J. Belsky and T. Nezworski. Hillsdale, NJ: Lawrence Erlbaum Associates, 327–51.
3. Fraiberg, S. (1959) *The Magic Years: Understanding and Handling the Problems of Early Childhood.* New York: Scribner.
4. *Flexible, Fearful or Feisty: The Different Temperaments of Infants and Toddlers* (video, written by David Donnefield). (1979) Sausalito, CA: State Department of Education, Center for Child and Family Studies, Far West Laboratory for Educational Research and Development.
5. Parens, H. (1994) *The Development of Aggression in Early Childhood.* Northvale, NJ: Jason Aronson.

Chapter 6: Slow-to-Warm-Up Toddlers: Taking One's Time

1. Kagan, J., and N. Snidman. (August 1991) Temperamental factors in human development. *American Psychologist* 46(8): 856–62.

2. Ibid.

3. Kagan, J., J. S. Reznick, and N. Snidman. (December 1987) The physiology and psychology of behavioral inhibition in children. *Child Development* 58(6): 1459–73.

4. Henderson, H. A., D. S. Pine, and N. A. Fox. (January 2015) Behavioral inhibition and developmental risk: a dual-processing perspective. *Neuropsychopharmacology* 40(1): 207–24.

5. Kagan, J., and H. A. Moss. (1962) *Birth to Maturity: A Study in Psychological Development.* Hoboken, NJ: John Wiley & Sons.

6. Kagan, J., J. S. Reznick, N. Snidman, J. Gibbons, and M. D. Johnson. (December 1988) Childhood derivatives of inhibition and lack of inhibition to the unfamiliar. *Child Development* 59(6): 1580–89.

7. Kagan, J., and N. Snidman. (1991) Infant predictors of inhibited and uninhibited profiles. *Psychological Science* 2(1): 40–44.

8. Kagan, J. (Winter 1991) The shy and the sociable. *Harvard Alumni Magazine.*

9. Chen, X., P. D. Hastings, K. H. Rubin, H. Chen, G. Cen, and S. L. Stewart. (July 1998) Child-rearing attitudes and behavioral inhibition in Chinese and Canadian toddlers: a cross-cultural study. *Developmental Psychology* 34(4): 677–86.

10. *Flexible, Fearful or Feisty: The Different Temperaments of Infants and Toddlers* (video, written by David Donnefield). (1979) Sausalito, CA: State Department of Education, Center for Child and Family Studies, Far West Laboratory for Educational Research and Development.

11. Helfinstein, S. M., N. A. Fox, and D. S. Pine. (May 2012) Approach-withdrawal and the role of the striatum in the temperament of behavioral inhibition. *Developmental Psychology* 48(3): 815–26.

Chapter 7: Early Anxieties

1. Larson, G. (1993) *The Far Side Gallery 4.* Kansas City, MO: Andrews McMeel.

2. Fraiberg, S. *The Magic Years: Understanding and Handling the Problems of Early Childhood.* New York: Scribner.

3. Bowlby, J. (1973) *Attachment and Loss, Vol. 2: Separation: Anxiety and Anger.* New York: Basic Books.

4. Humphrey, T. (1970) The development of human fetal activity and its relation to postnatal behavior. In *Advances in Child Development and Behavior,* vol. 5, eds. H. W. Reese and L. P. Lipsitt. New York: Academic Press, 1–57.

5. Field, T. (1990) *Infancy.* Cambridge, MA: Harvard University Press.

6. Humphrey. The development of human fetal activity and its relation to postnatal behavior.

7. Stern, D. N. (July 1971) A micro-analysis of mother-infant interaction: behavior regulating social contact between a mother and her 3½-month-old twins. *Journal of the American Academy of Child & Adolescent Psychiatry* 10(3): 501–16.

8. Ainsworth, M. D. S., M. C. Blehar, E. Waters, and S. N. Wall. (1978) *Patterns of Attachment: A Psychological Study of the Strange Situation.* Hillsdale, NJ: Lawrence Erlbaum Associates.

9. Graves, P. L. (1980) The functioning fetus. In *The Course of Life: Psychoanalytic Contributions Toward Understanding Personality Development, Vol. 1: Infancy and Early Childhood,* eds. S. I. Greenspan and G. H. Pollock. Washington, DC: US Government Printing Office, 235–56.

10. Ibid.

11. DeCasper, A. J., and W. P. Fifer. (June 6, 1980) Of human bonding: newborns prefer their mothers' voices. *Science* 208(4,448): 1174–76.

12. Field. *Infancy.*

13. Macfarlane, J. A. (1975) Olfaction in the development of social preferences in the human neonate. In *Parent-Infant Interaction.* Ciba Foundation Symposium 33. Amsterdam: Elsevier, 103–18.

14. Sander, L. W. (January 1962) Issues in early mother-child interaction. *Journal of the American Academy of Child & Adolescent Psychiatry* 1(1): 141–66.

15. Greenspan, S. I., and N. T. Greenspan. (1985) *First Feelings: Milestones in the Emotional Development of Your Baby and Child.* New York: Penguin.

16. Bell, S. M., and M. D. S. Ainsworth. (December 1972) Infant crying and maternal responsiveness. *Child Development* 43(4): 1171–90.

17. Ainsworth et al. *Patterns of Attachment.*

18. Winnicott, D. W. (1965) *The Maturational Process and the Facilitating Environment: Studies in the Theory of Emotional Development.* Madison, CT: International Universities Press.

19. Parke, R. D., and R. Buriel. (2006) Socialization in the family: ethnic and ecological perspectives. In *Handbook of Child Psychology: Social, Emotional, and Personality Development,* vol. 3, eds. N. Eisenberg, W. Damon, and R. M. Lerner. Hoboken, NJ: John Wiley & Sons, 429–504.

20. Lamb, M. E. (1997) Fathers and child development: an introductory overview and guide. In *The Role of the Father in Child Development,* 3rd ed., ed. M. E. Lamb. Hoboken, NJ: John Wiley & Sons, 1–18, 309–13.

21. Parke, R. D. (2002) Fathers and families. In *Handbook of Parenting, Vol. 3: Being and Becoming a Parent,* ed. M. H. Bornstein. Hillsdale, NJ: Lawrence Erlbaum Associates, 27–73.

22. Pruett, K. D. (1987) *The Nurturing Father: Journey Toward the Complete Man.* New York: Warner Books.

23. Dixon, S., M. Yogman, E. Tronick, L. Adamson, H. Als, and T. B. Brazelton. (Winter 1981) Early infant social interaction with parents and strangers. *Journal of the American Academy of Child & Adolescent Psychiatry* 20(1): 32–52.

24. Main, M., and D. R. Weston. (September 1981) The quality of the toddler's relationship to mother and to father: related to conflict behavior and the readiness to establish new relationships. *Child Development* 52: 932–40.

25. Main, M., N. Kaplan, and J. Cassidy. (1985) Security in infancy, childhood, and adulthood: a move to the level of representation. In *Growing Points of Attachment Theory and Research,* eds. I. Bretherton and E. Waters. *Monographs of the Society for Research in Child Development* 50(1/2): 66–104.

26. Roiphe, H., and E. Galenson. (1981) *Infantile Origins of Sexual Identity.* Madison, CT: International Universities Press.

27. Lozoff, B., G. M. Brittenham, M. A. Trause, J. H. Kennell, and M. H. Klaus. (July 1977) The mother-newborn relationship: limits of adaptability. *Journal of Pediatrics* 91(1): 1–12.

28. Erikson, E. (1950) *Childhood and Society.* New York: W. W. Norton.

29. U.S. Department of Health and Human Services, Administration for Children, Youth, and Families. (2009) *Child Maltreatment 2007.* Washington, DC: US Government Printing Office.

30. Fantuzzo, J., and R. Fusco. (October 2007) Children's direct exposure to types of domestic violence crime: a population-based investigation. *Journal of Family Violence* 22(7): 543–52.

31. Grossman, D. C. (Spring/Summer 2000) The history of injury control and the epidemiology of child and adolescent injuries. *Future of Children: Unintentional Injuries in Childhood* 10(1): 23–52.

32. Fraiberg, S. (1982) Pathological defenses in infancy. *Psychoanalytic Quarterly* 51(4): 612–35.

33. Tremblay, R. (2003) Why socialization fails: the case of chronic physical aggression. In *Causes of Conduct Disorder and Juvenile Delinquency,* eds. B. B. Lahey, T. E. Moffitt, and A. Caspi. New York: Guilford, 182–225.

34. Dix, T., A. D. Stewart, and E. T. Gershoff. (July/August 2007) Autonomy and children's reactions to being controlled: evidence that both compliance and defiance may be positive markers in early development. *Child Development* 78(4): 120–21.

35. Bowlby. *Attachment and Loss, Vol. 2: Separation.*

36. Ibid.

37. Baillargeon, R. H., C. L. Normand, J. R. Séguin, M. Zoccolillo, C. Japel, D. Pérusse, H. X. Wu, M. Boivin, and R. E. Tremblay. (January 2007) The

evolution of problem and social competence behaviors during toddler-hood: a prospective population-based cohort study. *Infant Mental Health Journal* 28(1): 12–38.

38. Carter, A., M. Briggs-Gowan, K. McCarthy, and L. Wakschlag. (April 2009) Developmental patterns of normative misbehavior in early child-hood: implications for identification of early disruptive behavior. Paper to be presented in the symposium. In *The Evolution of Disruptive Behavior Problems in Young Children,* ed. R. Baillargeon. Meetings of the Society for Research in Child Development, Denver.

39. NICHD Early Child Care Research Network and W. F. Arsenio (2004) Trajectories of physical aggression from toddlerhood to middle child-hood: predictors, correlates, and outcomes. *Monographs of the Society for Research in Child Development* 69(4): 1–143.

40. Tremblay, R. E., D. S. Nagin, J. R. Séguin, M. Zoccolillo, P. D. Zelazo, M. Boivin, D. Pérusse, and C. Japel. (July 2004) Physical aggression during early childhood: trajectories and predictors. *Pediatrics* 114(1): 43–50.

41. Fraiberg. Pathological defenses in infancy.

42. Einon, D., and M. Potegal. (1994) Temper tantrums in young children. In *The Dynamics of Aggression: Biological and Social Processes in Dyads and Groups,* eds. M. Potegal and J. F. Knutson. Hillsdale, NJ: Lawrence Erlbaum Associates, 157–94.

43. Carter, et al. Developmental patterns of normative misbehavior in early childhood.

44. Wakschlag, L. S., and B. Danis. (2009) Characterizing early childhood dis-ruptive behavior: enhancing developmental sensitivity. In *Handbook of Infant Mental Health,* 3rd ed., ed. C. H. Zeanah. New York: Guilford, 392–408.

45. Fraiberg. Pathological defenses in infancy.

46. Lieberman, A. F. (1985) Infant mental health: a model for service deliv-ery. *Journal of Clinical Child Psychology* 14(3): 196–201.

47. Lieberman, A. F., D. R. Weston, and J. H. Pawl. (February 1991) Preven-tive intervention and outcome with anxiously attached dyads. *Child De-velopment* 62(1): 199–209.

48. Lieberman, A. F., C. Ghosh Ippen, and P. Van Horn. (2015) *Don't Hit My Mommy!: A Manual for Child-Parent Psychotherapy with Young Children Exposed to Violence and Other Trauma.* Washington, DC: Zero to Three.

49. Ainsworth, et al. *Patterns of Attachment.*

50. Sroufe, L. A., B. Egeland, E. A. Carlson, and W. A. Collins. (2005) *The Development of the Person: The Minnesota Study of Risk and Adaptation from Birth to Adulthood.* New York: Guilford.

51. Matas, L., R. A. Arend, and L. A. Sroufe. (September 1978) Continuity of adaptation in the second year: the relationship between quality of attach-ment and later competence. *Child Development* 49(3): 547–56.

52. Sroufe, L. A. (1983) Infant-caregiver attachment and patterns of adaptation in preschool: the roots of maladaptation and competence. In *Minnesota Symposium in Child Psychology* 16, ed. M. Perlmutter. Hillsdale, NJ: Lawrence Erlbaum Associates.

53. Arend, R., F. L. Grove, and L. A. Sroufe. (December 1979) Continuity of individual adaptation from infancy to kindergarten: a predictive study of ego-resiliency and curiosity in preschoolers. *Child Development* 50(4): 950–59.

54. Lewis, M., C. Feiring, C. McGuffog, and J. Jaskir. (February 1984) Predicting psychopathology in six-year-olds from early social relations. *Child Development* 55(1): 123–36.

Chapter 8: Issues to Negotiate

1. Bowlby, J. (1973) *Attachment and Loss, Vol. 2: Separation: Anxiety and Anger.* New York: Basic Books.

2. Fraiberg, S. (1959) *The Magic Years: Understanding and Handling the Problems of Early Childhood.* New York: Scribner.

3. Brazelton, T. B. (1977) *Toddlers and Parents: A Declaration of Independence.* New York: Bantam/Doubleday.

4. Kagan, J. (1981) *The Second Year: The Emergence of Self-Awareness.* Cambridge, MA: Harvard University Press.

5. Brazelton. *Toddlers and Parents.*

6. Owens, J., and M. M. Burnbaum. Sleep disorders. In *Handbook of Infant Mental Health,* 3rd ed., ed. C. H. Zeanah. New York: Guilford, 362–76.

7. Ibid.

8. Daws, D. (1989) *Through the Night: Helping Parents and Sleepless Infants.* London: Free Association Books.

9. Minde, K., K. Popiel, N. Leos, S. Falkner, K. Parker, and M. Handley-Derry. (May 1993) The evaluation and treatment of sleep disturbances in young children. *Journal of Child Psychology and Psychiatry* 34(4): 521–33.

10. Guilleminault, C. (1987) Disorders of arousal in children: somnambulism and night terrors. In *Sleep and Its Disorders in Children,* ed. C. Guilleminault. New York: Raven Press, 243–52.

11. Devaney, B., P. Ziegler, S. Pac, V. Karwe, and S. I. Barr. (January 2004) Nutrient intakes of infants and toddlers. *Journal of the American Dietetic Association* 104(1): s14–21.

12. Carruth, B. R., P. J. Ziegler, A. Gordon, and S. I. Barr. (January 2004) Prevalence of picky eaters among infants and toddlers and their caregivers' decisions about offering a new food. *Journal of the American Dietetic Association* 104(1): s57–64.

13. Milano, K. (September 2007) Prevention: the first line of defense against childhood obesity. *Zero to Three Journal* 28(1): 6–11.

14. Johnson, S. L. (December 2000) Improving preschoolers' self-regulation of energy intake. *Pediatrics* 106(6): 1429–35.

15. Galloway, A., L. Fiorito, Y. Lee, and L. Birch. (April 2005) Parental pressure, dietary patterns, and weight status among girls who are "picky eaters." *Journal of the American Dietetic Association* 105(4): 541–48.

16. Johnson. Improving preschoolers' self-regulation of energy intake.

17. Gillman, M., S. L. Rifas-Shiman, A. L. Frazier, H. R. Rockett, C. A. Camargo Jr., A. E. Field, C. S. Berkey, and G. A. Colditz. (March 2000) Family dinner and diet quality among older children and adolescents. *Archives of Family Medicine* 9(3): 235–40.

18. Hart, S., and H. Carrington (July 2002) Jealousy in 6-month-old infants. *Infancy* 3(3): 395–402.

19. Buss, D. M. (2000) *The Dangerous Passion: Why Jealousy Is as Necessary as Love and Sex*. New York: Free Press.

20. The National Child Traumatic Stress Network (2016) Types of Traumatic Stress. https://www.nctsn.org/trauma-types.

21. Ibid.

22. Scheeringa, M. S. (2009) Post-traumatic stress disorder. In *Handbook of Infant Mental Health*, 3rd ed., ed. C. H. Zeanah. New York: Guilford, 345–61.

23. Lieberman, A. F., and P. Van Horn. (2008) *Psychotherapy with Infants and Young Children: Repairing the Effects of Stress and Trauma on Early Attachment*. New York: Guilford.

24. Lieberman, A. F., C. Ghosh Ippen, and P. Van Horn. (2015) *Don't Hit My Mommy!: A Manual for Child-Parent Psychotherapy with Young Children Exposed to Violence and Other Trauma*. Washington, DC: Zero to Three.

25. Blum-Ross, A., and S. Livingstone. (July 2016) Families and screen time: current advice and emerging research. London School of Economics Media Policy Brief 17.

26. Zero to Three. (March 2016) *Tips for Using Screen Media with Young Children*. https://www.zerotothree.org/resources/386-tips-for-using-screen-media-with-young-children.

Chapter 9: When Parents Divorce

1. Hetherington, E. M. (May 2003) Social support and the adjustment of children in divorced and remarried families. *Childhood* 10(2): 217–36.

2. Piaget, J. (1959) *The Language and Thought of the Child*. London: Routledge and Kegan Paul.

3. Macfarlane, J. A. (1975) Olfaction in the development of social prefer-

ences in the human neonate. In *Parent-Infant Interaction*. Ciba Foundation Symposium 33. Amsterdam: Elsevier, 103–18.

4. DeCasper, A. J., and W. P. Fifer. (June 6, 1980) Of human bonding: newborns prefer their mothers' voices. *Science* 208(4,448): 1174–76.

5. Fagan, J. F. (December 1973) Infants' delayed recognition memory and forgetting. *Journal of Experimental Child Psychology* 16(3): 424–50.

6. Nachman, P., and D. N. Stern. (1983) Recall memory for emotional experience in pre-linguistic infants. Paper presented at the National Clinical Infancy Fellows Conference, Yale University, New Haven, CT.

7. Grall, T. S. (December 2011) *Custodial Mothers and Fathers and Their Child Support: 2009*. US Census Bureau, Current Population Reports.

8. Ibid.

9. DeCasper, et al. Of human bonding.

10. Bretherton, I., and T. F. Page. (Summer 2004) Shared or conflicting working models? Relationships in postdivorce families seen through the eyes of mothers and their preschool children. *Development and Psychopathology* 16(3), 551–76.

11. Grall. *Custodial Mothers and Fathers and Their Child Support*.

12. Thompson, R., M. E. Lamp, and D. Estes. (February 1982) Stability of infant-mother attachment and its relationship to changing life circumstances in an unselected middle-class sample. *Child Development* 53(1): 144–48.

13. Lieberman, A. F., D. R. Weston, and J. H. Pawl. (February 1991) Preventive intervention and outcome with anxiously attached dyads. *Child Development* 62(1): 199–209.

14. Herzog, J. M. (1980) Sleep disturbance and father hunger in 19- to 28-month-old boys: the Erlkönig syndrome. *The Psychoanalytic Study of the Child* 35: 219–36.

15. McHale, J. P. (2010) Shared child rearing in nuclear, fragile, and kinship family systems: evolution, dilemmas, and promise of a coparenting framework. In *Strengthening Couple Relationships for Optimal Child Development: Lessons from Research and Intervention*, eds. M. S. Schulz, M. K. Pruett, P. K. Kerig, and R. D. Parke. Washington, DC: American Psychological Association, 77–94.

16. Lieberman, A. F., C. Ghosh Ippen, and P. Van Horn. (2015) *Don't Hit My Mommy!: A Manual for Child-Parent Psychotherapy with Young Children Exposed to Violence and Other Trauma*. Washington, DC: Zero to Three.

Chapter 10: The Toddler in Child Care

1. Provence, S. (1986) Presentation at the Symposium on Early Infant and Toddler Care, San Francisco Psychoanalytic Institute Extension Division, San Francisco.

2. Provence, S., A. Naylor, and J. Patterson. (1977) *The Challenge of Daycare.* New Haven: Yale University Press.

3. Kalmanson, B. (1990) Understanding responses to separation. In *Psychosocial Issues in Day Care*, ed. S. Chehrazi. Washington, DC: American Psychiatric Publishing, 159–75.

4. Pawl, J. H. (February 1990) Infants in daycare: reflections on experiences, expectations and relationships. *Zero to Three, Bulletin of the National Center for Clinical Infant Programs* 10(3): 1–28.

5. Provence et al. *The Challenge of Daycare*, 104.

6. Roemer, J. (1989) *Two to Four from 9 to 5: The Adventures of a Daycare Provider.* New York: Harper & Row.

7. Lally, J. R., ed. (1990) *Infant/Toddler Caregiving: A Guide to Social-Emotional Growth and Socialization.* Sacramento: California Department of Education.

8. Howes, C. (January–March 1983) Caregiver behavior in center and family day care. *Journal of Applied Developmental Psychology* 4(1): 99–107.

9. Howes, C. (October 1985) Sharing fantasy: social pretend play in toddlers. *Child Development* 56(5): 1253–58.

10. Nachman, P. A. (1990) A companion study of toddlers cared for by mother or by substitute caregivers. In *Psychosocial Issues in Day Care*, ed. S. Chehrazi. Washington, DC: American Psychiatric Publishing, 147–58.

11. Howes, C. (September 1987) Social competence with peers in young children: developmental sequences. *Developmental Review* 7(3): 252–72.

12. Ibid.

13. Howes, C., C. Rodning, D. C. Galluzzo, and L. Myers. (1990) Attachment and child care: relationships with mother and caregiver. In *Infant Day Care: The Current Debate*, eds. N. Fox and G. G. Fein. Norwood, NJ: Ablex, 169–82.

14. Belsky, J. (1990) The "effects" of infant day care reconsidered. In *Infant Day Care: The Current Debate*, eds. N. Fox and G. G. Fein. Norwood, NJ: Ablex, 3–40.

15. Clarke-Steward, K. A. (1990) "The 'effects' of infant day care reconsidered" reconsidered: risks for parents, children, and researchers. In *Infant Day Care: The Current Debate*, eds. N. Fox and G. G. Fein. Norwood, NJ: Ablex, 61–86.

16. Thompson, R. A. (1990) The effects of infant day care through the prism of attachment theory: a critical appraisal. In *Infant Day Care: The Current Debate*, eds. N. Fox and G. G. Fein. Norwood, NJ: Ablex, 41–50.

17. Sroufe, L. A. (1990) A developmental perspective on day care. In *Infant Day Care: The Current Debate*, eds. N. Fox and G. G. Fein. Norwood, NJ: Ablex, 51–59.

18. Laughlin, L. (October 2011) *Maternity Leave and Employment Patterns of*

First-Time Mothers 1961-2008: Household Economic Studies. US Census Bureau, Current Population Reports.

19. Howes, C. (1990) Current research on early day care. In *Psychosocial Issues in Day Care*, ed. S. Chehrazi. Washington, DC: American Psychiatric Press, 21–36.

20. Phillips, D. A., and A. E. Lowenstein. (2011) Early care, education, and child development. *Annual Review of Psychology* 62: 483–500.

21. Berk, L. E. (June 1985) Relationship of caregiver education to child-oriented attitudes, job satisfaction, and behaviors toward children. *Child Care Quarterly* 14(2): 103–29.

22. Howes. Current research on early day care.

23. Phillips and Lowenstein. Early care, education, and child development.

24. Whitebook, M., D. Phillips, and C. Howes. (2014) *Worthy Work, STILL Unlivable Wages: The Early Childhood Workforce 25 Years After the National Child Care Staffing Study.* Berkeley: Center for the Study of Child Care Employment, University of California.

25. National Institute of Child Health and Human Development (NICHD). (January 2006) *The NICHD Study of Early Child Care and Youth Development.* NIH publication no. 05–4318.

26. Whitebook et al. *Worthy Work, STILL Unlivable Wages.*

27. NICHD. *The NICHD Study of Early Child Care and Youth Development.*

28. Gould, E. (November 5, 2015) Child care workers aren't paid enough to make ends meet, Economic Policy Institute. Issue Brief 405.

Illustration Credits

Index

About the Author

Alicia F. Lieberman, PhD, is Irving B. Harris Endowed Chair in Infant Mental Health and professor in the department of psychiatry at the University of California, San Francisco. The author of *The Emotional Life of the Toddler*; *Psychotherapy with Infants and Young Children: Repairing the Effects of Stress and Trauma on Early Attachment*; *Don't Hit My Mommy!: A Manual for Child-Parent Psychotherapy with Young Children Exposed to Violence and Other Trauma*; and numerous other publications, she is world-renowned for her work on parent-child attachment. She is the recipient of the 2017 Whole Child Award from the Simms/Mann Institute, the 2016 René Spitz Award from the World Association for Infant Mental Health, and other honors.